Y0-BCG-512

General William Averell's Salem Raid

Breaking the Knoxville Supply Line

by
Darrell L. Collins

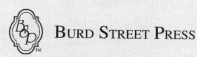 BURD STREET PRESS

Copyright © 1998 by Darrell L. Collins

ALL RIGHTS RESERVED—No part of this book may be reproduced in any form without permission in writing from the publisher, except by a reviewer who wishes to quote brief passages in connection with a review.

This Burd Street Press publication
was printed by
Beidel Printing House, Inc.
63 West Burd Street
Shippensburg, PA 17257-0152 USA

In respect for the scholarship contained herein, the acid-free paper used in this book meets the guidelines for permanence and durability of the Committee on Production Guidelines for Book Longevity of the Council on Library Resources.

For a complete list of available publications
please write
Burd Street Press
Division of White Mane Publishing Company, Inc.
P.O. Box 152
Shippensburg, PA 17257-0152 USA

Library of Congress Cataloging-in-Publication Data

Collins, Darrell L.
    General William Averell's Salem Raid : breaking the Knoxville
supply line / by Darrell L. Collins.
        p.   cm.
    Includes bibliographical references and index.
    ISBN 1-57249-111-6 (acid-free paper)
    1. Salem Raid, Salem, Va., 1863. 2. Averell, William Woods,
1832–1900. 3. Virginia--History--Civil War, 1861–1865--Cavalry
operations. 4. United States--History--Civil War, 1861–1865-
-Cavalry operations. I. Title.
E475.7.C65   1999
973.7'35--dc21   98-39878
                                                                      CIP

PRINTED IN THE UNITED STATES OF AMERICA

To Judy
who is my love and my life

Contents

Illustrations

MAPS

INTRODUCTION

Like an invasion, a raid is an incursion into enemy-held territory. But whereas an invasion relies on massive power to hold on to the territory by either pushing back an enemy or overwhelming him, a raid is a temporary thrust that uses limited force to achieve a specific objective; the raid is a tactic used in support of a grander strategy. And whereas an invasion usually develops around the strategy of bringing on a decisive battle, a raid, relying on speed to get in, secure the objective and quickly get out, generally tries to avoid contact with the enemy.

In the Civil War such speed and stealth could only be achieved by a mounted strike force—the cavalry. Troopers in such a strike force had to possess special qualities of endurance, determination, adaptive skills, teamwork, and have confidence in a leadership that had to be resourceful, flexible, daring, and intelligent.

The Civil War saw many mounted raids, most of which could be classified into one of three types, each with a different objective. The objective of the first type was the gathering of intelligence, such as enemy strengths and positions. An example of this type is Jeb Stuart's ride around McClellan's army on the Peninsula in the spring of 1862. The second type of raid sought to gather in much needed supplies. These raids could be quite prolonged as the strike force swept across the countryside in search of food and livestock. A classic example of this type is the weeks-long Jones-Imboden raid into western Virginia in the spring of 1863. The third type of raid had the most limited objective of the three, in that, like a modern cruise missile or stealth bomber, it sought to take out a specific target behind enemy lines, which usually meant disrupting enemy communications. One of the most daring and remarkable of this type was General William W. Averell's December 1863 raid to Salem, Virginia.

CHAPTER ONE

The Summons

1. The Fourth Separate Brigade

To some observers, Brigadier General Benjamin Franklin Kelley didn't look at all like a soldier. Tall and angular, with grayish hair and whiskers and "a thin hatchet like face," he dressed in plain, unassuming clothes that gave at least one witness the impression he "looked like a Quaker, run to seed." But it was those very qualities—that look of commonness and an obvious disdain of pomposity—that endeared him to the men of his command, men who, like himself, were indeed amateurs when it came to soldiering.[1]

Born in New Hampshire in 1807, Kelley had lived in Wheeling since the age of nineteen. There on the banks of the Ohio he had built up a successful mercantile business before becoming a freight agent for the Baltimore & Ohio Railroad in 1851. By the time the Civil War broke out a decade later Kelley's popularity and influence in the Wheeling area were such that he was largely responsible for raising the loyal, ninety-day 1st Virginia Infantry, for which deed he was named the regiment's colonel. He led the 1st at the war's first land battle, Philippi, where he sustained a severe chest wound. Thus his status as an early hero in the war, combined with his strong pro-Union activities in western Virginia, made Kelley the beneficiary of that peculiar nineteenth-century American political process whereby influential civilians were transformed into commanding generals (the reverse was also true—commanding generals were sometimes transformed into influential civilians—in both the nineteenth and the twentieth century). As a brigadier responsible for guarding the B&O, he commanded a division in the Middle Department's VIII Corps. Then with the creation of the Department of West Virginia in June 1863, he seemed the natural choice as commander. In that capacity, Kelley's one great ambition had been to clear out all Confederate forces from his adopted and beloved new state.[2]

By the late fall of 1863, that cherished dream seemed to have been realized. With the recent overwhelming defeat of the Confederates at the

Gen. Benjamin F. Kelley

Boyd B. Stutler Collection, West Virginia State Archives

battle of Droop Mountain, and their subsequent broken and demoralized retreat beyond Lewisburg and into Virginia, Kelley believed the enemy no longer posed a serious threat to the new, barely five-month-old state from which his department drew its name. So strong was his conviction in this regard that on 19 November 1863, thirteen days after the Droop Mountain triumph and a mere twenty-four hours after the return of the victors to their home base at New Creek on the Potomac, he transferred his headquarters out of West Virginia altogether and set up new offices in Cumberland, Maryland, 100 miles east of his former command post at Clarksburg. With the removal of the enemy from the Greenbrier Valley, their last stronghold in the infant state, the focus of the department, Kelley now reasoned, would fall mainly between the South Branch and Shenandoah valleys.[3] In short, he believed that the long struggle for control of the loyal counties of western Virginia had been won at last.

If Kelley's optimistic assessment was indeed true, it meant that decades of increasing strife and antagonism in Virginia had finally reached a climax, for the state, like the nation, had grown dangerously apart from itself during that period of time. But whereas the nation's two opposing sections were marked out by an imaginary line running east-west, the Old Dominion was divided from itself by the very real north-south spine of the Appalachian Mountains. East of that barrier lay Tidewater and Piedmont, Virginia, whose loyalty to the Confederacy was a natural consequence of the region's reliance on the plantation system of slave labor and its binding cultural ties to the deep South. Beyond the mountain chain lay the trans-Allegheny counties, with few slaves, strong economic links to states of the North and Midwest, and a firm commitment to the Union and the Federal government. And again like the nation, loyalties in Virginia were more mixed, more blurred and thus more hotly challenged in the "border" regions, which is to say, within those counties of the state that straddled the Appalachian spine or lay very near its western slope.[4]

Within a year of the firing on Fort Sumter, that border region had become an unofficial boundary between the two warring sides. The Federals, after easily gaining control of the Kanawha Valley and the northwest counties early in the war, had held back from the much more daunting task of penetrating the Appalachian spine from the west. They concentrated their energies instead on protecting the loyal population of the trans-Allegheny and in defending the B&O Railroad, possibly the nation's most important line, running as it did through northern West Virginia and connecting Washington with the Midwest's great wealth in men and supplies. This protection and defense came mostly in the form of large bodies of infantry posted at certain points throughout the region and along the railroad.[5]

But the relative quiet status quo of outpost and garrison duty that came with this more-or-less successful pacification process in western Virginia was suddenly shattered when thousands of rebel horsemen and infantry came thundering out of the Shenandoah on 21 April 1863, to begin what came to be known as the Jones-Imboden Raid. Sanctioned by General Lee as a means of disrupting the B&O while gathering in provisions and recruits, both of which he believed were bountiful in the region, the raid caught the Federals completely off guard. Moving with alarming speed, the hard-riding graybacks, some 2,500 under William "Grumble" Jones, hit the B&O at several vital points while John D. Imboden's 3,000 men of all arms marched into the central portion of the region to keep the various, scattered Federal commands off balance. Both rebel leaders moved through the western counties with relative impunity, scooping up cattle, horses, and other provisions as they went. Completing a round trip of several hundred miles in four weeks, they returned to the Valley virtually unharmed, having executed one of the most remarkable feats of its kind in the entire war.[6]

Such an embarrassing fiasco, occurring as it did on the eve of the admission of West Virginia to the Union and thereby essentially constituting an enemy intrusion into Federal territory, aroused the high command in Washington to take a much closer look at the situation beyond the Alleghenies. The Jones-Imboden raid had made it painfully clear that the region's most glaring need was for more cavalry. Heretofore, in keeping with a mostly defensive strategy, the high command had broken up into separate companies what scant cavalry there was in western Virginia and assigned them to various infantry units scattered throughout the region. Moreover, since assuming the post of commander in chief of the army the year before, Major General Henry Halleck had viewed western Virginia, with its rugged terrain, poor roads, and sparse settlements, as something of a military backwater, a suitable place for dumping troops and commanders of questionable value, not for squandering precious front-line cavalry. From this attitude, despite what had just happened, he refused to waver. If western Virginia wanted more cavalry, as the local commanders had been arguing for months, he decreed that they would have to provide it themselves.[7]

That meant only one thing—converting existing units of infantry in the area into troopers. In the face of Halleck's persistent refusals to send cavalry into the region, the local commanders, of "questionable ability" though they might have been, had just as persistently advocated such a solution. Halleck had always been opposed, arguing that "mounted infantry" was a "mongrel force," which in his opinion constituted "the poorest troops in the world." But in the wake of the Jones-Imboden raid, and the dangerous defense deficiencies it had exposed, the commander in chief relented and authorized the formation of an entire brigade of "mongrel" troopers.[8]

Having taken this step, Halleck desired that such a brigade should be a powerful strike force, capable not only of fighting off rebel raiders, but also of pursuing them into the mountains and destroying them there, if possible. Ideally, such a command would be composed of local West Virginians, men familiar with the region they were to defend. "Old Brains" was

Gen. John D. Imboden

General Imboden was one of Averell's pursuers.

Massachusetts Commandery, Military
Order of the Loyal Legion and the US Army Military History Institute

relieved that it wasn't necessary to scrape together regiments from around the state to create such a command, for the ideal candidate already existed—the Fourth Separate Brigade.[9]

It was so named because at the time of the Fourth's creation on 28 March 1863, the Middle Department, within which western Virginia was a district, already had three "separate" brigades. Composed of veteran units scattered throughout the region, the new brigade had originally been formed to protect the loyal counties of northwestern Virginia. The first commander of the Fourth had been fifty-two-year-old Benjamin Stone Roberts, a native of New Hampshire and a West Point graduate. He had landed the assignment to break his fall from grace for having been on the staff of John Pope, the author of the woeful disaster at Second Bull Run. Roberts, however, dramatically completed his fall when he stood by, perplexed and befuddled, during the Jones-Imboden raid, thereby losing the confidence not only of the administration in Washington, but of his own men.[10]

Obviously, to go forward in its new role, the Fourth needed a new commander.

2. Averell's Brigade

With curly but thinning light brown hair that framed a handsome, clear-cut face distinguished by a high forehead, a drooping mustache, a trim, pointed chin beard, and clear, wide-set piercing blue eyes, William Woods Averell certainly had the look of a dashing cavalry officer. Before the war had even begun, he had the reputation of one as well.[11]

His American roots went deep. Born in Cameron, New York 5 November 1832, Averell was the son of an early pioneer of Steuben County and the grandson of a Revolutionary War soldier from Connecticut. His great-grandfather, Josiah Bartlett, was the first constitutional governor of New Hampshire and a signer of the Declaration of Independence.[12]

One of five children by his father's second wife, William received a good public school education in his early years, and did so well in his studies that at the tender ages of fifteen and sixteen he did some teaching in the winter months and in the summer he learned to survey lands and roads. At seventeen he moved to nearby Bath where he became a drugstore clerk, an occupation that hardly satisfied his growing intellect and restless ambition. Too poor to afford a college education, he secured an appointment to West Point from Congressman David Rumsey of Bath.[13]

Though Averell enjoyed life at the Academy he was not a model cadet, and, despite lighthearted ways that earned him many friends, including Fitzhugh Lee, he occasionally suffered from bouts of loneliness and depression. He turned in only a fair academic performance, graduating twenty-sixth out of thirty-four in the class of 1855. This may have been a result, strangely enough, of an insatiable curiosity that was driven by a keen intellect. Averell found the classroom subjects at West Point interesting but limiting, and he admittedly allowed his studies to suffer somewhat in order to round out his education by using most of his spare time to pour over the books held at the Academy's great library. He succumbed to the "unrestrained habit of reading," as he described it, "I could not resist it." In one subject, however, he did finish at the top of his class—horsemanship. This was no doubt attributable, in part, to the fact that since early childhood he had been very fond of horses and was quite adept at handling them.[14]

Averell had originally viewed West Point as a means to an end, a way perhaps to eventually gain an executive position with a railroad company. But the order and discipline of military life quickly took hold of him and he chose to make his career in the army. After graduation, the new second lieutenant served as an adjutant at the cavalry school at Carlisle Barracks, Pennsylvania. His job, to which he fully dedicated himself, being meticulous almost to the point of obsession, was to prepare recruits for service in the mounted arm. "Going over and over again every line and precept of tactics and regulations," he recalled of his experience as a trainer, "and the use of my voice daily at parades and guard mountings was of the greatest service to me in after years when it became my duty to prepare regiments, brigades and divisions for the field—to feed, clothe, mount and drill, to arm, equip and command them on the march and in battle."[15]

At Carlisle Averell continued to enjoy the bachelor life; indeed, he would not marry until 1885. He became quite fond of various social entertainments, his charming personality winning him many friends. Those friends were quick to appreciate another major facet of his personality—ambition—in recognition of which they dubbed him with a name taken from a line in Shakespeare's Julius Caesar: "I have seen the ambitious ocean swell." Proud of the recognition, Averell did not discourage use of the handle, with the result that for years afterwards many of his closest friends often began their letters to him with "Dear Swell."[16]

In the autumn of 1857, Averell was sent, much to the satisfaction of his swelling ambition, to New Mexico Territory to join the "Regiment of Mounted Riflemen" (3rd U.S. Cav.). In that far-off region, where the culture was still predominantly Spanish, the young New Yorker found the customs and people strange. He was particularly intrigued by the women, who openly smoked cigarettes and danced at balls with men to whom they had not been properly introduced. The charming lieutenant was irresistably drawn to these fascinating ladies, a few of whom apparently became his lover.[17]

But along with the pleasures, New Mexico presented Averell with many trying hardships that put his mettle to the test throughout the time he spent there. And such tests began almost immediately.

Upon arrival, he discovered that the captain and first lieutenant of his new company were away on extended leaves, thus leaving command of the unit to him. Barely two months later, he led that company in combat against a band of Kiowa in the Rio Grande Valley. His first fight came close to being his last. With thirteen men he rode over to a nearby ranch to investigate reports of an Indian raid. As he and his men approached the ranch house on foot, about a dozen Kiowa burst out of the place and Averell quickly found himself in a fierce hand-to-hand struggle with the knife-wielding leader of the band. The deadly contest remained undecided for several anxious moments until a trooper got free from his own struggle, reached around Averell and shot the chieftain in the gut.[18]

During the following year Averell became a tough and hardened campaigner, taking part in no less than twenty-five fights against the Navajo. Many of the reports and general orders sent off to Washington in that time include his name among those cited for gallant conduct. On the night of 8 October 1858, however, his frontier experience came to an abrupt, near-tragic end when Navajos jumped his company while it was in camp along the Rio Puerco. By the time the attackers had been driven off, Averell lay in agonizing pain, a bullet having passed through his left thigh, shattering the femur. He spent the next two years on medical leave, hobbling around on crutches, mostly at home in Bath. His restless, ambitious nature found it very difficult to endure the inactivity and feelings of inadequacy. "He that was self-reliant and independent must now lean on others," he wrote of the experience. "He could once lend his strength and now he must always borrow . . . The most serious and immediate result is the enforced restraint. It is so hard to quit work." (Among his pastimes was the game of chess, "a beneficial mental exercise" at which he apparently became quite proficient. Inspired by the published exploits of the great master of the day, U.S. champion Paul Morphy, Averell challenged himself by playing blindfolded or by taking on several opponents simultaneously.)[19]

Though still walking with a cane on the eve of the great conflict, Averell, in anticipation of the war, rushed to Washington in February 1861, to offer his services. He was thus present in the capital to witness Lincoln's inaugural address. The young lieutenant came away very impressed with the new president. "Thrills of emotion swept over the sea of upturned faces as his mighty theme unfolded," Averell wrote in admiration of the speech, "exalted, illuminated and permeated with the ideas of an American nationality that would constitutionally defend and maintain itself. His frequent earnest emphasis, reinforced with striking attitude and forcible action, made him for the purpose of the hour seem to be American patriotism personified."[20]

A few weeks after the inauguration, "the momentous issue of civil war" having been taken up by the firing on Fort Sumter, Commander in Chief Winfield Scott gave Averell an unusual and daring assignment—to deliver dispatches to two regiments of loyal troops cut off and isolated at Fort Arbuckle in Indian Territory.

After a grueling 260-mile, "nearly blind" wilderness ride (because of his wound, he hadn't been on a horse in nearly two years) out of Fort

Smith, Arkansas, during which the rebels maintained a hot pursuit, Averell found the loyal command and went north with it to friendly Kansas.[21]

Though his arrival in Washington preceded the news of this daring exploit, Averell nonetheless returned to the capital as one of the army's most promising cavalry officers. After serving as a staff officer at First Bull Run, he was appointed colonel of the 3rd Pennsylvania Cavalry, a disorganized and ill-disciplined regiment scattered at various points across the Potomac in northern Virginia. Averell did so well in organizing and training this regiment that within a week the 8th Pennsylvania was turned over to him as well, his two regiments then forming the First Brigade of Volunteer Cavalry. With this brigade he won favorable notice for his skillful vigilance in covering McClellan's retreat from Malvern Hill to the James River.[22] But the praise came at a severe price. While on the Peninsula Averell contracted "Chickahominy fever." He later described the malady as "a malarial fever and sort of typhoid which exhibits itself in congestive headaches and in a general dislocation of all one's joints." The "fever" incapacitated him for about five weeks, during which time his sister Martha came from New York to help nurse him back to health.[23]

Returning to duty in mid-summer, Averell spent the next several weeks performing the usual frustrating tasks—picketing, guarding, running errands—assigned to the army's under-utilized cavalry. This typified the manner in which Union cavalry was often used early in the war. Fearing the acknowledged superiority of their Confederate counterparts, the Federal mounted arm was handled cautiously, and was not allowed or expected to fight its own battles independent of infantry. Underlying this caution was the general belief that the raw Northern recruit needed time to overcome his relative lack of skill in horsemanship, and that as much if not more time was needed to find good leaders for those boys, leaders who could eventually act alone and "be made a terror to the enemy." In the meantime, the fighting capabilities of the Federal mounted arm became so suspect as to give rise to a derisive saying in the army that no one had ever seen a dead mule or a dead cavalryman.[24]

Under constraints, then, that suggested the cavalry could not be trusted to perform important independent assignments, Averell had little chance to distinguish himself during the Fredericksburg campaign. (A relapse of "Chickahominy fever" caused him to miss the Antietam campaign.)[25] But because of his excellent training and organizational skills, his star continued to rise. On 26 September 1862, he received a promotion to brigadier general, and the following 12 February he was elevated to command of the Second Division of the Cavalry Corps, Army of the Potomac.

Averell's first great opportunity for distinction in the field finally came when "Fighting Joe" Hooker, commander of the Army of the Potomac, sent his division, some 3,000 sabers and six guns, to cross the Rappahannock and strike at the Orange & Alexandria Railroad near Culpeper Court House.

On 17 March at Kelly's Ford, Averell ran into his old friend Fitz Lee and 800 Confederate horsemen. In what has generally been conceded as the first real victory of Union cavalry in the war, or at least the first impressive showing by them, Averell's men held their own and fought off the rebels in a fierce struggle involving several classic charges and countercharges. With total victory in sight, however, Averell came down with a fit of overcaution. Instead of rolling over Fitz Lee, as he might have easily done, and riding on to the railroad—and unimagined heights of glory—he succumbed to rumors of advancing Confederate infantry and withdrew back across the Rappahannock.

Amidst all the promise and expectation, one now had to ask whether Averell had the killer instinct to go for the jugular and finish off his victim; was he content to merely hold on to and not jeopardize whatever success, however limited, he had initially gained? In the midst of all the acclaim now being heaped on Averell for the "victory" at Kelly's Ford, Hooker suppressed his disappointment with him for not completing the mission, but the seeds of doubt had been planted.

Six weeks later at the start of the Chancellorsville campaign, he gave Averell another chance when, with instructions to "fight, fight, fight," he sent the entire cavalry corps to get behind Lee's army. As part of what became known as the "Stoneman Raid," named for the corps commander who led the cavalry on its first large-scale independent action, Averell was to strike at Gordonsville in Lee's rear.

With his superbly trained and disciplined division, Averell eagerly set out on his great mission, and, despite detailed and sometimes conflicting orders coming in from both Stoneman and Hooker, he reached the Rappahannock on 29 April. Caution, however, soon started to creep in. The Rappahannock was swollen with rushing water, and, perhaps remembering his own crossing of the Poteau during his "blind ride" to Fort Arbuckle in early 1861, wherein his panicky horse nearly got him drowned, he did not wish to subject his men to a similar, horrifying experience. Instead he followed the safer course of riding up to the sight of his renowned fight at Kelly's Ford, crossed there and then rode on to the Rapidan. Despite this extra use of time, he still had a good chance to complete his mission. These successive river crossings, however, seemed to be humbling him to an almost irrational level that drained him of initiative. At the Rapidan he concluded that the enemy was too strong on the other side, and meekly returned to camp. On 3 May Hooker ordered him to go back out and find a suitable place on the right flank for the cavalry to operate. When Averell reported that there was no such place, "Fighting Joe," furious and in need of scapegoats for the failure of the overall campaign, accused him of not following orders and of displaying dilatory leadership. On 16 May he relieved Averell of his command.

It seemed ironic. Averell had always believed that the war had been caused by bungling politicians, who were continuing to mismanage things by not allowing the professional soldiers to prosecute it.[26] Now, the consummate professional soldier himself had bungled his chance.

Understandably outraged at Hooker's accusations, Averell asked for, and was denied, a court of inquiry. Dejected and humiliated, his once promising military career apparently near an end, he gave up command of his beloved Second Division and reported to the adjutant general in Washington to see what crumbs might be offered. To his surprise, Washington did have a crumb for him, one that would not only revitalize his career but send it to new heights.

Averell had arrived in the capital in the wake of the Jones-Imboden raid and the command shakeup in western Virginia. He had at first been sent into military exile with the unglamorous assignment of recruiting in Philadelphia and was on his way there when Robert Schenck, the commander of the Middle Department, requested his services for the Fourth Separate Brigade. Averell was thus conveniently and fortuitously on hand for Halleck to "dump" him in the mountains with the seemingly unenviable task of converting infantry into a brigade of cavalry. But Averell jumped at the assignment and gladly welcomed it, if only as a means to clear his reputation and win back a command in the Army of the Potomac, where lay the true path to glory.[27] Little did he know that, free from the constraints of overbearing commanding officers, he would achieve his greatest renown with an obscure semi-independent command in the rugged mountains of West Virginia.

On 22 May 1863, Averell arrived in Weston by rail with instructions to relieve General Roberts and assume command of the Fourth Separate Brigade.[28] He faced a daunting task, not only in converting infantry into cavalry, but in molding a true brigade out of what Roberts had allowed to lapse into a poorly equipped, widely scattered and ill-disciplined command. But Averell had been called upon, in part, because he was a superb organizer, having whipped the 3rd and 8th Pennsylvania into topnotch outfits, and later having won the respect of the entire Second Cavalry Division. Furthermore, the troops of his new command—tough, loyal, and determined men—would ease his difficulties considerably by willingly accepting their new role. Moreover, they were thrilled to be rid of the inept Roberts and to now have over them what they perceived was a proven fighter.

Averell's assumption of command was thus "hailed with demonstrations of genuine rejoicing by the officers and men of the Fourth Separate Brigade,"[29] observed one veteran. In contrast to the humiliation they had suffered under Roberts, the men of the Fourth were now imbued with such hope and optimism as to be unable to see any blemish at all on their new commander. "General Averell's reputation as a gallant and successful cavalry fighter had preceded his coming by several months," a veteran later declared, "and to be placed under such a leader was inspiring to these troops, who were at all times eager for the active operations of war."[30]

With such eager and willing students, Averell would have a great opportunity to mold this brigade into his own perception of what constituted a proper fighting unit. "The ruling principle of the time," wrote Major Theodore Lang of Averell's staff about the brigade's previous training and experience, "was to know how to make long marches, to endure hardships, and load and fire low in time of battle. The master hand of discipline and drill had not been a part of their military experience. Therefore, when General Averell assumed command of these troops, he found himself with a brigade of loyal, courageous fighters, scattered through half a dozen counties, but who knew little of discipline, or of regimental or brigade maneuvers—scantily supplied with approved arms, equipments, clothing, etc.

"They were inefficient for any reliable defense of the country, and the utter hopelessness of any effort to take the offensive . . . all of the officers and enlisted men alike, were war students with no teachers among them of skilled warfare." Having pointed out the brigade's many deficiencies, Lang concluded, with pride, "It will be seen, therefore, that he [Averell] came to the command of the 4th seperate brigade [sic] with a ripe experience that fitted him well to build up a splendid brigade out of the best quality of 'raw material.'"[31]

The potentially "splendid brigade" Averell inherited consisted of the 28th Ohio Infantry, the 2nd, 3rd, 8th, and 10th Virginia Infantry, the 14th Pennsylvania Cavalry, Gibson's Independent Cavalry Battalion and Batteries B and G of the 1st Virginia Light Artillery. Three of those commands—the 2nd, 3rd, and 8th Infantry—were designated for conversion into cavalry.

The 2nd Virginia had been the first loyal three-year regiment raised and mustered in by authorization of Francis Pierpont, governor of the "Restored Government of Virginia." Organized at Wheeling in the summer of 1861, the new command contained men from Wheeling, Parkersburg, and Grafton, and the counties of Ritchie, Taylor, and Wetzel. It also included a number of men from Ohio—the towns of Ironton and Bridgeport and the counties of Belmont and Monroe. And it had a huge contingent from Pennsylvania, men from Alleghany, Greenfield and Washington counties who had been turned away from service in their home state because of the quickly filled quotas there. After serving nearly a year on outpost duty—guarding the B&O and various other points in western Virginia—the 2nd was pulled east where it gave a good account of itself fighting Stonewall Jackson in the Shenandoah and at Second Bull Run. Then after sitting a few weeks in the defenses of Washington, the regiment returned to western Virginia in the fall of 1862, and the following spring it was attached to the Fourth Separate Brigade.[32]

Commanding the 2nd Virginia was forty-two-year-old Lieutenant Colonel Alexander Scott, a native Pennsylvanian who had dropped his study of music when the Mexican War began in order to join a local company called the "Rough and Ready Guards." After that conflict, marriage and the furniture business led him to Mississippi, where he maintained his military skills in a miltia company called the "Monroe Rifles." At the outbreak of war in '61, he turned down a commission in the Confederate service and returned to Pittsburgh, where he helped recruit what later became Company F of the 2nd Virginia. After serving as captain of that company for nearly a year, Scott took command of the 2nd in the early summer of 1862. With his bravery on the battlefield—a horse had been shot from under him at Second Bull Run—and his genuine ongoing concern for the welfare of the regiment, Scott quickly won the respect of his men. "They cheerily followed his leadership," one of them asserted, "though they knew that it meant danger, and perhaps death."[33]

The 3rd Virginia was the second three-year regiment brought in under Governor Pierpont. Organized at Clarksburg in July 1861, the regiment contained men from the counties of Harrison, Marshall, Monongalia, Preston, Ritchie, Taylor, and Upshur, with a smattering of recruits from across the Pennsylvania line. The service of the 3rd was much like that of the 2nd: outpost duty in western Virginia, fighting Stonewall Jackson in the Shenandoah and at 2nd Bull Run, holding the defenses of Washington, then returning to western Virginia to be incorporated into the Fourth Separate Brigade.[34]

The 3rd's commander, thirty-five-year-old Lieutenant Colonel Francis W. Thompson, had been born in Morgantown but in 1850 he went out to California to seek his fortune. Evidently finding no financial success there, he went two years later to Oregon, where, as a member of a battalion of rangers, he became involved in various Indian wars while managing to become fluent in a number of native dialects. With the secession crisis looming in the East, Thompson returned to Morgantown and was offered a commission in the Confederate service. Turning that down, he raised what later became Company A of the 3rd. Later that summer (1861), he became the regiment's commander, and like his counterpart Scott in the 2nd Virginia, Thompson's diligence and bravery—he had been severely wounded at Second Bull Run—earned him the respect and admiration of his men.[35]

The 8th Virginia Infantry had been organized in the fall of 1861 at Charleston, and was made up of men from the Kanawha Valley and the surrounding region. Its service on outpost duty, in the Shenandoah, at Second Bull Run and in the defenses of Washington, was quite similar to its sister regiments, the 2nd and 3rd Virginia. The commander of the 8th was thirty-three-year-old Colonel John H. Oley, a merchant and telegraph operator from Utica, New York. When the war began, Oley joined the 7th New York National Guard, in which he quickly earned a reputation, despite his lack of military training, as "a man of tremendous driving force," who was "fit to command." In desperate need of commanders, Governor Pierpont received Oley as one of six instructors sent upon request from the governor of New York. Oley helped raise and train the 8th, served for a time as its major, then became colonel just before the regiment joined the Fourth Separate Brigade. He was "a fine appearing officer," remarked one observer, "intelligent, a good disciplinarian, and in every respect thoroughly qualified to command." Moreover, Oley "endeared himself to the officers and men of his regiment and had the respect and confidence of his superior officers."[36] One such superior officer was fellow-New Yorker Averell, with whom he would build up a close and enduring friendship.[37]

Eager to begin molding the "raw material" of these three regiments, Averell set up a cavalry training camp at Bridgeport, near Clarksburg. From the immediate vicinity and as far away as Ohio and Pennsylvania, horses and equipment began to pour in. Training commenced the first week of June.[38] The men, tough veterans that they were, had never experienced such demands as were now placed upon them. "He was an excellent drillmaster," remembered one of the general's admiring soldiers, "with proper views of what constituted real discipline. Instruction in a systematic manner, with a view of preparing these men for the service expected of them, was commenced and persistently followed in the most industrious and painstaking manner . . . Squad drill, troop drill, battalion drill followed each other in such rapid succession as to make his head swim, and a detail for a scout or picket duty in the presence of an active and industrious enemy was hailed as 'a sweet day of rest.'"[39]

"And beyond all," Averell recalled of his training methods, "for without it everything else would have soon disappeared, they . . . learned how to care for their horses, arms and equipments."[40]

Though Averell believed that a new recruit needed at least three years of training and experience to reach his full potential as a cavalryman,[41] within a mere month, thanks largely to his own diligence and the eagerness of his pupils, the three regiments began to take on the look and feel of true cavalry. A look that no doubt included the new guidon Averell had designed for the 3rd Pennsylvania. To help prevent a recurrence of the confusion he had witnessed on the field at First Bull Run, Averell had

Col. Francis W. Thompson, 3rd W.Va. Mtd. Inf.

National Tribune, 8 Sept. 1887

given his command a distinctive guidon that would eventually be adopted for use throughout the cavalry: the fork-tailed U.S. flag.[42]

But Averell's three converted regiments lacked one other important item. As "mounted infantry," they were expected to fulfill a dual role, wherein they would ride to a fight, dismount and form up like infantry. As such, they were given a saber and navy colt revolver but not the cavalry carbine. They retained the short Enfield musket, an almost impossible weapon to load while in the saddle.[43]

In any case, the military transformation of these regiments coincided nicely with the political transformation of the region they were to defend. On 20 June Congress admitted West Virginia to the Union, and four days later the new state was made into a separate military department containing some 23,000 men, with "the thin hatchet like face" of Brigadier General Benjamin F. Kelley in command. Such momentous changes meant that the local regiments had to be renamed; "Virginia" was no longer acceptable. Reflecting their new political and military status, the three regiments became the 2nd, 3rd, and 8th West Virginia Mounted Infantry. Moreover, they now belonged to the First Separate Brigade, more commonly referred to from then on as "Averell's Brigade."[44]

3. First Operations

On 30 June 1863, that brigade contained 4,129 men present for duty, a larger force than the division Averell had commanded with the Army of the Potomac.[45] His assignment now was to keep the region of West Virginia between the B&O and the Kanawha clear of the enemy.[46] He did not have long to wait before facing that challenge. That same 30 June the brigade was called upon to repel a new "invasion" of the new state.

The invasion had been launched by Confederate troops from General Samuel Jones' Department of Western Virginia. Jones' command was the counterweight, so to speak, to the Union forces in the trans-Allegheny. In point of fact, the responsibilities of each side mirrored those of the other. Like the Federals' protection of the B&O, for example, Jones' "army" had the responsibility of guarding

Col. John H. Oley
National Tribune, 8 Sept. 1887

the Confederacy's equally vital rail link, the Virginia & Tennessee, stretching 204 miles from Lynchburg to Bristol. With well-built tracks and large, powerful engines, this line was perhaps the most modern and efficient in the Confederacy. Its route carried it by numerous vitally important lead and salt mines in southwest Virginia, and it was connected to most of the major supply lines coming up to Richmond from the deep South.[47]

And like the Federal mandate to protect the "loyal" counties of the region, Jones held a similar trust toward loyal Confederates in the trans-Allegheny, even if they lived in counties broken off from Virginia by the Federal congress. Indeed, some of those counties—Pendleton, Pocahontas, and Greenbrier, for example—were overwhelmingly Confederate in sympathy.[48]

On 20 June Jones' command consisted of about 7,000 men in five brigades. At Lewisburg in Greenbrier County was John Echols' First Brigade of 2,601 infantry, cavalry, and artillery. At Saltville in Washington County was the Second Brigade of 890 infantry, cavalry, and artillery. The Third Brigade of 814 infantry was stationed along the line of the railroad near Glade Springs, also in Washington County. The Fourth Brigade of 1,444 men of all arms was located at Piney just south of Raleigh Court House.[49] And Jones' extreme right was secured by the "Huntersville Line," which stretched thirty miles or so from southwestern Pocahontas County to Warm Springs in Highland County. The "Line" was under the command of Colonel William L. Jackson, derisively known on both sides as "Mudwall" by way of distinguishing him from his more renowned cousin "Stonewall." With a nebulous command of new, still somewhat disorganized companies that would eventually become the 19th and 20th Virginia Cavalry, Jackson had the responsibility of watching the mountain passes to the east so as to prevent a surprise push by the Federals into the Shenandoah. He also served as an early warning, or advanced picket line, against a Federal drive south toward the railroad. And finally, his "line" offered protection to the loyal Confederates of the Greenbrier Valley.[50]

It was Jackson's command of 1,200 men that had crossed over Cheat Mountain and by 2 July was threatening Colonel Thomas Harris' 971 men of the 10th West Virginia at Beverly. Jackson had done this in compliance with Lee's wish to create a diversion in order to prevent the Federals from moving into the Shenandoah while the Army of Northern Virginia was marching through the Valley en route to its great invasion of Pennsylvania.[51]

Averell responded by promptly riding down from Grafton with the 3rd and 8th West Virginia and 14th Pennsylvania (leaving behind the still undertrained and underequipped 2nd West Virginia). Though still feeling somewhat like "infantry hitching a ride," the two new mounted regiments handled the thirty-five mile journey like professionals. Then in light, dismounted skirmishing, they drove Jackson back across Cheat Mountain on 3 July.[52]

It had been a fine first showing by the two new regiments of mounted infantry, but the men barely had time to congratulate themselves when

Gen. Samuel Jones

Massachusetts Commandery, Military
Order of the Loyal Legion and the US Army Military History Institute

urgent orders came in from Washington the next day (4th). The mounted portion of Averell's brigade was to proceed at once to Hancock, Maryland on the Potomac to help cut off Lee's army in its retreat from Pennsylvania.

Averell got the command back to Grafton, from where he sent the 3rd, 8th, 14th Pennsylvania, Gibson's battalion, and Keeper's battery on by rail to Cumberland. From there on the eleventh, he led the men on a tough three-day, eighty-mile ride to Williamsport, only to learn upon arriving that Lee had passed through less than twenty-four hours before. The command then remained as a picket along the Potomac for about three weeks, during which time it occasionally skirmished with Confederate rear guard cavalry. Finally recalled by Kelley after Lee's army had escaped below the Rapidan, Averell's men rode into Winchester on the thirtieth and on 5 August they arrived back in Morefield, West Virginia.[53]

4. The August and November Raids

Encouraged by this recent impressive showing of the new mounted regiments, General Kelley now believed he had at hand the instrument by which he could accomplish one of his most cherished ambitions—clearing the rebels from the Greenbrier Valley, their last real stronghold in his beloved West Virginia. He wasted no time in drawing up an aggressive plan to do just that.

Averell's assignment was simple—march to the southern end of the 170-mile long Greenbrier Valley and take Lewisburg, and as sort of a trophy of that achievement, he was to bring back from there the new state's law library, used for sessions of the Virginia Supreme Court of Appeals and recently purchased for "the western part of the state."[54] Leaving behind the 28th Ohio, 10th West Virginia, and Keeper's battery, Averell would take all of his mounted units, about 1,300 men altogether. Always reluctant, as he had been since his days out west and particularly since witnessing the debacle of First Bull Run, to begin a mission until his command was fully prepared, Averell had reservations now, especially since supply problems decreed that his men would be carrying only about thirty-five rounds of ammunition apiece. Nonetheless, on 18 August he set out from Petersburg and headed south.

Two days later he entered Monterey, where he surprised and captured a session of the quarterly court. From there he went after Jackson at Huntersville in Pocahontas County, chased him east over to Warm Springs, broke off and continued south to Callaghan's, entering there on the twenty-fifth. The next morning he turned west onto the James River pike and headed for Lewisburg. Coming through Rocky Gap east of White Sulphur Springs, he was intercepted by Echols' brigade (under Col. George S. Patton; Echols was in Atlanta on the court of inquiry regarding the surrender of Vicksburg) of 1,900 men. A vicious fight developed that lasted all day and into the next. Faced with depleted ammunition and stubborn resistance from superior numbers, Averell pulled out and headed back on the morning of the twenty-seventh. Pushing his men relentlessly to avoid capture, he safely reached Beverly on the thirtieth.

Though they had lost the battle of Rocky Gap (also known as White Sulphur Springs), losing some 218 men, the command had held its own against superior numbers (who had lost 166), and withdrew mainly because of low supplies of ammunition.[55] Moreover, they had maintained a disciplined retreat, wherein they outrode the much more experienced pursuing Confederate cavalry. And though their mission had been a failure, their thirteen-day, 250-mile march gave promise of better things to come. All in all, the expedition gave a tremendous lift to the men's pride and confidence, both in themselves and their new leader.[56]

But Kelley's dream—clearing the Greenbrier Valley of rebels, and removing, once and for all, the constant fears and rumors of Confederate raids against various points in the new state—remained unrealized. In late October he thus drew up new plans for another try at Lewisburg, though this time, on prompting from Halleck, Averell was to have the additional task of hitting the Virginia & Tennessee Railroad. To ensure success, this expedition was to have a much more powerful force than the one in August. This time Averell was to take his entire brigade, rendezvous at Lewisburg with a support column coming in from Charleston, then ride fifty miles on to the railroad with the mounted portion of each command.

With about 3,300 men, Averell marched out of Beverly on 1 November. Again, he went after Jackson, who this time did not scoot east out of the way but stayed in front of Averell and backed up before him south to Droop Mountain in southern Pocahontas County. Echols in turn marched up from Lewisburg to make a stand with Jackson on the 3,100-foot summit. On 6 November Averell came up and decisively defeated them (about 1,700 men) after executing a brilliant flanking movement around their left. He chased them to Lewisburg, met the support column there from Charleston the next day, but then, like at Kelley's Ford eight months before, he held back from jeopardizing, and completing, his victory. Citing fatigue in the command as well as the fear of Confederate reinforcements, he pulled back, all the way to New Creek on the Potomac.[57]

Once again, at a critical moment, Averell gave in to overcaution—the jugular of his enemy had been exposed and he did not rip it open. His intense ambition had a flip side—the fear of failure, which often expressed itself as an unwillingness to put success, however limited, at risk. "And if his sphere of activity be contracted," he had written about his convalescence from the leg wound received in New Mexico, "so perhaps will he be spared the memory of many little regretful mistakes of life."[58]

Moreover, this ambition and its flip side had need of seeing others as rivals for success and scapegoats for failure. In his report on Droop Mountain, Averell made a veiled attempt to shift the blame for the expedition's incomplete success onto the commander of the support column from the Kanawha. This element of his complex character did not endear him to

Gen. John Echols

He cut Averell off at Sweet Springs Mountain.

Massachusetts Commandery, Military
Order of the Loyal Legion and the US Army Military History Institute

many of his peers and superiors.[59] But Averell made no apologies. "In the course of some twenty years I have had some steep hills to climb," he had written his sister Martha on 5 April 1863, "there is no man of my position in the army who has had as much to contend against—

"My youth, want of influential friends and wealth have conspired against me, but I believe I am now a few lengths ahead of all competitors—and I am not at the end yet—

"Now the secret of my success is this. I have been blessed with a little foresight and I have fixed purposes and notwithstanding the efforts of my rivals and enemies I manage to row my own boat—Men with great political influence closely connected with the Administration, men of wealth and genius have been pitted against me, but through everything I have seen and worked my way."[60]

Thus surrounded by "rivals" and "competitors," Averell lived by a go-it-alone attitude, which had its roots in the inspirations of his pioneer father, Hiram, whom he had always admired and looked up to. "I owe all my education and improvement (little enough)," the young cadet wrote his father from West Point in 1852, "to the ambition you inspired in me by well chosen stories of persons who made themselves by their own exertions &c."[61]

And now, having indeed managed to "row my own boat" and "seen and worked my way," Averell's most recent expedition, despite its incomplete success, had been a significant achievement. At a loss of 127 men, his brigade had inflicted a decisive defeat on the enemy, who had suffered a much greater loss of about 275, and pushed him out of the Greenbrier Valley. Moreover, in eighteen days the command had executed another impressive march, this time of 296 miles.[62] Averell and his men were justifiably proud of what they had accomplished.

Kelley was extremely pleased at last. "The recent success of Brigadier-General Averell at Lewisburg," he gleefully wired Washington on the nineteenth, "has cleared the new state of West Virginia of any organized form of rebels." Kelley even went so far as to conclude that his job in West Virginia was done and he accordingly shifted his headquarters east to Cumberland, Maryland.[63]

Everyone was pleased except Commander in Chief Halleck.

Brig. Gen. William W. Averell

Massachusetts Commandery, Military
Order of the Loyal Legion and the US Army Military History Institute

Chapter Two

The Strike South

1. The Plan

Unlike Kelley, General Halleck was not that impressed with Averell's "recent success." Though pleased the rebels had been driven from the Greenbrier Valley, the commander in chief was disappointed Averell had not accomplished a primary goal of the mission—severance of the Virginia & Tennessee Railroad. In Halleck's mind the Greenbrier Valley was of minor military importance, while the railroad, stretching 204 miles from Lynchburg to Bristol, then another 100 miles or so to Knoxville, was a vital Confederate link between two major theatres of war. As such, "Old Brains" concluded that Averell's expedition had achieved only a minor success while leaving a major disappointment.

That disappointment became especially acute on 17 November when Knoxville came under siege by rebels supplied by the Virginia & Tennessee. This deplorable situation developed after the Confederate high command, desperate for success upon Lee's disastrous invasion of Pennsylvania, had transferred two of James Longstreet's divisions from Virginia to Braxton Bragg's Army of Tennessee. The results of this daring move had thus far been quite stunning. At Chickamauga, Georgia in September, Bragg and Longstreet inflicted a crushing defeat on the Federal Army of the Cumberland, then chased it up to Chattanooga and laid it under siege. In November, Longstreet, after picking up Jones' troops in east Tennessee, set out to complete the triumphal sweep by going after Ambrose Burnside's IX Corps, which he promptly drove into Knoxville. To the high command in Washington, complete disaster in the West seemed imminent.

Longstreet, however, looked vulnerable. It might be possible to break his grip on Knoxville by cutting his main supply line—the Virginia & Tennessee Railroad. Especially since the railroad's protector, General Jones' command, was widely scattered, most of his troops having been sent over to Longstreet (Robert Ransom's new, makeshift division and the 16th Va. Cav.

were with Longstreet and the 45th Va. Inf. was at Saltville). This meant that for a short stretch fifty or so miles west of Lynchburg the Virginia & Tennessee had very little protection. Halleck, persistent if nothing else, knew that there was still only one man who could get to that stretch of line and break it. On the morning of 29 November he sent Kelley a simple, one-sentence dispatch: "The greater part of Jones' force is now at Knoxville, Tenn., and there can be very little opposition to a movement against the Virginia and Tennessee Railroad."[1]

It is interesting to note that Halleck did not order "a movement against the Virginia and Tennessee Railroad," he merely suggested that it could be done. After the war Kelley maintained that the commander in chief, desirous as he had been to see the railroad severed, was nonetheless fearful of the blame that would be heaped upon him should such an attempt to cut it fail with heavy losses, as he thought was most probable given the time of year. At any rate, by way of an "intimated wish" from on high, the seed for a new expedition had once again been planted.

Six days later, on 5 December, the seed had grown into a new plan, devised by Kelley, to do one thing and one thing only—strike at the railroad. With no cities to take or valleys to clear, Kelley kept the single-minded plan extremely simple. With fifteen days' rations, the mounted portion of Averell's brigade was to leave New Creek and plunge about 200 miles south to hit the railroad at either Salem in Virginia's Roanoke County, or Bonsack's Station in Botetourt. From Beverly, Colonel Joseph Thoburn would go as far as Monterey with two infantry regiments of Mulligan's division and mind Averell's train until his return.[2]

It was too simple. Kelley presumably thought that because of Averell's "recent success" in November, and the current disbursement of Jones' command, the expedition would encounter little resistance. Either that or he took the unlikely position that to achieve success Averell's command was expendable. Averell, after perusing the details of the plan that same 5 December, would have none of it.[3]

Since arriving in New Creek in Hampshire County (now Keyser in Mineral County) on 18 November, following his Droop Mountain triumph, Averell had devoted his considerable energies to revitalizing his command and preparing it for future operations, operations that both he and the humblest of his privates assumed would not occur until the following spring, at least. Expecting to go into winter quarters, the command had begun to settle down. "The Campaignes Ended for the fall," Sergeant Benjamin Hughes of Company F, 3rd West Virginia wrote his wife, Ellen, on 5 December, "and We Will goe into Winter quarters Some Where Soon."[4] The men applied for leaves, and many of the officers sent for their wives and families. No one expected the command to be asked to take on the mountains in the harsh December weather. And, the season aside, few believed the brigade would be called upon so soon, while it was still recovering from the last raid and when even its most basic needs, such as horseshoes and nails, had not been met. And Averell, at least, had not expected to be given such a disagreeable and dangerous assignment.[5]

From that year's previous expeditions he had learned important lessons. When trying to take Lewisburg in August he had met the enemy head-on, and, being without support, he was turned back. In November, with the help of a column from the Kanawha, he had taken Lewisburg but was still unable to reach the railroad. Now Kelley was again asking him to ride out alone and place his main trust in speed and good fortune.

For Averell, these were not enough. The August and November expeditions had been designed with the expectation that a direct, major confrontation with the enemy was inevitable, even desirable. This raid, relying on speed to achieve its purpose, would need to avoid such a confrontation. But even with the greatest of speed, the very length of the raid would allow the enemy plenty of time to react. Thus Averell realized that even if fortune and the weather smiled broadly upon him, and he hit the railroad at a record pace, the enemy, however dispersed, would still have time to coalesce behind him and block the return route. Moreover, he also knew that many of Lee's troops, then or soon to be wintering in and about the Shenandoah, would also be in striking distance of that route. Important as he believed support was or should have been to the August and November expeditions, Averell was convinced it was absolutely crucial to the type of raid now being contemplated.

Unprepared as he believed his command to be, and awed as he was by the prospect of dealing with the merciless mountain weather, Averell was nonetheless willing to undertake the expedition, but he wanted that support—lots of it. At his own headquarters that same day, 5 December, he expressed these feelings to Kelley in person.

Kelley had apparently come to New Creek on a tour of inspection, whereby he hoped to have a look at Averell's command before it set out on its mission. He was no doubt surprised to be presented with vehement objections to the design of that mission.

Averell probably had little use for Kelley. It must have galled the young New Yorker, a graduate of the Academy and a dedicated professional, to have to serve under an inexperienced and untrained politician-general. Nonetheless, Averell made sure that the department commander was shown proper respect, which on this occasion took the form of a review. At 10 a.m. the next morning (6 Dec.), the 2nd, 3rd, and 8th West Virginia, the 14th Pennsylvania, Gibson's battalion and Ewing's battery were drawn up on a vacant lot just south of town. "Of course it was no 'big thing,' compared with the Army of the Potomac or that of the Cumberland," reported the *Wheeling Intelligencer*, but the mile-long review of "well disciplined troops was exceedingly attractive and interesting." Many of the townspeople, including "a fair share of ladies," were on hand to watch, thus giving the proceedings something of a festive air. The review over, Kelley retired to Averell's headquarters for "a capital dinner," after which the two men boarded a special train for Kelley's headquarters at Cumberland, twenty-five miles northeast of and downriver on the Potomac from New Creek. Naturally, the day's unusual proceedings were not lost on Averell's veterans, whose speculations on their meaning would prove quite prophetic. "Rumor," concluded the *Intelligencer*, "says that this review was preparatory to a grand scout of twenty days' duration, in what direction, the General knows."[6]

Despite transferring the argument up to the supposed security of his own turf, Kelley, to his credit, viewed Averell's objections with an open mind. So open, in fact, that a convincing persuasiveness had little trouble gaining entrance. At Cumberland the two men worked out a much grander and more elaborate plan whereby troops from throughout the department would come flowing to Averell's support. Unlike the November expedition, which had only one supporting column, this raid was to have four, each with the responsibility of confusing the Confederates and diverting their attention from Averell's main strike force.[7]

And the intended area of operations certainly contained enough enemy troops, despite Kelley's boast to the contrary, to give Averell a hard time, if not destroy him altogether. In September, Jones' authority had been extended into eastern Tennessee, and accordingly, his command was now called the Department of Southwestern Virginia and East Tennessee, the troops therein constituting the army of the same name. A major portion of that "army" was Robert Ransom's makeshift division of about 7,000 men, who were now with Longstreet. Though much of his command had thus been sent to Knoxville, as Halleck correctly observed, Jones still had Echols' Brigade[8] on hand, whose 1,500 survivors of the Droop Mountain disaster had pulled themselves together and returned in defiance to the vicinity of Lewisburg. Also, at the Narrows on New River in Giles County, about thirty miles southwest of Union and within supporting distance of Echols, Jones had Colonel John McCausland's brigade of about 1,700 men.[9] And finally, Jones had Colonel Jackson, who was at Warm Springs with about 600 men, with another 350 or so on detached duty at Mill Point and near Huntersville in Pocahontas County.[10] Thus, despite Droop Mountain, Jones had virtually reestablished the status quo in and around the Greenbrier Valley—Echols had returned to Lewisburg and Jackson had more or less reoccupied the Huntersville Line.

But that was not all. Outside of Jones' authority, but within striking distance of Averell's intended line of march, was the commander of the Valley District, General John D. Imboden, who had his Northwest Brigade of more than 1,500 men at Krautzer's Spring, five miles north of Harrisonburg in the Shenandoah.[11] Moreover, an untold number of Lee's troops were expected to be wintering soon somewhere in the same valley.[12] All in all, Averell had good reason to fear for the safety of his command, and with justifiable concern did he hope for as much support as he could get.

Under the new plan, diversion and protection would come from nearly every direction; Averell's back and both flanks were to be covered. Watching his right, as he rode south, would be a column from the Kanawha, marching 100 miles to confront Echols' brigade at Lewisburg. To prevent the enemy from coming out of the Shenandoah on Averell's left, another column would march up the valley from Harper's Ferry and threaten the vital Confederate supply base at Staunton. And to protect Averell's back, a force from Beverly would descend on Marlin's Bottom (present day Marlinton, the county seat of Pocahontas), while another would march east to Monterey to both keep an eye on Jackson and pose an additional threat to Staunton. Finally, the planners agreed that the target of the expedition would be either Bonsack's or Salem, preferably both. Information from various reliable sources indicated that the Confederates had accumulated at these places a huge cache of supplies destined for Longstreet's troops, and thus in hitting these spots, fifty miles west of Lynchburg, Averell would not only be cutting Longstreet's main communication line, he would also destroy perhaps several days' of his supplies.[13]

Thus in one day had the scope of the plan evolved from a simple, daring raid executed by a single column, to a major complex operation involving five separate commands. Yet, in the end, Averell would rely very little on these supports, and a great deal on the courage and determination of his own men, the speed of their movements, his own wits and sheer good fortune. Thus, in a sense, the execution of the plan would ironically revert to Kelley's original simplistic version, and in so doing become one of the most spectacular raids of its kind in the entire war.

2. The First Half—New Creek to Monterey

"If my plans and orders are promptly and faithfully executed," Kelley confidently wired Halleck on the eighth, "I hope to accomplish important results. It will certainly cut off all communications by railroad and telegraph between Lee and Longstreet."[14]

Ironically, by the time Kelley sent that wire to Washington, the siege of Knoxville had been over for four days. Longstreet had broken it off on 4 December when he learned that Bragg had been beaten and driven back into Georgia and that a Federal army under William T. Sherman was advancing from Chattanooga to the relief of Knoxville. Unable to reunite with Bragg, Longstreet swung around north of Knoxville and marched to Rogersville in northeast Tennessee near the Virginia border and went into winter quarters. But there he still relied on the Virginia & Tennessee Railroad,[15] which meant that Averell still had a chance to deliver a serious blow by destroying a substantial amount of Longstreet's supplies while also cutting him off from Richmond and Lee's army, thereby making it difficult to either reinforce him in Tennessee or bring him back to Virginia.

Crucial to the success of that chance would be the coordination of the support-column movements to the timing of Averell's advance. On the morning of 8 December, after only a single day of preparation, all but one of the various movements began. Leading a brigade of about 1,000 men of all arms from his own Third Division,[16] Major General Eliakim P. Scammon pulled out of Charleston and headed east on the James River pike. His instructions called for him to double his strength by picking up two more infantry regiments[17] on the tenth at Sewell Mountain that had come in from Fayette County, then seize Lewisburg on 12 December and remain there until the eighteenth, taking every opportunity in the interim to deceive and detain the enemy by making forays south toward Union.[18]

From Beverly forty-nine-year-old Colonel Augustus Moor, a native of Leipzig in Saxony,[19] started south with Averell's infantry, the 10th West Virginia (Col. Thomas M. Harris) and his own 28th Ohio, perhaps a thousand men altogether. They were to reach Marlin's Bottom on the eleventh, go on to Frankfort the next day and remain in the vicinity until the eighteenth, then return, bringing off the wounded left behind after the battle of Droop Mountain.[20]

Also leaving Beverly on the morning of the eighth was Colonel Joseph Thoburn with about 700 infantry.[21] He was to march east to a rendezvous with Averell at Petersburg, go south with him as far as Monterey, then hold there until Averell's return, all the while watching his train and posing threats to Staunton.[22]

The Shenandoah movement would not begin until the tenth. At that time a brigade of infantry and cavalry under Colonel George D. Wells of Jeremiah Sullivan's First Division was to march south from Harper's Ferry and reach Strasburg on the twelfth. He was to hold there until the sixteenth, take Harrisonburg on the eighteenth, then move toward Staunton "and threaten the same boldly on the 20th and 21st."[23]

Basically then, each supporting column was to reach its menacing destination point by the twelfth and hold until the eighteenth, thereby giving Averell a ten to twelve day window of opportunity. "It was thought that between the two demonstrations of the Kanawha and Shenandoah forces," Averell explained of the plan he had helped devise, "I might pass the enemy's lines without delay, and that the threatening of Staunton on the 20th and 21st, with the operations in the direction of Union, would divert the enemy from offering any great resistance to the return of my fatigued command."[24]

Averell had all he could possibly ask for. Still, he remained apprehensive. On the eve of the raid he admitted to "many misgivings on account of our poor condition to overcome the weary distances and confront the perils incident to such an expedition."[25] But the "poor condition" of the command may have been a reflection of his careful, if not obsessive nature. "Averell is the most particular man for detail," Colonel David Strother of Kelley's staff wrote in his journal about what the 8th West Virginia's Colonel John Oley had told him back on 19 October, "and takes personally a rigid account of everything pertaining to his command, even to the horseshoe nails. The routine and discipline of his camp is most rigid and exact."[26]

Though seemingly in a questionable frame of mind for someone about to lead an important mission, Averell, his obsessive nature aside, was simply being a realist. An experienced, veteran "raider" now, he knew that, despite all the careful planning and the elaborate support, great risks remained. The distance alone—about 200 miles one way—was daunting. Those miles passed through rugged mountain country over tough roads and numerous deep, bridgeless streams. Along the way there was sure to be severe, punishing weather—mountain storms, sleet and snow, rain and floods. And even if all the diversionary movements succeeded in pulling the Confederates away from the strike force, there would remain one other deadly, merciless foe to contend with—the bushwhacker. Getting through all this without a hitch would be nearly impossible. Averell knew this would be a highly dangerous undertaking requiring a grueling test of endurance and skill.

The return for 30 November put the strength of Averell's brigade at 3,663 men present for duty.[27] Almost two-thirds of that number, the mounted portion, would be going on this mission.[28] With mobility being the crucial element of almost any raid, this would be a rather large strike force, but such numbers were deemed necessary to accomplish all that was to be done. The strike force included the 2nd West Virginia Mounted Infantry under Lieutenant Colonel Alexander Scott, the 3rd West Virginia Mounted Infantry under Lieutenant Colonel Francis W. Thompson, the 8th West Virginia Mounted Infantry under Colonel John H. Oley, the 14th Pennsylvania Cavalry under Lieutenant Colonel William Blakely, Major Thomas M. Gibson's Independent Cavalry Battalion, the four guns of Captain Chatham T. Ewing's Battery G, 1st West Virginia Light Artillery, and about 120 wagons and ambulances.[29]

Unlike the 2nd, 3rd, and 8th West Virginia, which had all been organized within months of the firing on Fort Sumter, the 14th Pennsylvania Cavalry did not come into being until the second summer of the war. The new command was originally intended to be a battalion of five companies, but so many volunteers poured in—from Philadelphia and the counties of Alleghany, Armstrong, Erie, Lawrence, Warren, and Washington—that it quickly grew into a regiment of twelve companies. Under the command of twenty-year-old James Schoonmaker, possibly the youngest colonel in the army, the 14th completed its organization in November 1862, and the following month it was sent to Harper's Ferry. It remained there on outpost duty until the following May, when it was sent to Grafton to become a member of the Fourth Separate Brigade. The regiment's first real combat came at Rocky Gap, where it lost just over a hundred men while stubbornly holding Averell's right flank. In a more limited role at Droop Mountain the command performed well in holding the left

**Col. John H. Oley,
7th W.Va. Cav. (8th W.Va. Mtd. Inf.)**

Massachusetts Commandery, Military
Order of the Loyal Legion and the US Army Military History Institute

**Col. John H. Oley and Staff,
8th W.Va. Mtd. Inf. (7th W.Va. Cav.)**

Boyd B. Stutler Collection, West Virginia State Archives

flank. All in all, the 14th Pennsylvania was now an excellent outfit of seasoned veterans, though Schoonmaker, their young colonel, had fallen ill, leaving command of the regiment on this raid to Lieutenant Colonel William Blakely.[30]

Blakely's former comrade in the 14th, twenty-one-year-old Major Thomas Gibson, a native of Alleghany County, Pennsylvania, commanded the brigade's Independent Cavalry Battalion. It consisted of three companies—E, H, and I—of the 3rd West Virginia Cavalry, Company A of the 1st West Virginia Cavalry, Company C—the "Chicago Dragoons"—of the 16th Illinois Cavalry, and, from Cincinnati, the 3rd Independent Cavalry Company of Ohio. Such an odd mix reflected the haphazard manner in which cavalry companies had been strewn about western Virginia early in the war, these six finally being grouped as a remedy into a battalion early in the summer of 1863. Prior to this all the companies had seen hard service on outpost duty fighting bushwhackers and guerrillas, and later the battalion gave a good account of itself at both Rocky Gap and Droop Mountain. Of the battalion's leader, Major Gibson, it was said he had "inherited the Irish courage and daring," and as a recent graduate of Pittsburgh's Western University, he was considered by some observers to be "a gentleman of culture and ability." He had at first served as a major in the 2nd (West) Virginia but upon the formation of the 14th Pennsylvania he transferred to that regiment, and the following summer he gladly accepted the challenge when command of the Independent Battalion was offered to him.[31]

Averell's artillery on this raid consisted of the four guns of Battery G, 1st West Virginia Light Artillery. The battery boasted an unusual beginning, in that it had been formed out of the 2nd West Virginia's Company G. Originally organized in Pittsburgh as an infantry company, the men of the "Plummer Guards" found their true calling nearly a year later, in the spring of 1862, when they displayed surprising proficiency at handling some old brass six-pounders that had been left in their care, a proficiency that led to the conversion of the men into cannoneers. Though separated from the 2nd, the new battery remained close to its parent regiment, participating with it in both the Shenandoah and Second Bull Run campaigns, then doing good work at Rocky Gap and Droop Mountain. Commanding the battery was the same man who had led it when it was a company of infantry, twenty-four-year-old Captain Chatham T. Ewing. Having just passed the bar exam in early 1861, Ewing had barely enough time to begin his law practice in Pittsburgh when the war broke out. As a captain of infantry and later of artillery, he had gained the respect of his men, many of whom regarded him as "a splendid officer and a gentleman of culture." At Rocky Gap Ewing took a severe wound in the leg and was captured. He was fortunate enough, however, to be exchanged about a month later, and after a brief furlough he returned to duty and was now generally credited with having the battery "in great condition and well prepared."[32]

Such, then, was the makeup of the splendid command Averell would lead on this raid. And though that command did have deficiencies—the West Virginia troops, for example, still carried the out-of-date muzzle loading Enfield musket, and the command in general still lacked horseshoes and nails—the men possessed one other asset of inestimable value: confidence. Complete confidence, in themselves and in "Fighting Billy," as many now reverentially referred to their commander.[33] This asset could measure up to almost any challenge and they knew it. That, more than anything, made them ready. "This was a command of veterans," boasted the 8th West Virginia's Captain Jacob M. Rife, "[that] had made two successful raids before; had met the enemy in numerous skirmishes and cavalry battles, and had made the name of Averell and his raiders both famous and to be feared in all Western Virginia from the Virginia & Tennessee Railroad to the Ohio River."[34]

Moreover, the officers and men of the command were now tough, experienced, well-trained veterans possessed of invaluable qualities necessary for dealing with the dangers and uncertainties of a long raid into enemy territory. Those qualities included an "enduring spirit," crucial skills of adaptability, and an implicit faith in their commander, who had molded them into an efficient, unified team capable of performing their work with deadliness and precision.

From Cumberland, meanwhile, Averell returned to New Creek on the seventh and issued orders to the effect that the command would move out the next morning. Such short notice was indicative not only of the urgency of the situation but of the desire to maintain secrecy and squelch the spread of rumors. The men, however, probably had little trouble figuring out that since only the mounted portion was going, they were to complete the work left unfinished after Droop Mountain. They spent the rest of the day in a beehive of activity, putting their gear in order, stocking rations, drawing ammunition, examining weapons, grooming and outfitting their mounts.[35]

That evening, with preparations efficiently completed (save for the shoeing of the horses) and with a little time on their hands, the men were granted those few precious moments of quiet contemplation that in these pre-raid hours naturally led to considerations of the possible dangers that lay ahead. Such considerations invariably turned many a heart and mind toward home and loved ones. Around campfires that night or beside a candle in the pre-dawn hours of the next morning, pencil and paper met to record thoughts and feelings that for many a family would be the last word from their soldier son, brother, or husband. The men obviously found it very comforting to write home by way of remaining connected with what, in the end, really mattered to them. But they also took pencil in hand to provide comfort to those who might be worried, to assure them, among other things, that although, in accordance with the feelings of young men everywhere, they did not expect to die, they were prepared to make the supreme sacrifice for a cause they believed was right and just.

Thirty-two-year-old Lieutenant Colonel John Polsley, second in command of the 8th West Virginia, sought to comfort his wife by assuring her, "It is not expected that we will have any or much fighting this trip." But his tender letter went on to express another concern that had been troubling him for some time. The lieutenant colonel had been a sad witness to the anguish suffered by the widow of the 14th Pennsylvania's Major John McNally, killed at Rocky Gap in August and left in the hands of the enemy during one of the many desperate and futile cavalry charges Averell had ordered to break the Confederate center. Upon learning of her husband's fate, Mrs. McNally came down from Pennsylvania and spent three traumatic weeks at Beverly in the vain hope of passing through the lines to claim his remains. Polsley wished to spare his own wife from such an agonizing ordeal. "Do not come to camp to find out what has become of me," he pleaded with her, should he fall, one way or another, into the hands of the enemy. The plea would turn out to be prophetic, for Polsley would not return from "this trip." (Polsley did not limit his letter to the theme of comfort. He used the occasion to express resentment of his superior officer, Colonel Oley. Though forced by a severe toothache to miss November's Lewisburg expedition, Polsley somehow got it in his head that Oley had shown cowardice at Droop Mountain by refusing to order the 8th W.Va. forward at a critical moment. Consumed with bitterness, Polsley now wrote his wife that many men in the 8th would consider reenlisting only if he—Polsley—were in command of the regiment. "Officers that I thought were perfectly blind to his [Oley's] faults have expressed themselves to me in this way." Although those "faults" went unsubstantiated, Polsley and Oley remained bitter rivals, and on this march they would often ride at opposite ends of the regiment.)[36]

At 6 a.m. on the morning of the eighth, the rousing yet distressing sound of reveille broke the predawn silence and called out for the men to take their place in history. Having made sure the command had been supplied with enough ammunition to provide each man with 150 rounds,[37] Averell left his acting inspector general, the 10th West Virginia's Major Theodore Lang, in command at New Creek[38] (which would essentially be defenseless, save for a few dismounted troops left behind from the 14 Pa. Cav.). With the 14th Pennsylvania Cavalry in the lead carrying seven-shooter carbines,[39] Averell pulled out an hour later on a deceptively "beautiful and bright" morning that many men thought was more characteristic of October than December.[40] The fine weather reflected the high spirits of everyone in the column. "The officers, men and horses," proclaimed Captain Rife, "looked fresh and eager for whatever the days might bring."[41] Private William Slease of the 14th Pennsylvania would have fully agreed. The men and animals, he believed, "looked well and were eager for the fray, the skirmish, the charge or whatever the next few days and nights might bring . . . The boys were all in fine spirits, ready to chase a thousand or be chased by the thousand, ready to empty the saddles of the enemy or have their own emptied by the enemy." Then he added a touch of foreboding: "It was a merciful Providence that veiled the future, else many a brave, loyal heart might have quailed."[42]

For maximum protection and safety while moving through enemy territory, it was essential for the command to stay closed-up, marching in column down a single road. At the head or "point" of the column rode numerous "scouts," who prowled several miles to the front, or on the flanks, in search of potential danger and useful information. Averell sometimes allowed his scouts to disguise themselves in civilian or even Confederate clothing, though capture in such garb could mean execution as a spy. Behind the scouts came the advance guard, perhaps a half mile to a mile in front of the main column. Averell preferred to give this assignment to a single small company. The main purpose of the advance guard was to absorb any nasty surprises before they reached the main column. Thus being so stressful, this duty was rotated among different companies, usually on a daily basis. Likewise with the rear guard, whose one or two companies had the similar responsibility of preventing the column from being surprised from behind. Unless there was an urgent need for him elsewhere, Averell, with his staff, aides, and couriers, generally rode in the center of the main column, along with the battery of artillery. The wagons and ambulances usually traveled in the center as well, but on this expedition Averell assigned them to the regiment bringing up the rear of the main column. He apparently did this in order to enable the entire column to move out on the double in the event of an emergency.

On good roads in flat terrain such a column could average between three and four miles per hour. The usual pace was a sustained walking gait, though that tedium was occasionally broken by a trot or even a brief gallop. To give the animals some relief, Averell occasionally had the men dismount and walk, or, time permitting, he allowed a few minutes of complete rest every hour or two.[43]

Riding down along Patterson's Creek (south 7 miles on current U.S. 220, then east 6 miles on the same route to Burlington, then south on county road 11 following Patterson's Creek), the column moved slowly, despite the fair weather.[44] "Constant exertions were made to complete the shoeing of the horses," Averell subsequently complained.[45] But the good roads—another deceptive opening feature of the campaign—enabled the shoeing-on-the-run command to make eighteen miles that day. They stopped about seven miles north of Williamsport. (Throughout the expedition Averell would always try to secure what he considered were the three essentials of a cavalry camp: wood, water, grass.)[46] In camp that night, Corporal George Washington Ordner of the 2nd West Virginia took out his small, leather-bound diary and made a simple entry: "We are on a raid."[47] Over in Gibson's battalion Lieutenant N.N. Hoffman scribbled in his diary,

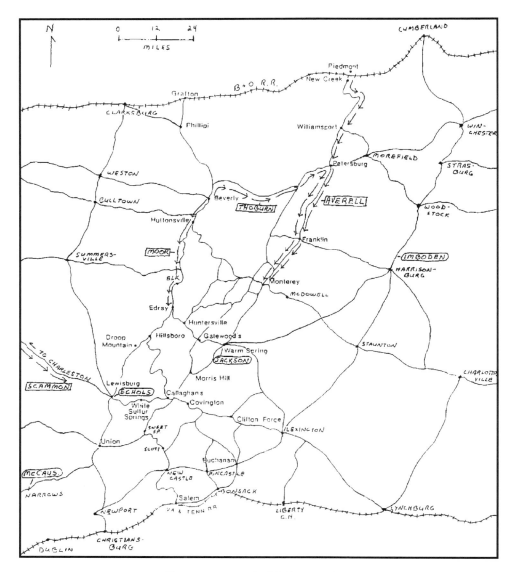

Movements, 8–11 December

Compiled from *Official Records Atlas*, Plate 135c, No. 1. Stephen Z. Starr,
The Union Cavalry in the Civil War. Author's notes.

"we put all our blacksmiths to work to shoe up some of our horses," and he later added, "the forges were kept going all night."[48]

The next day, after reveille sounded at daybreak and the order "forward" rang out an hour later, about 7 a.m.,[49] the command, having finished most of the shoeing, picked up the pace and made twenty-four miles to ride into Petersburg at around three-thirty that afternoon (9th). Shortly afterwards Colonel Thoburn came in from Beverly.[50]

Averell was now beyond his own outposts, the ones he had thrown out around New Creek, and he had come within range of the usually active rebel scouts. Yet, strangely, there hadn't been the slightest sign of enemy activity. The rebs, evidently not expecting any action this time of year, seemed to have retired to their distant camps.

Averell and Thoburn set out from Petersburg at 5 a.m. on the tenth. With the early start, Averell's men made very good time, marching thirty-two miles that day before going into camp near Franklin.[51] Now, already, everyone agreed that they were in enemy territory, for Pendleton County was overwhelmingly Confederate in sympathy. "The citizens looked daggers at us," Lieutenant Hoffman observed. From now on the men would have to be extra diligent, the stress of which, however, they frequently found ways of off setting. "We squatted on the farm of a rich old man of strong rebel proclivities," Hoffman noted in his diary that night, "and corn, hay, sheep, geese, ducks, chickens, cabbage, 'taters, and 'other feathered insects' were pressed into service with a rush."[52] Notwithstanding these compensations, while on picket that night, twenty-one-year-old Corporal Benjamin Starr, Company K, 3rd West Virginia, became the expedition's first casualty when a bushwhacker shot him in the leg.[53]

From Franklin the march resumed at 4 a.m. the next morning (11th), on a day that brought with it another harbinger of misfortune—the temperature plummeted and the fair weather turned bitterly cold. Nonetheless, the combined commands marched twenty-three miles to reach Monterey around 3 p.m.[54]

3. Monterey to Callaghan's (12–14 Dec.)

So far, so good. The first four days had been relatively easy. At Monterey Averell, having marched ninety-eight miles, stood near the approximate half-way point between New Creek and the Confederate railroad. Now he prepared for the swift execution of the second half of his advance by ordering a general shakedown of the brigade. The dangers from now on would be increasing every day, every hour; the command could not afford any unnecessary encumbrances. The column would have to march in the lightest possible order. Captains, lieutenants and sergeants hustled through their outfits, urging the men to keep their saddle loads extremely simple, consisting of no more than a few camp utensils, saddle bags, extra horse shoes and nails, grooming tackle, and ammunition. "Here we stripped ourselves for the race," one soldier characterized the shake-down.[55] Moreover, the weak and disabled of the command were weeded out. "All men and officers unfit for severe duty were sent back to New Creek," recalled Private Frank Reader.[56]

Francis Smith Reader, whose observations will figure prominently in these pages, had been born near Pittsburgh in 1842. A farmer by trade and teacher by profession, "Frank" eagerly sought to enlist at the war's out-break, only to discover, like so many others in the Pittsburgh area, that there was no room for him in the quota-filled inn. And like so many of those fervently patriotic Pennsylvanians, he found his way over to Wheeling, where he joined what became Company I of the 2nd West Virginia. Because of his education and writing skills, he later became a clerk at Averell's head-quarters.[57] Now at Monterey, Reader quickly passed inspection and pre-pared to move out on the second half of the strike south.

Weeded out from the column were those who had succumbed to the chilling temperatures and come down with severe colds or other respira-tory ailments, as were those with intestinal disorders and "saddle galls." "Only well-mounted men who were able bodied went on," declared Captain Rife.[58] How many men were sent back is uncertain, but the number could not have been great; most would have considered it a disgrace and were eager to prove themselves fit to continue. About 2,500 men won the honor to go on.[59]

The train, too, was "stripped." The horses, some 3,000, received the last of the forage and would henceforth subsist entirely off the country; the men were left with just enough rations to supposedly last until the return to Monterey. Only the most essential items were kept, and they were crammed into just a few wagons that, with a handful of ambulances, would comprise a train of only about thirty-five vehicles. The remaining eighty-five or so were given over to Thoburn's care.[60] Still, thirty-five wagons was a signifi-cant number that could eventually drag the column down to a dangerously slow speed. Most raiding columns went without any wagons whatsoever, preferring instead to live off the land and carry their ammunition on swift pack animals. But Averell's men would be going into a rough mountain wilderness that, for the most part, could provide little sustenance. More-over, the men would need tents if they hoped to survive the bitterly cold nights in the mountains. The wagons were deemed necessary—and they would cause serious problems.

"Stripped," trim and eager, the command in a few hours was ready to move on—"where, we did not know," Rife speculated, "possibly to death, certainly to danger and suffering . . ."[61] With the 14th Pennsylvania again in the lead,[62] the column pulled out of Monterey at 5 a.m. the next morning (12th)[63]—though not before the dreaded bushwhacker had struck again. Sometime during the night three men of the 3rd West Virginia were shot while on picket.[64]

Thoburn set out on the Parkersburg pike for McDowell, ten miles to the east. Averell took the main road (present day U.S. 220) south. His men, still in excellent spirits, moved quickly down the firm, dry road. At Bulltown (present day Vanderpool), four miles south of Monterey, Averell surprised them. Instead of continuing on south for Warm Springs, as they expected, he turned off the main road onto a country lane heading west (present day Va. 84).[65] He had made an important tactical decision.

Though he knew speed was crucial to the success of the mission, and at Monterey the command had accordingly been "stripped for the race," he also believed the formula for success included one other absolute necessity—stealth. The longer he avoided detection by the enemy, he reasoned, the greater his chance for sneaking into their den unharmed. For that chance, Averell chose to sacrifice some speed by avoiding the main roads and following obscure paths and hidden country lanes.[66] A calculated risk, to be sure, not only because of the lost speed, but because Averell, to make his way, would need to rely heavily on the cooperation of local citizens. This last, however, was not such an unknown quantity. From the previous raids through this country, he had learned that there were many loyal citizens "willing to give us information about the roads, mountains, streams and bridges. . . ."[67] And so at Steward Station, three miles west of Bulltown, Averell turned south again and headed down Back Creek (Va. 84 to current county road 600), into the wilderness.[68]

Almost immediately, it seemed he had made the wrong choice. Around 10 a.m. that morning (12th) it began to rain—a cold, hard, steady rain mixed with sleet and snow.[69] It marked the beginning of a week of heavy intermittent downpours that would cause the worst flooding these mountains had known for decades.[70] The poorly maintained country lane turned into thick mud, the streams began to swell, and the men became wet, cold and miserable. "It rained steadily and had become intensely cold," Frank Reader subsequently declared, "the wind blew hard from the north, and snow and sleet, and the elements, air and water, seemed to be against us."[71]

"The temperature had fallen," recalled Captain Rife, "the wind blew a gale from the north, and from the dense clouds a storm of rain, sleet and snow pounded down upon us. . . ."[72] That night the cold, wet command camped beside Back Creek near the Ruckman farm.[73]

For two agonizing days the men put up with this, during which their wilderness trek forced them to wade across icy, swollen Back Creek a total of thirteen times.[74] Moreover, at two of these crossings bushwhackers took occasion to peck away at the column, apparently with no effect except for the added stress placed on the men.[75] Under conditions that would make even the most ardent soldier grumble, the column made only thirty-three miles in those two days. In the evening of the thirteenth, Averell brought them safely into the tiny hamlet known as Gatewood's.[76]

Six days into the mission now, and, incredibly, they had been undisturbed, aside from bushwhackers, and, as far as anyone knew, undetected by the enemy. Thus despite the miserable, harsh weather and the suffering it had caused, Averell's side-lane gamble seemed to be paying off.

But the rebels knew something was up. Imboden, for one, had gotten wind of Averell's movement around 7 a.m. on the tenth. It seems a Miss Sallie Cunningham, an "enthusiastic Confederate" and a "beautiful and accomplished" young lady from one of the wealthiest families in Hardy County, had been visiting friends in Petersburg when Averell's men rode into town back on the ninth. Realizing the Yankees were making a significant move of some kind, she sneaked out of town on horseback and rode fourteen miles to Morefield, where she turned her mount over to a convalescing rebel soldier and sent him on to Imboden's camp near Harrisonburg. Imboden, astonished at the news, assumed Averell was headed for Staunton, and immediately set his own horsemen riding south in that direction.[77]

And at Warm Springs Colonel Jackson, too, knew the Federals were on the move. When he learned of the strength of the Federal column that was coming down from Petersburg, however, he decided to step aside and let it pass, much as he had done the previous August. To prevent his detachments in Pocahontas County from being cut-off, he sent instructions on the twelfth for them to proceed at once for Warm Springs.[78]

Thus it was part of the Marlin's Bottom detachment (Capt. Jacob W. Marshall's Co. I, 19 Va. Cav.), moving east on the Huntersville road, that Averell's pickets, men of the 14th Pennsylvania, caught sight of outside Gatewood's on the morning of the fourteenth. The pickets opened fire, scattering the surprised rebels. The Pennsylvanians gave chase and captured a handful of rebs before the rest got away (compelling Marshall to fall back into the mountains and remain isolated there for two more days). They left behind, however, four wagons loaded with ammunition and commissary— Averell's first trophies of the expedition.[79]

But along with the trophies came the anxiety of knowing that this encounter had to mean the rebels were now aware of the column's location. Under this reasonable assumption, Averell returned speed and vigilance to the top of his list of priorities. Going back on the main road, he pulled out of Gatewood's on the fourteenth and continued heading south.

Nature, however, seemed to be a vicious ally of the enemy. That wretched, cursed cold rain that had begun two days before, refused to let up. Despite their rubber ponchos, the men were getting drenched. In such wretched conditions, a cold soaking could be extremely dangerous to one's health. And the men were catching it from above and below. Thirteen times they had had to cross Back Creek, usually getting wet up to their knees. Now, below Gatewood's, they had to face swollen Jackson River, which soaked them up to their armpits. Mild hypothermia, whereby the core body temperature drops below ninety-five degrees Fahrenheit, was starting to be a problem, leaving men exhausted after intense bouts of shivering. Signs of frostbite started showing up, too, along with complaints about painful, swollen feet. But the men endured, pressed on and made twenty-two miles

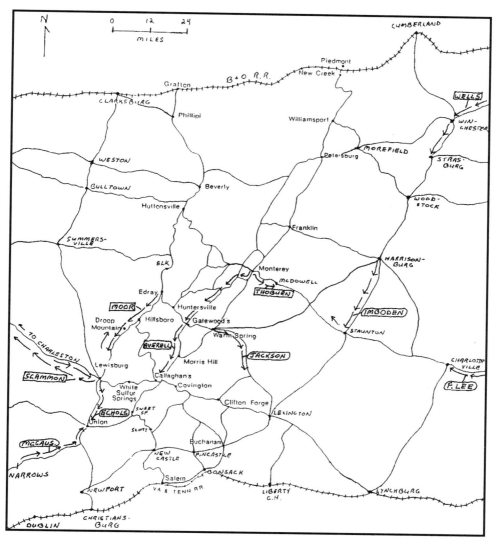

Movements, 12–14 December

Compiled from *Official Records Atlas*, Plate 135c, No. 1. Stephen Z. Starr,
The Union Cavalry in the Civil War. Author's notes.

to reach Callaghan's around 4 p.m. that afternoon (14th). Strangely, they had seen no further sign of the enemy—something must be keeping him busy elsewhere.[80]

4. Callaghan's to Potts' Mountain (15–16 Dec.)

The overall plan was working, almost to perfection. At Callaghan's that afternoon (14th) couriers brought Averell the welcome news that Scammon had taken Lewisburg on the twelfth, as planned, and that Echols had retired south toward Union.[81] This most reassuring information did much to put Averell's mind at ease.

The Confederates hadn't put up a fight for Lewisburg because Jones (at his headquarters in Dublin, about 45 miles south of Union on the Va. & Tenn. RR and sight of the New River bridge) had instructed Echols not to risk his small command against so large a force. Besides, Jones reasoned, the Federals were probably just making another temporary foray. "Their late raid," he had written Echols concerning Averell's November expedition, "shows how reluctantly they venture into this country."[82]

Virginia-born forty-four-year-old Samuel Jones, a West Point graduate of 1841, had spent nearly his entire military career in the artillery, his crowning achievement coming as Beauregard's chief of artillery at the glorious victory of First Manassas. His promising career broke down, however, when his stubbornness, jealousy, and reluctance to cooperate by sharing his own troops led to removal from field command and reassignment to various administrative posts. He landed the Department of Western Virginia on 25 November 1862. But his old stubbornness persisted, leading to frequent arguments with Lee over troops loaned to him in Virginia and to Longstreet in Tennessee.[83] Now, in addition to pleading with Richmond for reinforcements and pestering Lee for the return of his troops, Jones planned to deal with Scammon by bringing up McCausland from the Narrows to a rendezvous with Echols at Pickaway, four miles north of Union. He would hold the two there in good defensive positions should the Federals "venture" beyond Lewisburg. But, largely because of the success of Averell's side-lane gamble, Jones did not yet know that another Federal column had advanced south of Monterey.[84]

But despite the pay-off of that gamble so far, and the good news from Lewisburg, Averell remained uneasy. For although the right flank now seemed secure with Echols' retreat south, there had been no word from the Shenandoah. He interpreted this to mean that the expedition had reached a major crossroads. His orders called for him to strike at Bonsacks or Salem, preferably both. If he still intended to hit Bonsacks, he would have to turn southeast now toward Covington and Fincastle. But he didn't know what was out there. He did know that, with Echols' retreat south, the way had been cleared on his right. He thus chose to bear right, march south down Dunlaps Creek and make for Salem.[85]

Uncertain, then, about the threat to his left, Averell decided to toss the rebels a bit of confusion in that direction. Shortly after 4 p.m. he sent about 200 men riding east out of Callaghan's on a "false advance" toward Covington, the idea being, of course, to create the impression the expedition was headed that way. The remainder of the command rested and waited until the 200, having completed their mission without mishap, sneaked back into Callaghan's after dark, around 8 p.m.[86]

The "false advance" made up the first part of the new deceptive measures Averell adopted for the final drive to Salem. The second part was the return to stealth—a different stealth, not found on country lanes, but in pushing the column on through the night. This was very risky, not only because of the additional strain placed on the men and their mounts, but because of the near impossibility of sustaining a cohesive movement in total darkness. Going deeper and deeper into enemy territory, it became ever more essential to keep the command together. But Averell obviously believed the risks were worth it, and, just as obvious, he had great faith in the ability of his men to overcome those risks. He also knew this was no time to relax and get careless. Their good fortune thus far, despite the harsh weather, could run out at any time—nothing must be taken for granted. With the prize finally starting to loom up before him, Averell became infused with an extra sense of urgency—to move quickly now, and "push forward day and night."[87]

After giving the command, especially the 200 who had ridden toward Covington, some additional time to prepare, Averell pulled out of Callaghan's at 2 a.m. on the fifteenth and continued south on the Sweet Springs road (present Va. 159) following Dunlap's Creek,[88] a twenty-five-mile-long stream that enters Jackson River at Covington. Though the rain had mercifully stopped to finally grant the men some relief from that misery, the rough road, the night's intense darkness and the bitterly cold air made the going slow and difficult nonetheless. Eight hours they plodded on before Averell at last allowed them, around 10 a.m., to stop. They advanced twenty-one miles in that time.[89]

They had reached Sweet Springs at the intersection of the road (Va. 311) with the Kanawha pike, which led to White Sulphur Springs about twenty miles to the northwest, and they were now in the lush valley of the Sweet Sulphur. Averell granted a two-hour pause to allow his cold, sleepless and increasingly hungry men and their tired mounts to prepare for the ascent of Sweet Springs Mountain, the first of four alpine barriers between themselves and Salem. While the horses took advantage "of the plentiful forage found there," the men enjoyed a meager breakfast of dry hardtack and black coffee. According to Lieutenant Hoffman, they "also laid in a lot of tobacco, an article that the men were particularly short of."[90]

While the men and their mounts were thus refreshing themselves, Averell received some astonishing news. Word came in that Scammon, instead of holding Lewisburg until the eighteenth as planned, had already

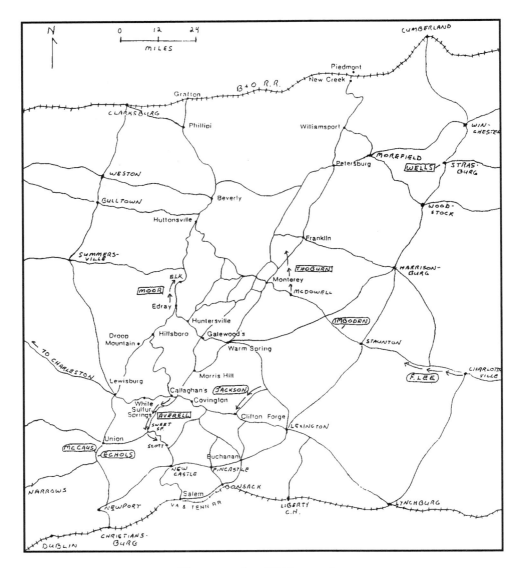

Movements, 15 December

Compiled from *Official Records Atlas*, Plate 135c, No. 1. Stephen Z. Starr, *The Union Cavalry in the Civil War*. Author's notes.

withdrawn. This meant that Echols, only about fifteen miles west at Pickaway, was now free to turn his attention elsewhere. Averell was not only alarmed, he was outraged.[91]

Eliakim Parker Scammon, a forty-seven-year-old native of Maine, had been a teacher before the war. That profession, however, he had entered into very reluctantly upon the collapse of his first career choice. His nineteen years in the military came to an abrupt end when he was cashiered from the service in 1856 for disobeying an order while serving on the western frontier. Jumping at the chance the Civil War provided to revive that career, he reentered the army and promptly rose from Colonel of the 23rd Ohio to command of the Third Division of the Department of West Virginia. But now as he marched his command back along the James River pike toward Charleston, he was definitely jeopardizing that revival by once again disobeying his superiors.[92]

Scammon had simply lost his nerve. After dutifully taking Lewisburg on the twelfth, he had done little to pursue, harass or come to grips with the southward fleeing Echols. He merely sat and waited, getting more nervous by the hour as he did so. Working on his composure was an unwarranted concern for the safety of Charleston, his fear of guerrilla activity in his rear, and the grumbling of his men over the lack of food (their supply train had been left at Meadow Bluff).[93] The final straw came the next day (13th) when he learned that two Confederate regiments (McCausland's 36th and 60th Va.) were coming up from the Narrows to reinforce Echols. At 2 p.m. Scammon pulled out and beat a hasty retreat westward, having held Lewisburg for only twenty-four hours. At that time, Averell was at Gatewood's, a very long eighty-seven miles from Salem. His right flank was now dangerously exposed.[94]

But that was not all. Scammon's premature exit had undercut Averell's support in the center. With the 10th West Virginia Infantry and the 28th Ohio Infantry, the German-born Colonel Moor had reached the vicinity of Frankfort on the thirteenth as planned, having made good time, about sixty miles, with little resistance from the enemy (Moor's pickets skirmished briefly with Captain Marshall's Co. I, 19 Va. Cav. on the night of the 11th at Marlin's Bottom, and with the companies of William McNeel and Edmund Jarvis at Mill Point on the 12th). That night Moor sent couriers to open communications with Scammon at Lewisburg, but their return early the next morning (4 a.m. on the 14th) with the startling news that Scammon was gone, left him bewildered about what to do next. He finally concluded that his own mission had been seriously compromised and, with Scammon gone, he felt isolated and exposed. Fearing the rebels might now blockade the roads in his rear and cut him off, he pulled out that morning (14th) and headed north. Carrying the wounded left behind after Droop Mountain, fulfilling that part of his mission at least, Moor would easily reach the safe confines of Beverly on the afternoon of the seventeenth.[95]

Thus while his men savored their brief rest period at Sweet Springs, Averell must have realized his mission had been placed in serious jeopardy. Though only about forty-five miles separated the command from Salem, Echols was now a mere fifteen miles to the west and would thus have plenty of time to get across the rear of the column and block its return. But if Averell considered turning back, he gave no indication of it to his men. Perhaps remembering what had happened to him after turning back from the Rapidan the previous April, his resolve stiffened; as if to cast aside the demon of overcaution that had plagued him in the past, he overcame and got beyond this critical psychological point in his road to redemption. At noon the command moved on—southward.[96]

An hour later they turned southeast onto the road to New Castle (still on Va. 311), and began the ascent of Sweet Springs Mountain. For days the men had been plunging downward, through numerous creek and river crossings. Now they had to start moving upward, climbing steep, rough mountains. The road to the top of Sweet Springs wound around for five tough miles, the temperature dropping dramatically as they climbed, but the summit graciously rewarded the men with stunning views of the surrounding countryside. "From the top of the mountain," Averell recorded, rather eloquently, "a sublime spectacle was presented to us. Seventy miles to the eastward the Peaks of Otter reared their summits above the Blue Ridge, and all the space between was filled with a billowing ocean of hills and mountains, while behind us the great Alleghanies, coming from the north with the grandeur of innumerable tints, swept past and faded in the southern horizon."[97]

Again, Averell allowed a brief rest. Again, word came in from the west—but this time the news was good. His scouts had captured and brought in a rebel quartermaster—who belonged to Echols' command. The man was quite possibly one A.W.G. Davis, a native of Kentucky and resident of Greenbrier County. Noted for his generosity, having once paid from his own pocket for needed supplies, Davis had adamantly refused to extend any such similar kindness to his captors when they demanded he give up his horse. "You can kill me," he told his new hosts, "but you can't make me walk." Having thus been allowed to ride into Averell's presence, Davis, who before his capture had evidently been prowling the area for supplies, now professed great astonishment at the presence of Yankees on Sweet Springs Mountain, an astonishment he guaranteed would be equally great in the mind of his commander, General Echols.[98]

It seemed preposterous, but it just might be possible Echols had no knowledge of the command's location. If so, Averell's "luck" was holding; his stealth was still working.

Though Averell did not know it at the time, his luck was holding elsewhere. His support in the Shenandoah was still in place and had not yet let him down.

On the tenth, two days after the start of everyone else, Colonel George D. Wells had left Harper's Ferry and Charlestown with about 1,800 men of all arms.[99] Shadowed but not hindered by the rebels, Wells reached Strasburg on the twelfth, his worst enemy being the cold rain that began the day before. Then, according to plan, he set up a strong defensive position, sent probes south toward Woodstock on the thirteenth and prepared to hold until the appointed time to threaten Staunton.[100]

Not knowing any of this, however, Averell had no assurances from any direction. With little choice but to assume he was on his own, he now resolved to push his men relentlessly, driving them as never before. He was becoming like a man possessed. If necessary to achieve success, he was prepared to demand that his men, and himself, go to the very limits of physical and mental endurance. Just before dark, probably around 4 p.m., he started them down the southeast side of Sweet Springs Mountain and began the ascent of Potts' Mountain.[101]

Sweet Springs, Potts' and the other nearby "spurs of the Alleghenies" were wild and rugged, with very few souls living among them. In these inhospitable regions the sight of a home was cause for comment among the soldiers, especially at night when the light from a mountain cabin would shine like a beacon in the void. Invariably, some of the soldiers would pay a visit to such a place, time permitting, if only out of curiosity.

One such visit came from the 8th West Virginia's Captain Jacob Rife, who, as Officer-of-the-Day, had just enough time to stop at a cabin somewhere between the summits of Sweet Springs and Potts', and "warm while the line was closing up." Rife found the couple inside, who were "sitting by the fire, [with] a number of children in bed at the other end of the room," to be a hospitable, friendly pair of "lively talkers" with a rough, almost primitive edge that comes with living in such isolation. Rife introduced himself and explained further that he was "a Yankee soldier from Ohio." Before the war the twenty-five-year-old Rife had been a mercantile clerk in his native Piketon, Ohio (after the war he would go into the ministry and become an itinerate preacher). Upon the first call for volunteers he had signed up with the three-month 18th Ohio, after which he joined the 8th (West) Virginia. Intelligent and hard working, he had worked his way up through the ranks, finally being appointed captain of Company A two months before the start of the Salem Raid. Despite a "halt" in his gait that had been caused by a horse falling on and breaking his right leg some three years before, the five-foot-nine-inch Rife, with gray eyes, a fair complexion and a sweeping moustache that joined his sideburns, presented a striking figure to these simple mountain-folk he now stood before. The husband seemed especially curious about the young captain's appearance, and asked him several questions about articles of his clothing and equipment. Finally, after further careful scrutiny, the man blurted out what was really on his mind—"Stranger, whar is your horns?" The wife, however, somehow possessed a much higher degree of sophistication than her husband, and with a thump to his shoulder she reminded him that Yankees were "human critters like the rest of us." Unamused by any of this, Rife came away convinced that "The ignorance of the average inhabitant of these mountains was appalling."[102]

Somewhere else in that wilderness area, between the two summits (probably on Potts Mountain), yet another cabin would receive a visit from Yankee "human critters." Riding a mile or so in front of the main column was the advance guard of about twenty men, who, in addition to leading the way this night (15th–16th), would take on an extra, unexpected duty. They had ridden off into "one of the darkest nights I ever saw," remembered their leader, twenty-one-year-old Quartermaster Sergeant Elias F. Seaman of the 2nd West Virginia.

As a steel-worker in the dungeonlike factories of Pittsburgh, Seaman saw the war not only as a patriotic calling, but as a chance to escape the drudgery of his existence. In the spring of '61 he was one of the first to show up at the recruiting office, but his then tender age and slight build caused him to be turned down by recruiters who had more than enough candidates to choose from to fill their Pennsylvania quotas. Hearing correctly that standards were not so high across the state line, he went to Wheeling and joined what became Company D of the 2nd West Virginia. As if to prove the recruiters in Pittsburgh wrong, Seaman worked extra hard as a soldier and by September of '63 he had risen in rank to become quartermaster sergeant of the entire regiment.[103]

Now on the cold night of 15–16 December he was leading a squad into a void so dark the men had to use extreme care to probe their way down the mountain. "Almost the only light we could see," Seaman declared, "was the sparks made by our horses' feet striking the rocks." After some time, however, another light appeared, emanating in the distance from the windows of a mountain cabin. Cautiously moving closer, the men could hear festive music "and the shuffling of feet in the dance." With two or three men (one of whom supposedly wore a Confederate uniform), Seaman crept up to the cabin and peered through a window. Inside he saw a wedding celebration with perhaps a couple dozen guests, including, Seaman quickly noted, a handful of rebel soldiers—one of whom was the groom. The sergeant motioned for the rest of the squad to come up and surround the cabin.

Capt. Jacob M. Rife, 8th W.Va.
National Tribune, 8 Sept. 1887

Then, with colts drawn, he and several men burst in. The festivities came to an abrupt, stone-faced halt. "You never saw a company more completely thunderstruck," Seaman declared. The sergeant then announced that the house was surrounded and the Confederate soldiers present were now prisoners of war. "Fall in line!" he barked.

In stunned disbelief, the rebels quietly filed out of the cabin. All except one. Lewis Scott, at home on furlough from a Virginia regiment, bolted out the back door, ran past the Yankees behind the cabin, and zigzagged down the mountain to successfully avoid a number of pot shots.[104]

The bride, meanwhile, Mary (Polly) nee Tucker, a stout but hand-some young woman, refused to let go of her new husband. "We have just been married, sir," she suddenly cried out, "and you are not going to take [John] away from me now, are you?" Though visibly touched by this pas-sionate plea, Seaman gently reminded her "that war was a sad thing, and that as soldiers there was nothing left for us but to do our duty." He went on to assure her, however, that her husband would be well treated, and he would probably be exchanged and be back with her in a few short months.

Resigned to their unhappy fate, the sorrowful young couple gave each other one last tender, sobbing embrace. "A silence had fallen upon us all," Seaman confessed, "and I saw many of the old weathered-stained men draw their sleeves quickly across their faces." But then, with the cabin cleared, the mood quickly changed and Seaman's ravenous comrades swooped down on the still-untouched wedding dinner and consumed ev-ery scrap, leaving "only some vinegar on the table."[105]

The story of John Starks, at whose home the wedding had taken place, and Mary became especially tragic when John, while traveling with Averell's column as a prisoner of war, was swept off his horse and drowned in one of the river crossings. Always feeling somewhat guilty about this, Seaman went back to the Potts' Mountain area in 1884 to find out, if pos-sible, what became of John's widow, Mary. To his dismay, he discovered that she still mourned for her lost bridegroom, and had not remarried.[106]

Starks was not the only member of the wedding party to meet a tragic end. In January 1865, Jacob Huffman, Company F of the Thirtieth Battal-ion of Virginia Sharpshooters, would die at Camp Chase of chronic diar-rhea. There was, however, at least one "happy" ending. Also taken prisoner was the reverend who had performed the ceremony, Andrew Jackson Elmore. He engineered a remarkable escape by feigning insanity. At one of the Craig's Creek crossings he commanded, Moseslike, the parting of the water to allow safe passage. With no desire to keep company with such a "lunatic," the Yankees promptly let Elmore go.[107]

The main column, meanwhile, safely made it down Sweet Springs Mountain that evening (15th), then climbed to the top of Potts' Mountain, arriving there about 9 p.m. Averell allowed another brief halt. They had gone seven more miles for a total of thirty-three since mounting up seven-teen hours ago at 2 a.m. in Callaghan's. They were now twelve miles short of New Castle and thirty-four shy of Salem.[108]

5. The Final Lunge

Still, there was no news from the Shenandoah. For all Averell knew, Imboden, Jackson or some other Confederate commander was rapidly closing in on him from the east. It was time for another "false advance"—to either learn something about the enemy, or deceive him as to the direction of the expedition. From the top of Potts' Mountain Averell sent a squadron riding east into the darkness toward Fincastle, about fifteen miles distant (on present county road 611). As before at Callaghan's, the rest of the command waited. In a short time, the squadron returned, bringing in sixty precious horses and a few locals suspected of bushwhacking, but there was no new information. The march resumed.[109]

At the tavern (a favorite stopping place for Southern visitors on their way to White Sulphur Springs to the west or to Fincastle in the east) of Elisa Scott, widow of Oliver Scott, on Barber's Creek, Averell acquired a new guide, a local farmer named William Paxton, whom the scouts had brought in as one of those suspected of bushwhacking. Paxton, however, not only proved his loyalty by producing a letter of endorsement written by four Massachusetts officers in gratitude for the hospitality he had shown them some months before, he agreed to help guide the column on to Salem.[110]

The command thus came down from Potts' Mountain, and around midnight passed through the small town of New Castle, the Craig County seat with a population of about 225, where Private Slease maintained "the boys found loads of Confederate money and carried it away in large quantities."[111] From New Castle the men pressed on into the early morning hours of the sixteenth.

With virtually no sleep now for more than thirty hours, and very little in the past few days, and with cold, frostbite, hypothermia and hunger tormenting them, the men and their mounts came under an increasingly severe, unbearable strain. "The exhaustion of the command began to show fearfully," testified Captain Rife.[112] One by one, horses collapsed or pulled up, and the sad process began of shooting them. "Many horses were lame or broken down," Reader declared. And he added, "Some men were obliged to walk, having killed their horses when they gave out."[113] A man on foot had to do his best to somehow keep up. If he failed to do so, he faced the prospect of freezing to death or of being captured by the enemy. Riding double with a comrade was no solution, except as a guarantee of death to the horse. Some men shared their mounts by taking turns walking. Others took horses from the locals whenever possible, undoubtedly not always providing the "proper vouchers" for them as specified in Kelley's orders.[114] But in general, a man on foot kept up with the column by maintaining his own, fairly brisk pace.

And so, like their horses, many of the men, too, were starting to "give out." "The condition of the troops was bad," Frank Reader flatly declared. "We were in sore need of food and sleep, but the march never ceased on that account."[115]

"The cry for sleep and food," Rife added, "was for a while hushed by the stinging cold we endured. What precious sight a little fire was. How we wanted to stop just a moment and warm the icy currents of blood."[116]

With more than half the expedition, and untold suffering, still in front of them, many of the men, even the toughest among them, began to doubt they would get through this alive, and some were quietly agreeing with the rebel prisoners who taunted them about never seeing "Yankeeland" again. "Any prediction of evil could be safely risked of us now," Rife admitted, "for we were a miserable set of patriots."[117]

Miserable as they were, they kept going, in large measure because of their leader. Here Averell was at his best. In sharing their suffering on an equal footing, he inspired the men, and by pressing on without murmur he stiffened their resolve; with constant words of encouragement he led them on and got the most he possibly could from them.[118] But then, just before dawn, news finally came in from the Shenandoah, news that compelled Averell to drive his tired men on even harder.

The news was brought in by a squad of the 2nd West Virginia's Company B, which had been the point guard of the column after it passed through New Castle. Riding out in front of the squad had been twenty-seven-year-old Sergeant Oliver P. Bower and Corporal Will Shirley. About to drop from exhaustion, Shirley and his mount had pulled over for a brief rest. Bower rode on alone. About four miles from Salem, he came upon four riders approaching from the opposite direction. The strangers stopped in the road and demanded from Bower his name and unit, the darkness conveniently concealing the true color of his uniform. Assuming the four to be Confederates, Bower shrewdly told them he belonged to Early's (Echols'?) command, and with further chatter he detained them until four of his own men came riding up from behind. Bower then dropped his friendly tone, drew his pistol and demanded the surrender of the four supposed-Confederates. Shots rang out. A wild melee erupted. Horses reared in fright, curses ripped the cold night air, men tumbled out of their saddles. In a moment, it was over. One Confederate lay dead on the ground, another had been wounded. The other two had surrendered. Miraculously, Bower and his friends had not been hurt.

Despite their fatigue, the men hurried these trophies back to Averell. (Bower also "got a splendid horse in the capture.") The prisoners carried startling information—Fitzhugh Lee's cavalry division had left Charlottesville on the fourteenth and was moving rapidly to intercept the column. If true, it meant that, as feared, Confederate troops from the Army of Northern Virginia—an entire division of cavalry, no less—had been taken out of their winter quarters and sent specifically to catch the strike force. Averell could only assume the disheartening information was true, and hope that his support in the Shenandoah might be able to delay or detain Fitz Lee long enough for the command to complete its mission and safely get the hell out. But of more immediate concern—the prisoners also said that a troop-train was expected in Salem at any moment.[119]

Facing Averell, then, was the unpleasant prospect of finding Salem well defended. Moreover, with Echols free to the west and Fitz Lee coming in from the east, the dreaded major confrontation with the enemy now seemed inevitable. There was reason enough to turn back, before it was too late and disaster overwhelmed him. But Averell, still resolved to expel the demon of overcaution, would not have it. While there was still the slightest chance of success, he remained determined, remarkably so, to press on.

But there was no time to lose. At dawn on the sixteenth he began the final push for the great prize. He sent ahead "vigilant scouts, armed with repeating rifles [probably men from Gibson's battalion], mounted upon fleet horses, who permitted no one to go ahead of them." About four miles from town, Averell made his final lunge. With 350 men and a pair of three-inch guns, he sped forward and at 10 a.m. they dashed into Salem.[120]

6. Six Hours in Salem

They had made it! Eight days and 219 miles; they had eluded the enemy, fought the weather and the terrain and safely reached their goal. "We had suffered much to get there," Captain Rife proudly recalled. "With little sleep and little food, in the midst of the most fearful mountain storms of wind and rain and sleet, a constantly-falling thermometer, and swelling streams—amid all these we had moved forward and gained our purpose."[121]

The purpose they had so proudly gained, the town of Salem, had originally been laid out as a few small lots lining a single street some sixty years before by an entrepreneur named James Simpson, who had envisioned the area becoming prosperous as a stop-over for travelers passing through the Roanoke Valley. Named for a city in New Jersey, the young town grew slowly over the years until 1847, when it suddenly and unexpectedly became the new home of the Virginia Collegiate Institute. About to go bankrupt in rural Augusta County, the college officers had loaded all the school's property onto a single wagon and rode down to the Roanoke River to set up shop in Salem. Under the name Roanoke College, the school soon prospered, as did the town that was its new and grateful host. Five years later, in 1852, another important visitor arrived when the wood-burning locomotive, the "John R. McDaniel" came chugging into town on the freshly laid tracks of the Virginia & Tennessee Railroad. The arrival of the line led to a brief spurt in land values and the addition of a few minor businesses, but in general Salem remained a small town, the 1860 census crediting it with only 590 whites and twenty-two slaves.[122]

With the outbreak of "The War" in 1861, there was little doubt as to the fervent loyalty of these few people, blacks excluded, to the new Confederacy. The town and surrounding area promptly furnished the Southern armies with four companies, including the Salem Flying Artillery.[123] This left the community so depleted of young men that the fall 1861 semester at Roanoke College opened with only about twenty students. College president, Dr. David Bittle, sought to remedy this by arranging with the government to have students exempted from military service on condition that they form into a home guard for the protection of Salem. Thus was born the Roanoke College Home Guard, officially designated as Company E, First Regiment, Virginia Reserves, which by late 1863 contained some 100 boys, aged fourteen to eighteen.[124] It was the general feeling in the community, however, that the boys, though diligent and eager in their training and drill, were in little danger of having their newly acquired military skills put to the test. For although the war had made Salem an important post on the Virginia & Tennessee, first as a supply base for the Department of Western Virginia then as a collection point for stores destined for troops in Tennessee, the town was considered too remote for the Yankees to disturb.

That false sense of security came to an abrupt end on Tuesday, 15 December 1863, eleven years to the day after the "John R. McDaniel" had launched Salem on its career as a railroad town. From General Jones at Dublin, a wire came in at about 11 p.m. that night for Major J.C. Green, the officer in charge of all the military stores in Salem. The major could hardly believe his eyes as he read that a large number of Yankee troopers had passed Sweet Springs and were headed his way.[125]

Green's immediate concern was for the safety of the commissary and quartermaster supplies that had been placed in his charge. Vast as those supplies were, he believed there was a chance they could be saved if only he could get them on the train coming in from Lynchburg the next morning. But there was the rub. The supplies were scattered all over town, in government warehouses, stores, mills and stables, and a tremendous, time-consuming effort would be required to collect and transport them to the railroad depot, three-fourths of a mile west of town. Furthermore, such efforts could be hampered by the panicky reactions of citizens who had every right to know of the impending danger. These tremendous obstacles notwithstanding, Green, his assistant, Captain M.B. Porteaux, and the handful of men at their disposal, "went to work."[126]

Lamp lights came on and the town roused itself as news of the Yankee peril spread through the streets. But there was no panic, only a determined, controlled frenzy of activity, as people everywhere hid their valuables or packed them in trunks to be carried away to safety, along with themselves, on that morning train from Lynchburg. Apparently, a number of citizens pitched in to help Green and Porteaux. Using wagons, buggies, horses and whatever else was available, they worked feverishly through the night transporting government supplies to the depot and its two adjoining warehouses. As the hours passed and the buildings bulged to capacity, supplies had to be stacked up outside by the tracks.[127]

More could have been done. Apparently no one thought of sending a wire to Lynchburg to request that a train be sent immediately or as soon as possible. Nor did anyone think to delay the Yankees by blockading the approaches to Salem, particularly the road coming in from New Castle.[128] And finally, only one small patrol had gone out to provide advance warning of the Yankees' approach. Some of these responsibilities would have been taken up by the College Home Guard, but most of the boys had already left town to begin their semester-break, Christmas vacations.[129]

And though General Jones had put all the local home guards on alert, from Liberty to Lynchburg, none responded to the emergency in Salem.[130] Such a lack of defense left many of the citizens very bitter. "The utter worthlessness of that branch of our defenses termed the 'home guards,'" J.J. Moorman angrily wrote his friend, Governor John Letcher, two days later, "here in our midst, & along the whole line from & including Lynchburg to this place, had been made perfectly clear." Then he added, "Lynchburg did nothing although fully notified—[other communities] did less than nothing—worse yet, they did not try to do so . . . I really believe that such an organization of 'home guards' & militia as we have is vastly worse than no organization at all, in as much as it causes some reliance on the part of the Country that never has been, & never will be realized."[131]

The one patrol that did ride out that cold, dark night contained but four men, led by twenty-six-year-old Thomas J. Chapman. A native of Salem, having been born at the family home a block northeast of the courthouse, Chapman was an alumnus of Roanoke College, and currently owned a small hotel in town.[132] Unable for some reason to enter Confederate service, he had taken it upon himself this night to act as a scout.

In the darkness about four miles north of town, Chapman and his men came upon a suspicious-looking lone stranger approaching from the opposite direction. That stranger was Sergeant Oliver P. Bower of the 2nd West Virginia, the same man who had stalled the civilian-patrol with small talk until more of his own comrades came along, one of whom then shot Thomas Chapman dead when he did not immediately surrender.

With the loss of the Chapman patrol went any possibility for the Salem citizens to be warned of the enemy's final approach. Thus when the cry "Yankees!" rang out around 10 a.m. that morning, panic struck at last. Main street had been thronged with people, who were generally moving in a westerly direction toward the depot, where dozens of others anxiously stood about waiting for the train from Lynchburg. Upon the thunderous approach of two hard riding blue coats, followed closely by a yelling column of fours, all with pistols drawn, the townspeople "took to their heels, and wagons, horses, and every living thing joined in the general stampede."[133]

The townspeople "gave us a wide berth," stated Captain Rife, flatly. Then with a touch of humor, he added, "I do not remember that one came out to welcome us, and I am sure no banquet was spread for our hungry command."[134] Most of the people quickly took to their homes or shops. A few, including some intrepid ladies "whose curiosity exceeded their fear,"

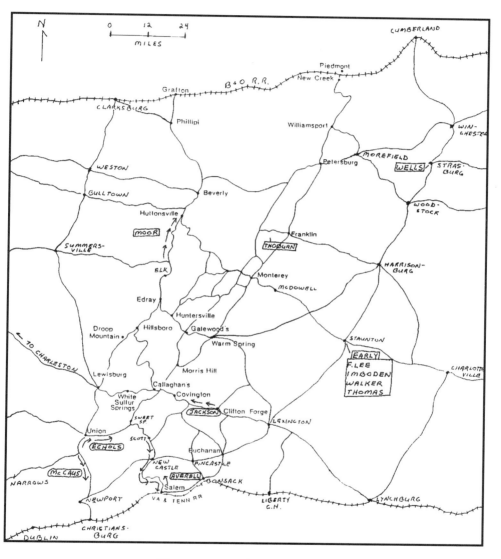

Movements, 16 December

Compiled from *Official Records Atlas*, Plate 135c, No. 1. Stephen Z. Starr,
The Union Cavalry in the Civil War. Author's notes.

remained on the street, apparently in stunned disbelief at the unholy sight of Yankee troopers in their town[135]—a further testament to the success of Averell's "stealth" tactics.

One of Salem's citizens, however, did seem glad to see the boys in blue. On the road just north of town a young woman stopped Captain Ewing and asked if he might unfurl the flag for her. The artillerist thought the young lady's request strange, even for a patriot. "We saw the flag every day," he later explained. "It got to be old with us. Its stars gleamed only in a matter-of-fact way, and the unfurling of its folds only stirred us on extraordinary occasions." Thinking then that she somehow meant to insult the flag, Ewing hesitated before consenting to have it unfurled. Her response astonished him. "I can never forget her look as she eagerly and passionately folded it to her bosom as a mother would her long-lost child," and with tears in her eyes she gave thanks for being allowed to see the noble banner for the first time "in years."[136]

In a similar incident in town, "an old lady" apparently told one of the soldiers, "When they took the old flag down from the University, I can't describe the distress that I felt; and I felt much worse when they put the new flag in its place; but now that you have come, the old flag looks as bright and beautiful as ever."[137]

"Union sentiments," Averell later acknowledged, "are quietly entertained by many in the country through which we passed."[138] In the depths of Confederate Virginia such expressions of "Union sentiments" could be

dangerous; in the previous year as many as twenty-nine persons were held in the Roanoke County jail at one time for "offenses against the Confederate States of America and against the Commonwealth of Virginia."[139]

In Salem, meanwhile, Averell's first order of business was to cut off the town from outside communication. He sent squads to surround the town and catch any civilians trying to escape, and another squad he sent to cut the telegraph line, which came into the post office. There the men burst through the door, found the place empty (the operator, William Oakley had fled—without sending any wire) and ripped out the wire that was attached to the post office window.[140]

Capt. Chatham T. Ewing

National Tribune, 8 Sept. 1887

Next, Averell prepared to meet the "troop train" expected to come in from

She Pressed the Flag to her Bosom.

National Tribune, 8 Sept. 1887

the direction of Lynchburg to the east. But the concern was basically unnecessary. The members of the Chapman patrol had misled their captors;
the train was the regularly scheduled run from Lynchburg, which this morning carried nothing more threatening than a small provost guard of home
guards under Captain Van R. Otey.[141] But Averell, expecting the worst,
ordered the lead column to dismount and deploy for battle, three lines deep.
From his engineer staff he sent Lieutenant John R. Meigs, the twenty-one-
year-old son of Quartermaster General Montgomery Meigs, to find a good
position from which one of the three-inch guns could fire directly into the
train as it arrived.[142]

The gun, under thirty-year-old Corporal A.G. Osborne, set up just in
time. "I put in a percussion shell as soon as I heard the train coming,"
Osborne recounted, "and had made up my mind to disable the engine, if
possible, and was waiting until I could get a good view when Lieut. Meigs
rushed up and asked me why I did not fire. I told him I was waiting for a
better view so that I could put a shell into the machinery or boiler of the
engine so as to disable it; but he ordered me to fire, when I could not see
anything but about two feet of the top of the smoke-stack. Of course I had
to obey orders, and the result was no damage to anything but the smoke-
stack."[143]

The smokestack-damaged locomotive began to slow. Osborne's crew
hurriedly reloaded. The train crept into full view, but the engine was past
them by the time they were ready. Osborne ordered the gun to fire directly
into one of the cars. After a tremendous boom, the shell crashed through
the wooden wall of the car, did untold damage within, then burst out the
other side. The engine came to a jolting halt, then immediately spun its
wheels in reverse. Osborne's crew hurried to get in one more shot. The
train, going backwards now, quickly picked up speed. Osborne fired and
missed. The train chugged around a curve and disappeared.[144]

Relieved to have won the "Battle of Salem" so easily, the men in blue
let out a rousing cheer, though the "victory" had left some a bit disappointed.
"We always felt bad that we did not get that locomotive and train," Captain
Rife recalled, rather fancifully. "It would have been so nice to have gone up
the road and had a chat with Longstreet. . . ."[145]

That the victory occurred at all was due in large measure to the mis-
information planted earlier that morning by the captured members of the
Chapman patrol. Their attempted ruse backfired when, instead of scaring
off Averell, it caused him to make the final, precipitate lunge that brought
him into town a bare half-hour before the arrival of the Lynchburg train—
the train Major Green and many of the townspeople had been anxiously
awaiting all night long. Now the train was gone and the citizens had dispersed, leaving behind at the trackside and at the depot with its two adjacent
warehouses, all the government stores, and personal belongings, Major
Green and those townspeople had worked so hard through the night to
accumulate. Averell and his men must have stared in wide-eyed disbelief

Lt. John Meigs as a Cadet

He ordered the first shot fired at the "Battle of Salem."

US Army Military History Institute

at the undefended treasures that now lay before them. Literally tons of commissary and quartermaster supplies, all of it conveniently stockpiled in one labor-saving location, were at the mercy of the blue invaders. There was far too much to accurately count. Quick estimates, quite possibly a bit high, revealed that there were about 1,000 sacks of salt, 2,000 barrels of flour and 2,000 of meat, 10,000 bushels of wheat, 50,000 bushels of oats, and 100,000 bushels of shelled corn. There were boxes of clothing, bales of cotton, harnesses, saddles, shoes, tools, oil, tar, rice, 100 wagons, 1,900 pounds of sugar, even seventy pounds of soap and 225 pounds of candles. . . .[146] (Estimates of the loss varied from one extreme to the other. "I feel perfectly confident that there were 300,000 bushels of grain destroyed," Lieutenant Hoffman wrote in his diary, "so I estimate the rebel loss, at Salem alone, leaving out the damage done the railroad, at not less than ten million dollars."[147] On the other hand, in a report submitted to Richmond on 3 January 1864, Confederate Assistant Commissary of Subsistence, Captain James Wade, calculated the value of the loss at $107,537.57, clearly a vast underestimate.[148]) After the count came the destruction.

Averell's men were dead-tired, hungry and exhausted, having had little food or sleep in five days, yet they knew why they had come here and they knew what must be done, not only to make the mission a success but to avenge the suffering they had endured to make it so. With a new-found, almost super-human energy and resolve, they eagerly set about their work. "They were on a mission of destruction and appropriation," declared Captain Rife, "and things were made to hum during the few hours we were in Salem."[149] Moreover, it seemed to Rife and his comrades that the rebs hadn't believed it possible they could get to so valuable a cache, or it wouldn't have been left so unprotected. The stores at Salem must have seemed perfectly safe to the Confederates, "as no Union force was within 200 miles of there," reasoned Rife, "nor did it seem possible that anything less than a large and powerful army could get there."[150] Knowing this, Averell's men took even greater satisfaction in their work.

Quickly, the men scrambled through the stockpiles one last time, pulling out anything they thought might be useful on the return trip. They rescued several barrels of coffee and sugar, but there wasn't room in their wagons for much else. They also rifled through the dozens of trunks and other personal items the panicky citizens had abandoned at the trackside. Articles of clothing, papers, photos, even furniture, were soon strewn about in one huge mess.[151] Then the torchers moved in.

Within minutes, the whole was a mass of roaring flames, with dense, black smoke billowing up, filling the sky and covering the town with a thick, dark canopy.[152] The total scene produced such an eerie effect as to cause many a soul to step back and simply watch it all with awestruck fascination.

Including many of the townspeople, who felt, in addition to awe, a measure of stunned disbelief. "The only happy faces we saw," said Captain Rife of the people he encountered, "were the blacks who were permitted to carry away food from the burning buildings, and who were exulting at the great reduction in the cost of flour. It was very dear in the morning, but cheap now."[153] The exultation went much further, for with the arrival of the bluecoats, many of the blacks in town now considered themselves ex-slaves. About twenty-five of their number, male and female, eagerly attached themselves to the command, though local newspapers, in an attempt, no doubt, to lessen the anxiety of whites over the willingness of slaves to run away, would assure their readers that "the negroes were carried off."[154]

In truth, it was many of Salem's whites who "were carried off." The squads Averell had sent to surround the town had netted, with the aid of several warning shots, about forty citizens trying to escape, among which were a number of furloughed soldiers and six of the Roanoke College students. Also taken was the Assistant Quartermaster, Captain Porteaux. (Voluntarily included in that number was a Mr. & Mrs. Hearns, apparent Union sympathizers.)[155]

Meanwhile, Averell had turned his attention to another of his, and his government's, priorities—busting up the track of the Virginia & Tennessee. He wanted at least fifteen miles of it. A bit much, perhaps, but his troops were pouring into town now and he had plenty of men to work with. He sent a destruction crew four miles out to the east and another, larger, gang twelve miles to the west.[156] He then turned the rest of his men loose on the town.

The water tower and turntable soon went up in flames, as did three cars standing on the track and "a large pile of bridge timber and repairing material."[157] They burned both Pitzer's and Martin's large flour mills (though the soldiers graciously allowed the miller to remove three or four barrels of flour), McClanahan's store, and "about 75 old Government wagons." Out on the edge of town they set ablaze the Snyder barn, which contained large quantities of tallow, leather, and oil. The Chapman barn, used as a government stable, and the "Salem Mills" also contributed to the inferno. One private stable, however, from which government grain had been removed and destroyed and the horses confiscated, was apparently spared the torch when the owner, Thomas Hough, arrived in time to successfully plead for mercy. Hundreds of horses, both government and private, were confiscated, the wagons to which they were attached being set ablaze. Helping the blue soldiers find much of the government property that had not been transported to the depot, was a man named Hall, who had been ordnance officer at Salem for General Jenkins the past spring while apparently harboring secret Union sympathies awaiting the proper moment for expression.[158]

Guiding all of this destruction were Averell's strict orders against vandalism; he demanded that private property be respected. "It may be outrages were committed," Captain Rife admitted, "but it is not likely that many of them occurred, as the discipline was very rigid; and those that may have occurred were more the outburst of a dare-devil spirit that was momentary in its impulse, and that meant no harm and probably did little."[159]

Among those "outrages" were the number of private stores and businesses along Main Street that the men broke into, and the goods inside that they either destroyed or carried away.[160] Private residences, however, were generally respected, the most notable example being a house the soldiers carefully preserved from the nearby flames of the burning depot.[161] But there were exceptions. Some years after the war, one townsman sought redress for his loss by publicly inquiring into the names of the "dogs" who had looted his house in Salem. In general, however, "discipline was very rigid," as Rife maintained, and there appear to have been few instances of pure vandalism.[162]

A number of places in town were "visited" without being destroyed. The jail was opened and the prisoners released, including, apparently, two Yankees, "who had been captured by the Enrolling officer the night before." (Perhaps it was these two Yankees Captain Otey's provost guard had come from Lynchburg to pick up.) The bank, too, was "visited," but the soldiers, disappointed at finding little money in the vault and cash drawers, had to content themselves with mischief. They strewed all the papers about and stole the bed clothing of the officers who slept at the bank.[163]

The most prominent building in town, Roanoke College on High Street north of Main, was spared any destruction upon the successful intercession of the institution's president, Dr. David Bittle. "Not to palliate the conduct of the Yankees," Professor William McCauley would write the *Richmond Examiner* a few days later in an anxious effort to squelch rumors the college had been destroyed, "but to give a correct statement of the matter, which is due the interests of the college, I shall say that they did not enter the college building, nor molest, in the least, anything on the premises." Professor McCauley went on to admit that the students waiting at the train depot had been the victims of unfortunate luck when "the Yankees came down on our quiet little village like a wolf on the fold," but he quickly added that the "property of the students which had been left in the college building, remained in perfect security. . . . Everything in and around the college building remains in status quo, and the exercises of the institution will be resumed after the usual interval for holidays on the 1st of January."[164]

As the afternoon wore on, meanwhile, the wrecking crews began streaming into town from both ends of the rail line. The men had been somewhat delayed in their work when the rails proved too strong for the "Yanks" they had brought to twist them out of shape. But, relying on the old, more time-consuming method of building huge bonfires to heat the rails, then twisting and bending the hot iron around the nearest tree or telegraph pole, they still managed to do enormous damage in just a few hours. Averell got his fifteen miles of destruction. In addition, the men had burned several culverts and five small bridges, including the seventy-five-foot span over Mason's Creek three miles east of town and the 150 footer over the Roanoke near the Joseph Deyerle farm. They cut, coiled and burned half a mile of telegraph wire and destroyed a number of small warehouses that contained leather "and other valuable articles."[165]

It was now about 4 p.m., six hours after Averell first rode into Salem.[166] In that time his men had done the incredible. They had punched a huge hole in the Virginia & Tennessee Railroad and they had made sure Longstreet's men would be denied a substantial amount of food and supplies.

Averell's men were dragged-out dead-tired, but spending the night in Salem was out of the question—Fitz Lee was out there somewhere and was no doubt heading this way; Echols, too, could very well be closing in from the west. With the enemy on alert all around him, Averell knew he was now entering the most critical phase of the operation and he accordingly turned his every thought to making an escape. The men, beat as they were, had to start moving out.

If that escape were to succeed, Averell would need to rely on and utilize to the fullest every resource available to him, foremost of which would be the courage and determination of his men as well as his own skills in leadership. And of this last, there could be little room for error.

While the evidence of his destruction was still swirling in smoke through the skies above Salem, Averell was planning and calculating. Deep in enemy territory, outnumbered and outgunned by those in pursuit of him, his best weapons remained speed, stealth, and deception. And no opportunity, however trivial, to deceive the enemy could be overlooked. He began immediately.

Since there was no time for a false advance, he turned to the "false rumor," which he spread among "some inquisitive ones" in town, hoping to convince them he eventually intended to return northeast by way of Buchanan then north through the Shenandoah. Apparently, he also let it be known that his command consisted of some 12,000 men, who were split up into a number of columns that were returning by several different routes.

Having done his best to plant the seeds of deception, Averell ordered the sounding of the recall. Within moments his smoke-grimed men choked Main Street with a long column of fours. Upon the signal, the command lurched forward. Riding east along Main, they turned left on Cove Street and rode out of Salem heading north on the same route they had used to enter the town.[167]

The men ached with fatigue. They were nearly delirious with exhaustion. And if that were not enough, a cold rain began to fall soon after they left Salem. After going only seven miles, Averell realized they could take no more. Mercifully he called a halt and allowed the men to collapse in camp on a Mrs. Smith's farm at the foot of North Mountain near Mason's Cove. "The last 80 miles had been marched in about thirty hours," Averell subsequently explained. "Little sleep had been enjoyed by my men during five days and nights; it was necessary to pause and collect our energies for the return." (More accurately, the distance was closer to seventy miles and the time thirty-two hours.)[168]

Energies that could mean the difference between life and death, for the agonies and suffering endured on the march down would not compare to those awaiting the men on their return.

Chapter Three

The Great Escape

1. Situation on the Morning of 17 December

The cold, wet morning of the seventeenth marked the beginning of the expedition's tenth day. Ten days, 226 miles—and the command had been virtually untouched by the enemy. To Averell and his men, it must have seemed too good to be true.

Averell's masterful combination of speed, cunning, and stealth accounted for much of the good fortune, but the various diversionary movements, even those that failed to complete their mission, must also be given credit for throwing the Confederates off balance—at least initially. By the seventeenth the rebels had fully regained their equilibrium and were swiftly closing in for the kill.

Off to the west of Averell were the brigades of Echols, about 1,500 men, and McCausland, about 1,700 men, of Jones' command. In response to Scammon's advance from Charleston, Jones, as we have seen, had pulled Echols out of Lewisburg on the twelfth and the next day he united him with McCausland at Pickaway, which lay four miles north of Union, eighteen miles south of Lewisburg and nineteen miles west of Sweet Springs. Jones had intended to hold these two in good defensive positions at Pickaway as a way of dealing with any "venture" the Federals might make south of Lewisburg. But upon receiving the startling news on the fourteenth that Averell had advanced south of Monterey, he concluded the Federals were moving in a pincers upon Union and he accordingly pulled Echols and McCausland back a few miles south of there. Jones finally gained a clear view of the situation when he learned the next day that Scammon had started back for Charleston, and Averell had turned southeast at Sweet Springs and was headed for the railroad. Forced to accept the bitter pill that it was too late to prevent Averell from striking the rail line, Jones set his mind to capturing or destroying the daring raider by cutting off his escape route.

A glance at the map made it plain that if Averell hoped to safely get back north to his own lines, that escape route would have to go in one of three directions—either on a swing out to the west, a march directly north, or a move around to the east. Jones, his blood up for the chase, made plans to block all three.

To block the route to the west along the rail line, he started McCausland on the sixteenth for Newport, which lay about thirty miles south of Union and the same distance southwest of New Castle. Jones also sent instructions for the 45th Virginia to proceed by rail from Saltville seventy-five miles east to New River Bridge at Dublin, which is about forty-five miles south of Union. He even tried to retrieve Ransom's division from Tennessee but Longstreet refused to give it up.

To block the northern escape route, down which Averell had just come, Jones, also on the sixteenth, started Echols for Sweet Springs Mountain. Though it meant a tough march of twenty miles for Echols' ragged troops, Averell, then at Salem, was more than twice that distance from Sweet Springs.

To prevent the Federals from getting out by going east then north through the Shenandoah Valley, Jones wired Jackson at Warm Springs to position himself on Jackson River near Clifton Forge.

Jones knew, however, that by itself Jackson's small command could not hope to overwhelm Averell. The idea was to tie up the Yankees until the hoped-for troops from Lee's army could arrive and finish them off.[1]

But Lee, unconvinced as late as the eleventh that the Federals had undertaken any serious operations in that region, had not been willing to pull any of his worn troops out of their just-established winter quarters in order to subject them to further strenuous, and possibly useless, exertions in western Virginia. Somewhat irritated by Jones' incessant demands for reinforcements, he had at first tried to put off the alarmist department commander by suggesting he turn to Longstreet for help. But Lee finally became alarmed himself when he learned on the twelfth that, in addition to the move against Lewisburg, a Federal force had also occupied McDowell and another had advanced south of Harper's Ferry to Strasburg, thus making it clear in his mind that "those people" were threatening his army's vital supply base at Staunton. This the gray commander would not tolerate.

The only substantial Confederate force in the Valley was Imboden's "Northwest Brigade," which was currently frozen in place at Buffalo Gap keeping an eye on the Yankees at McDowell and guarding the Parkersburg pike approach to Staunton. Obviously, more troops were needed to meet the growing emergency. With the current lull along the Rappahannock following the failure of Meade's Mine Run campaign, Lee believed he could afford to send a powerful force from his own army to defend Staunton. On the fourteenth he set his plan in motion.[2]

That morning two of the three brigades of Fitz Lee's cavalry division, about 1,800 men, pulled out of their just-established winter quarters near Charlottesville and began the ride to Staunton, some thirty-five miles to the west. (John R. Chambliss commanded one of the brigades and W.C. Wickham the other. The third brigade, Lunsford L. Lomax's, remained on the Rapidan as a picket.)[3]

Though only twenty-eight years old, and mindful of a youthful appearance he thought so inappropriate for a major general that he tried to conceal it under a massive, flowing black beard, Fitzhugh Lee, nephew of the army commander, suffered terribly from arthritis and he did not relish the prospect of aggravating that affliction by riding into the bone-chilling climate of the western mountains. But he did look forward to paying one more "visit" to his old friend Billy Averell. The two had held each other in high regard since their days together as cadets at West Point, Lee graduating the year after Averell. "Fitzhugh Lee was a sturdy, muscular and lively little giant as a cadet," Averell fondly recalled of him. "With a frank, affectionate disposition he had a prevailing habit of irrepressible good humor which made any occasion of seriousness in him seem like affectation." In early 1861, the two friends had parted with great sorrow in order to follow their separate loyalties. "The tears which suffered his eyes," Averell remembered of the occasion, "and the lamentations that escaped his lips betrayed a depth of feeling which revealed a sincere character beneath his habitual cheerfulness." Two years later, on 25 February 1863, the two renewed their acquaintance somewhat when Fitz Lee surprised and captured about 150 of Averell's men along the Rappahannock. Lee's "irrepressible good humor" then came out in a note he left behind for his friend: "If you won't go home," it read, "return my visit and bring me a sack of coffee." A month later at Kelly's Ford Averell obliged by driving Lee's troopers from the field. "Dear Fitz," he now replied in a note of his own, left behind in the same manner, "Here's your coffee. Here's your visit. How do you like it?" Undoubtedly, Lee did not like it, and he would soon be looking forward to yet another "visit" with his old friend.[4]

At Orange Court House, meanwhile, another 3,000 men—the infantry brigades of Henry H. Walker of Henry Heth's Division and Edmund Thomas of Cadmus Wilcox's Division, both of A.P. Hill's Corps—were boarding the cars of the Virginia Central for their ride to Staunton, some sixty miles to the west. And finally, from Wade Hampton's cavalry division, about 800 men of Thomas Rosser's famed Laurel Brigade (7 Va., 11 Va., 12 Va., 35 Va. Bn.) left their camps near Fredericksburg and began the ride to swing behind Wells to cut his communications north of Strasburg.[5]

Once these massive forces converged in the Valley, they would need an over-all commander. Lee gave that urgent assignment to one of his toughest and ablest division commanders, Major General Jubal Early.[6]

Like Fitzhugh Lee, Early looked older than his years, but unlike his newly acquired subordinate, "Old Jube" had not intentionally designed that impression, being instead the victim of a balding head, a graying beard and an arthritically induced stooped posture. The forty-seven-year-old, an

1837 graduate of West Point, had for ten years prior to the war been the commonwealth's attorney in his native Franklin County, Virginia. He had fought in all the major battles of the army since First Manassas, building up along the way an excellent combat record that had elevated him to division command while also making him a prime candidate for a lieutenant generalcy should such an opening ever arise. There were some in the army, however, who were convinced Early would be held back from further advancement because of an irascible nature, attributable perhaps to his painful arthritis, that left him devoid of the crucial skills of ingratiation. The army commander, however, was now obviously placing great trust in him, and Early no doubt welcomed the break from the anticipated tedium of winter quarters as he did the opportunity to demonstrate what he could do with an independent command.

Swaddled against the arthritically aggravating cold, the irascible former lawyer arrived in Staunton by rail from Orange at 1 a.m. on the sixteenth wearing a skull cap, leggings, and a full-length overcoat. He immediately set to work formulating plans to deal with the Federals at McDowell.[7]

Those plans, however, he quickly dropped when the startling news came in later the same day (16th) that a Federal column under Averell had struck the railroad at Salem. This made everything embarrassingly clear— the threat to Staunton had been a mere diversion. But any concerns Early may have had as to whether this meant the cancellation of his assignment were dispelled that evening when instructions came in from General Lee to remain in the Valley with the forces at hand and "make arrangements" to capture and punish the impertinent Federals who had dared to strike at one of the Confederacy's most vital rail links.[8] Early went to work.

His immediate inclination was to send the cavalry, both Fitz Lee and Imboden, directly against Averell to the south, and this preference he held on to despite a rather daring proposal submitted by Imboden.

A native of the Valley, having been born near Staunton where he had practiced law before the war, thirty-year-old John Daniel Imboden, a professional widower who would accumulate five successive wives, had almost single-handedly raised the force that became the nucleus of the "Northwest Brigade" and which now, under his command, had the responsibility of guarding the Shenandoah. Though a modest man, who had once remarked in explanation of why he did not seek promotion to major general, "I really feel I have as high a military rank as I am qualified for," the proposal he submitted to Early on the evening of 16 December was anything but modest. Don't go after Averell, he advised, but let the Northwest Brigade swing around to Franklin while Walker and Thomas advance directly upon McDowell, thereby trapping and bagging the Federals in between. After this success, Imboden proposed to ride north to New Creek and "turn the tables on Averell," as he explained it to Early, "and teach him a lesson to stay closer about home." To Imboden, this seemed like a can't-lose proposition.

Gen. Jubal Early

Massachusetts Commandery, Military
Order of the Loyal Legion and the US Army Military History Institute

"If I can't bring anything away from New Creek," he went on, "I can destroy as much as Averell and we will be even."[9]

Early apparently liked the daring plan; indeed, its execution could very well have brought a great deal of grief not only to Averell but to the entire Department of West Virginia. However, he preferred to stick with his original, more direct, and, to his mind, more practical course of sending the cavalry south to get Averell. Furthermore, he decided that should the wily Federal commander somehow elude the cavalry and come on down the Valley, he would have the infantry in place to snare him as he went by ("It was useless," Early explained in his memoirs, "to be sending them [infantry] after cavalry over such a track of country.")[10]

Thus on the morning of the seventeenth, while holding Walker's brigade at Staunton to keep an eye on the Federals at McDowell, Early started Thomas' brigade for Warm Springs, about fifty miles by rail to the west. Fitz Lee and Imboden he sent by different routes to rendezvous in Lexington, thirty-five miles to the southwest, from where they were to dash another thirty-five miles west over to join Jackson, whom he had ordered to cover Clifton Forge and Covington. There they would be in a good position to catch Averell should he use the Shenandoah, or they could easily slide over to Callaghan's, Gatewood's or even Huntersville if he went up further to the west.[11]

As Averell's men thus roused themselves in their camps at Mason's Cove at the start of the expedition's tenth day, little did they realize that the Federal bluffs against Union and Staunton, bluffs that had served their purpose so well at first, had begun to backfire, for the Confederate troops sent in reaction to those bluffs had been set loose to track Averell down and destroy him. From Union in the west to Staunton in the east, some 11,000 Confederates were now either rapidly closing in on him or setting themselves up to smash him as he went by.

2. The Battle with Craig's Creek

Some of this Averell knew. He knew his Droop Mountain opponent, John Echols, was free to the west but not that he was moving to cut him off at Sweet Springs Mountain. He knew his old friend Fitz Lee was in the Shenandoah but not that both he and Imboden were riding to a rendezvous with Jackson at Covington. Nor did he know that two infantry brigades were waiting for him farther down the Valley.

He did know his men were tired, cold, and hungry. Their rations, scant to begin with, were about to run out and he wanted to get the men back to their supply wagons in Monterey as quickly as possible. Monterey, however, was a very long 113 miles to the north, miles that would mostly likely be a gauntlet through which his tired command would have to outrun and possibly even outfight the enemy.

After a brief, but precious, sound sleep, Averell's men awoke at 5 a.m. on the morning of the seventeenth to the disappointment that one of their most detested enemies—the cold rain—was still dogging them.[12] Yet, eager to get "home," they quickly and efficiently prepared for a resumption of the march. And if their leader was worried about their chances, he gave no outward indication of it.

Always mindful of the great role morale played in determining success or failure, Averell was very careful about how he presented himself to the men. Even in the dreariest of circumstances, such as now, he maintained an outward cheerfulness and sense of humor that endeared him to the men, as did his fondness for music. A skillful guitar player, he was known on previous expeditions to have occasionally led the men in song.[13]

And on this especially dreary morning, with his command having yet to face unknown but certain dangers, Averell seemed in a particularly good mood, as revealed in part by an interview he conducted with the six college boys his men had captured trying to escape from Salem the day before. The "prisoners," not knowing what to expect, were obviously a bit nervous as they stood before their daring captor. Averell, sensing their anxiety, began in a friendly, reassuring manner by inquiring after the hometown of each boy. He then asked his audience for an opinion of the Confederacy and of its chances for survival. When some of the boys, relaxed and emboldened by the friendliness of their host, expressed confidence in the Southern republic, Averell gently rebuked them. "O now, boys, you know it is most played out," he said. "You all go back to your books and study your best." He then released them.[14]

With no desire to drag along any unnecessary encumbrances, Averell also released the forty or so civilians caught, like the students, trying to escape from Salem the day before; he kept only the handful of rebel soldiers who had been taken in the town while home on furlough. The civilians and the students then endured the indignity and strain of having to walk seven miles back to Salem in the cold rain.[15] Furthermore, Averell had allowed his former guests no food, either last night or this morning, nor did he give them any of the 400 or so horses confiscated in Salem, even though he had reached the conclusion that he now had more of the animals on his hands than his command could possible care for. In what would later prove a controversial move, Averell apparently directed that about fifty of the less capable beasts be disposed of by having their throats slit open. These unfortunate horses, their grisly carcasses left to mark the spot of the Mason's Cove campsite, would be sorely needed later on.[16] Moreover, as much as anything Averell had done so far, this act aroused the indignation of the Southern press. "The cutting of the throats of the horses which he was compelled to abandon," growled the *Richmond Sentinel*, "will end to attach undying disgrace to his name. There is something so disgustingly low and brutish in such a proceeding toward so noble an animal that it must fill every generous mind with odium for him who could commit it. It seems as if such a creature had but one step further to go, and that is to cut the throats of the prisoners whom he may not be able to carry off."[17]

For the moment, Averell's men had little concern for the captured rebel horses and even less sympathy for the beasts' former owners. Unlike the just-released grumbling civilians, the men would probably have welcomed a muddy seven-mile walk to Salem, if that was all it took to get back home. But nearly twenty times that distance stood between them and another town that would welcome them as friends. With the 14th Pennsylvania Cavalry taking the lead, the command broke camp and pulled out of Mason's Cove in that relentless, cold rain and headed north. Turning west at Mason's Creek, they made the strenuous two-mile climb to the top of North Mountain, where the rain became freezing—the howling, moaning wind blowing directly into their faces—then came down the other side and headed north again for New Castle. Sometime before noon, they came up against the greatest enemy they had faced thus far—Craig's Creek.[18]

During the column's trip down, the rain had begun around 10 a.m. on the twelfth and remained fairly steady until the afternoon of the fourteenth. Thus by the time the command reached Craig's Creek in the early morning hours of the sixteenth, a day-and-a-half after the rains had stopped, the stream was swollen but fordable. Gorged with another fifteen to sixteen hours of rain, however, it was now an angry, raging torrent. Full of slush, ice and driftwood, the normally quiet stream now had a current strong enough to "uproot trees and carry them away."[19] The sight of it brought the men to a humble standstill, and in some it struck more fear than did the prospect of charging the enemy's line. Because the banks were so narrow, sometimes butting right up against the steep mountainside, the creek was impossible to go around. "Here was a dilemma," Lieutenant Hoffman frankly admitted to his diary, "and we did not know which horn to lay hold on; to try to cross and escape, or to wait and go home via Richmond was the question. The men were troubled."[20] Averell had a ready answer—waiting or going back were out of the question; there was no other way to New Castle, the men must go forward. "The road crossed the creek seven times within a distance of ten or twelve miles," Frank Reader sadly recalled, "and there was no alternative but to ford the wild stream."[21]

But at that first crossing the prospect seemed too daunting to the men of the lead 14th Pennsylvania. Bewildered, tired and confused, they stood along the bank, refusing to go in. Averell rode up. Sensing that in this situation example would speak much louder than exhortation, he left his aides behind and without saying a word he plunged in alone with his mount. Though it might seem unduly risky, even foolish, for the commander to so jeopardize himself, and the expedition, Averell disregarded such risk as if determined to cast aside the demons of the Poteau and the Rio Puerco, the Rapidan and the Rappahannock, and in so doing he was displaying the kind of inspirational leadership that even his severest critic would have to admire. Anxiously, the Pennsylvanians watched their commander's valiant struggle through the water, until, after what seemed like an eternity, he came out safe on the other side. Raising his hat, Averell shouted, "Come on, boys!" The example had the desired effect. With a new and unbounded respect for "Fighting Billy," the boys cheered his accomplishment and plunged in after him.[22]

Though Averell's heroic example had gotten the men into the water, it did not reduce the difficulty of the crossing. "The water was mid-rib deep on the large horses," observed one soldier, "and the current so strong that the animals had to be kept with their breast up the stream and worked across sideways."[23]

Luckily, everyone in the 14th made it safely over. But Averell realized the unlikelyhood of that luck holding for the entire command at every crossing. The danger had to be lessened in some way. When the turn of the 2nd West Virginia came at another vicious-looking crossing, he called out for a volunteer to take a rope across to be used as a pull for the other men. From Company D Private John Woods, a mere boy from the Pittsburgh area, rode forward. "My boy," Averell asked, "do you think you can land your horse?" Woods gave a simple answer: "I will try, sir." The brave lad plunged in. His friends gave a cheer and continued to shout encouragement until he came out safe on the other side. But Woods paid dearly for his heroic act. From this and the other crossings, his feet froze and became so severely frostbitten as to eventually require amputation at a hospital in Grafton.[24]

Though the rope added stability to the crossing, it slowed the process considerably, and it was by no means fail-safe. Inevitably, tragedy struck. A man would lose his grip, or a horse would be struck by ice, stumble or otherwise be overtaken by the current. Then "horse and rider were carried downstream," a soldier recalled in horror, "and a number of men were drowned"[25] (including Pvt. Charles Peterson, Co. C, 16th Ill. Cav.[26] who was probably buried by the side of Catawba road, on the Anderson farm.)[27]

The artillery was another matter altogether. At some crossings the guns went completely under water. "Heavy caissons were swept down stream," Averell reported, "and great exertion and skill were required to save them."[28] Twenty-one-year-old Lieutenant Howard Morton, "a brave officer," declared one admiring soldier, "and thoroughly qualified for the position he held,"[29] finally resorted to attaching a long rope to the collars of the two lead horses of each gun, getting the rope across the stream, then "putting a hundred or more men to it, and literally dragging horses and guns into the raging torrents and through to terra firma."[30] But not before shots rang out from bushwhackers hidden in the brush along the streambank. Ten men of the "Chicago Dragoons"— the 16th Illinois' Company C of Gibson's battalion—raced toward the sound of the firing and promptly scattered the troublesome rebels.[31] The crossings proceeded without further interruption.

Inevitably, however, not everything could be saved. A fair amount of equipment and ammunition seems to have been lost. As a young girl playing in Craig's Creek near the Anderson farm in the 1890s, Allie Brickey often found minie balls at the sight of one of the crossings.[32]

There were other losses. Like his comrade Private Woods, twenty-five-year-old Private Martin Hope of Ewing's battery suffered terribly from the crossings. Hope's fate was typical of many who did battle this day with Craig's Creek. His feet became so frozen as to later blacken and swell, causing the young private to cry out in agonizing pain. Like Woods and many others in the column, Hope would eventually require treatment in Grafton, though unlike the unfortunate Woods, Hope would be spared amputation. His military service, however, was over, and his health would never be the same.[33]

Wagons, too, were a special problem. Not all of them made it over. The wagon carrying the signal rockets, for example, had to be destroyed. Averell had hoped to use the rockets to inform Thoburn at McDowell, hours, perhaps even days, ahead of the time it would take couriers to do so, of the column's return to Monterey. Thoburn, in turn, was to use his rockets to inform Averell that he was still safely on the job, awaiting his return. From the mountain tops of this region, it would have been a clever and effective way of communicating. But the rains and Craig's Creek had put an end to that hope. The rockets, much to the chagrin of Averell's chief signal officer, Captain Ernst Denicke, were now soaked and totally useless. Now carrying a worthless cargo, the signal wagon was destroyed by Averell's order, and the doomed vehicle's horses were put to work pulling other loads.[34]

But a more tragic loss, as far as the men were concerned, was the coffee and sugar taken from the supply depots in Salem. The barrels were simply too heavy, and porous, to get across the raging creek. In an almost mournful state, a detail of men with axes busted open the barrels and dumped out the precious contents onto a hillside. All was not lost, however, for after the Yankees departed, a number of locals descended on the spilled cargo and scooped up what they could, even being so thorough as to later pour water on the soiled sugar, thereby

Lt. Howard Morton

National Tribune, 8 Sept. 1887

allowing the dirt to settle and leave a usable "sugar water."[35]

Crossing after miserable crossing, the dreadful march continued, as did that damned cold rain. Some men lost their lives in the creek, many others suffered permanent, severe damage from frostbite. "The men felt the cold piercing them to the marrow," Captain Rife later declared.[36] "The weather was so cold," another trooper recalled, "part of the time below zero, that the clothing of the men was frozen stiff soon after leaving the water."[37] It was even worse for the poor animals. "The horses were covered with icicles and trembling from the cold," a soldier observed. "After a few crossings . . . it was with difficulty the horses were forced into the stream, and they were whipped and spurred to compel obedience."[38]

"I know it was cold," nineteen-year-old Private Charles E. Shanks, the 8th West Virginia's future chief bugler recalled many years later, "for I froze my feet and when we wanted to get off our horses we had to ride to a tree and kick our feet loose from the stirrups." The young Shanks' service record was probably unique in the regiment, in that he had deserted from the 36th Virginia after serving a full year in a Confederate uniform, apparently as a substitute for his father. Now in the retreat from Salem, Shanks had a special reason for wanting to stay mounted—at the battle of Rocky Gap the previous August a horse had kicked him in both legs, breaking the left knee cap and leaving him stiff and sore for months afterward. But though his knee might be spared the torment of walking, it could not escape an agonizing cold that pierced the skin and reawakened old torturous injuries to the bones, ligaments, and joints.[39]

Though it might seem heartless, even cruel, Averell allowed no time to stop and build a fire to dry out clothing or thaw human flesh. But the men understood this. "This was a chase for life," Rife conceded. "We had much to fear if the enemy was vigilant."[40] Even greater than the pain of freezing, then, was the fear, and dishonor, of being shot or captured by the enemy.

Thus sustained and inspired, the men performed countless untold acts of heroism in their battle with Craig's Creek until late that afternoon (17th), when they crossed it for the seventh and last time to finally leave this freezing hell behind them. By then "the men and horses were almost paralyzed," Frank Reader declared, "and suffered intensely from the cold as well as from hunger."[41]

The "creek" had taken its toll, immeasurable in terms of suffering but easy to calculate when adding the distance the command had moved closer to home. It had made only eight miles all day, and camped that night eight miles short of New Castle. In recovering from their ordeal, the men took all the next day to get through those eight miles, during which time the cold rain continued, fatigue and misery increased while stamina and the food supply rapidly dwindled. Moving at its slowest pace since the raid began, the column finally dragged itself into New Castle around sundown of the eighteenth.[42]

A good portion of the command set up camp outside town on the Britts farm, in an area known locally as Scratch Ankle. The Britts' young son George, a drummer boy with a Virginia regiment, had just come home on furlough to recover from a battle wound. Fearing the Yankees might take George prisoner, his parents hurriedly concealed him in a loft above the kitchen. This saved the young lad, but not before he had given his fretful parents a few anxious moments they would never forget. With the overnight stay of the Yankees, George's "exile" lasted longer than expected and he eventually became quite famished. By frequently whispering "I'm hungry" through a crack in the loft floor, and within earshot of the Yankees, he "kept the hair of the family standing on end."[43]

But Averell's men would have had little interest in young George Britt anyway. Among their many more pressing concerns was transportation. The attrition in horses the past two days had been frightfully more than anyone expected. Dozens of the animals had died or been killed since leaving Mason's Cove, and now hundreds had perished since the raid began. The 400 or so taken in Salem had barely made up the difference, and there were now open expressions of regret over the fifty horses intentionally destroyed on the morning of the seventeenth. The result was that, as soon as their camps were established in the evening of the eighteenth, many of the men went on the prowl for fresh mounts. In this way, New Castle and the surrounding region were forced to give up eighty to a hundred of its animals.[44]

That the haul in horses was not greater was because many local farmers had quickly taken precautions to save their property. The Britt family, for example, after stashing young George in the kitchen loft, took to hiding everything they considered valuable, including their precious few horses, which they sent deep into the woods. Out on Meadow Creek, meanwhile, Fannie Leffel quickly and successfully saved her beloved little gray mare by hiding it in the cellar of her log home. Near Craig's Creek, the Anderson family saved their supply of meat by taking it out of the smoke house and hiding it under a straw "tick" or mattress. For added security, Mrs. Anderson lay on the tick with her new baby.[45]

As the night wore on, however, and the temperature continued to drop until it eventually fell below zero,[46] Averell's men turned their search from horses to anything that could feed and sustain a warm fire. They stripped the region bare of fence rails, taking about 10,000 from the Spessard farm alone.[47]

But there were some "legitimate business transactions" that night— Corporal George Ordner of the 2nd West Virginia paid the unheard-of-price of seventy-five cents for a few oranges.[48]

3. New Castle to Barber's Creek

Meanwhile, the death trap kept steadily closing in. In the past two days, from the sixteenth to the eighteenth, Averell's command had made only about twenty-three miles, going from Salem to New Castle. In that same time, Echols had reached Sweet Springs Mountain and now blocked

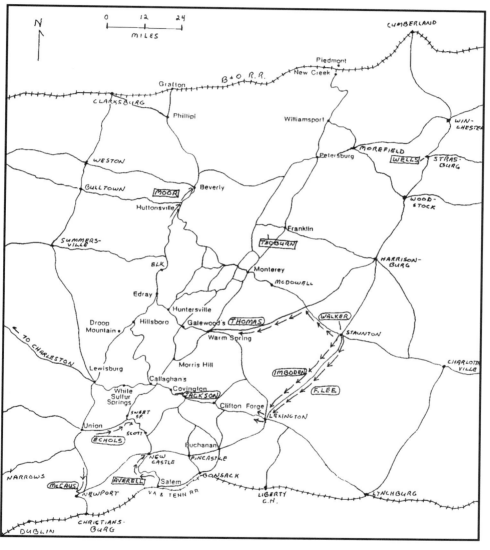

Movements, 17–18 December

Compiled from *Official Records Atlas*, Plate 135c, No. 1. Stephen Z. Starr, *The Union Cavalry in the Civil War.* Author's notes.

Averell's escape route seventeen miles to the north. Standing six-feet-four-inches tall and weighing 260 pounds, the forty-year-old John Echols was an imposing man who now straddled one mountain in eager anticipation of avenging the disaster he had sustained on another.[49]

Fitz Lee, meanwhile, starting from Mt. Crawford and going by way of Greenville, had driven his men and their mounts a grueling sixty-eight miles, wherein he had rendezvoused with Imboden at Lexington and ridden on with him to Collierstown, a mere twenty-five miles east of Covington, where Jackson had arrived the day before (17th).[50] (Waiting for Lee at Lexington was a battery and 260 infantry of Lieutenant Colonel Skipper's VMI cadets, and from Goshen per Early's orders, Colonel Massie's Rockbridge Home Guards. They all remained in Lexington.)[51]

That evening (18th) in New Castle Averell gained some idea of how grim the situation was. Shortly after dark his efficient scouts, whom he kept out on the roads twenty-four hours a day in search of useful information, began to bring in the distressing news. Echols' position on Sweet Springs Mountain (Jones had arrived there from Dublin the same evening) had been easily discovered because the rebels there, without shelter and cold and miserable themselves, had built up huge fires to keep warm[52] (Lt. Col. Andrew Barbee of the 22nd Va. wrote home that Sweet Springs Mountain was "the coldest place in Virginia," while Echols reported that his men were "poorly clad and without shoes, a condition which seriously tested the morale of the mountaineers.")[53] And although Fitz Lee's position was inaccurately reported as Fincastle,[54] the danger on the right was no less real.

Having crossed Craig's Creek, Averell was now up another creek. As he saw it, he now had three options. He could get around Jones by swinging on a wide arc to the west, going through Monroe and Greenbrier counties, then heading north. But this would require enormous time and take his exhausted men through country even more rugged than what they had already come through. Next, he could march to Sweet Springs Mountain and fight his way through. But this wasn't really an option anymore. A new, serious problem had arisen. Thanks to the steady rains and the Craig's Creek crossings, nearly all the ammunition, both in the wagons and the men's pouches, was ruined. Many of the firearms had also been severely damaged–a frightening dilemma this deep in enemy territory. If at all possible, a fight had to be avoided.

That left the third option—to somehow sneak between Jones and Fitz Lee by going northeast to Covington (Averell did not yet know Jackson was there), cross the swollen Jackson River on the two bridges he knew to still be intact there, then race northwest to safety through Pocahontas County to Beverly.[55] It seemed the only viable choice, but it carried great risks. Both Jones at Sweet Springs Mountain and Fitz Lee at Fincastle (actually Collierstown) could easily beat him to Covington should they become aware of his intentions. Thus to win that deadly race, he would have to deceive his enemies, delay alerting them, and move faster than them. That meant using his three favorite stealth tactics—the false advance, the all night march, and the use of side roads and country lanes—all at the same time.

But how to find those side lanes? Averell was unfamiliar with this region; there was no time for extensive reconnaissance and he could not rely on the decidedly pro-Confederate local citizenry. Pacing about the small, cold hotel lobby in New Castle (the "Old Brick Hotel," built in the 1840s) where he had established his headquarters, he quietly wrestled with this dilemma through much of the evening.[56] The situation looked grim, but his confidence and determination refused to allow him to consider it hopeless. There must be a way out to safety.

Then it struck him—if anyone could lead the way through on back lanes it would be the local country doctor, who should know the region well because of his travels to see patients. It was a long shot—a very long shot—but he had to try.

Averell inquired if the town had a doctor. When told that New Castle did indeed have its own physician, a Dr. Wylie, he insisted the man be brought to him at once.

Thirty-three-year-old Dr. Oscar Wylie lived in a fine home out along Sinking Creek, not far from town. A widower raising two small boys—nine-year-old Archer and seven-year-old Frank[57]—Wylie had worked hard to earn the respect the area residents now held for him. When he heard on the night of 18 December that the Yankees had sent for him, the young doctor, evidently believing his medical services were required, came to town promptly and without suspicion.

Averell, as he had done with the boy-prisoners at Mason's Cove, put his guest at ease by acting the friendly, gracious host. With a reassuring manner, he asked Wylie general questions about his experience, his practice, his family. When the doctor seemed sufficiently comfortable, Averell closed in. "You know most of the roads through these mountains, I guess?" he asked, innocently enough. "Yes, I know every road and path for many miles around," Wylie naively replied.

Averell slammed the trap shut. "Then you must guide me and my men out of here!" he suddenly demanded. Realizing at last that he had been set up, Wylie sat for a moment in stunned silence, then muttered, "Oh I can't do that." But Averell was not about to let go. He offered the doctor $500 in gold and conveyance for him and his family to Federal territory. Wylie, perhaps weighing the inevitability of Averell's capture anyway, still refused. Averell then bluntly threatened to shoot him. Convinced the general incapable of so monstrous an act, Wylie held firm. Averell sternly assured the doctor that he would indeed have him shot and consider it not only a justifiable act of war but an example for the next person he would ask for help. Then to prove his sincerity, Averell rose, called in a guard of troops, pulled out his watch and coolly informed Wylie that he had five minutes to choose between life and death.

With the ticking of the watch the only sound in the room, one minute passed and then two. Under Averell's piercing glare the doctor began to perspire and become restless. At three minutes, Wylie could take no more. He broke down and agreed to lead the men out.

This was an incredible stroke of luck for Averell, and an impressive display by him of cleverness and resourcefulness. But was he bluffing? Would he have had Dr. Wylie shot if he hadn't agreed to cooperate? When asked that very question by a family friend, a Mrs. Braxton, in 1899, Averell replied emphatically and without hesitation, "Indeed I would, madam." We shall never know, but considering how desperate the situation appeared to be, Averell probably did consider the shooting of Dr. Wylie "a justifiable act of war."[58]

Now, Averell believed, the command might have a chance to escape. But it remained a slim chance. Their new guide was a reluctant one, at best, and could prove untrustworthy; and there was still the matter of deceiving Jones and Fitz Lee long enough to allow the command to reach Covington first.

At 9 p.m. that night (18th), the detested rain having finally stopped, Averell started his "false advances." It meant extra, hard duty for the men, but he firmly believed their lives now depended on it. For Lee he sent a force riding toward Fincastle, which lay about fifteen miles to the east (6 miles northeast on county road 615 to county road 606, then 9 miles east), and for Jones he sent Lieutenant Colonel Polsley with the 2nd and 8th West Virginia north for Potts' Mountain.[59]

At "Mrs. Scott's place" (the widow Mrs. Oliver Scott's tavern) on Barber's Creek, about five miles north of New Castle, the 2nd West Virginia ran into Jones' advance pickets and chased them seven miles to the top of Potts'.[60] During the chase, Sergeant O.P. Bower, the same who had encountered the Chapman patrol three nights before, Joseph Walton, W.A. Wiley of Company B, and another soldier from Company D caught up with some of the rebs and got into a scrape with them. During the close-in fighting in the dark a rebel knocked the pistol out of Wiley's hand then raised his own to shoot him. Bower shot the rebel (quite possibly Pvt. Saunders Gray of Co. K, 22 Va. Inf.)[61] in the shoulder before he could fire, then called out for a charge. Though Bower was bluffing, the Confederates quickly broke off the fight and scampered away.[62]

On Potts' Mountain Polsley, as instructed by Averell, had the men build huge campfires that could be easily seen by Jones across the valley on Sweet Springs Mountain. The West Virginians were to "make all the bluster and noise possible," remembered Captain Rife, "and make the impression that we intended to force our way."[63] (Jones responded by having Echols' men sleep on their arms.)[64] Then around 1 a.m. on the nineteenth, they quietly slipped back down Potts'. "We left our campfires burning," Averell wrote, "and went forward in the darkest and coldest night we had experienced."[65] Once again, he was leading them on through the night. At Mrs. Scott's on Barber's Creek, seven miles back from Potts', he met up with the men who had ridden toward Fincastle. Waiting there, too, was Dr. Wylie. The fate of the command now rested in his hands.[66]

4. Confederate Confusion

As the cold, crisp predawn hours of the nineteenth thus unfolded, Dr. Wylie led the column down a country lane that ran northeast along Barber's Creek and into the Rich Patch Valley of Alleghany County.[67] If he betrayed them now, despite the threat of instant death should he do so, or if Averell's luck should otherwise run out, then Jones, Fitz Lee, Jackson, and Imboden would have their chance to destroy the column. But Wylie led them on at a steady pace, and Averell's luck was not only holding, it was taking a fantastic, unbelievable turn for the better.

Just a few hours before, the situation was even worse than Averell knew. He had assumed Fitz Lee was at Fincastle, about thirty miles southeast of Covington, when actually he was at Collierstown, a mere twenty-five miles east of Covington. It is doubtful Averell would have considered a march to Covington had he known this. But fate now intervened anyway to pull Fitz Lee even further away. The orders came from General Early.

During the night of the eighteenth–nineteenth, Early became convinced Averell had been cut off by high water on his retreat northward and was returning to Salem to find a new escape route through the Shenandoah. A number of factors contributed to this belief, but Early's acceptance of them was the most amazing fact of all.

It began with the rumors Averell had left in Salem regarding his return through Bonsack's. At Mason's Cove the next day the Federal commander cleverly reinforced these rumors by periodically sending scouts back toward Salem, not only to make sure the enemy was not following but to also give the impression the column had turned around. The locals readily accepted this impression and, with the quick repair of the telegraph line in Salem, the "news" was sent on to General Francis Nicholls, commander of the local militia at Lynchburg.[68] Averell's false advance toward Fincastle on the eighteenth caused the same reaction. But the Federal commander's most effective deception was his least intentional— the march back down Potts' Mountain after leaving his campfires burning there for Jones to see on the night of the eighteenth. Averell had tried to sneak down the mountain unnoticed, but within a short time, news of it, too, was on its way to Lynchburg. Thus early on the nineteenth, Nicholls received two messages from Bonsack's (one from Capt. D.C. Booth, acting commander at Bonsack's of the Roanoke Home Guards, and the other from L.E. Faucher, manager of Bonsack's telegraph office),[69] each of which claimed, in effect, that Averell had been cut off and was returning to Salem. Nicholls, in turn, passed all this on to Early at Staunton. For some reason, Early accepted it at face value.

Though it might have been reasonable to assume that Averell, cut off by Jones or high water, would try to find a different escape route, it stretches the imagination to think he would return all the way to Salem and sink back deeper into enemy territory. But by his own admission, Early "took it for granted that it was true,"[70] and he thereby assumed that Averell would return to Salem then try to escape down through the Shenandoah by way of Buchanan, Lexington and thence on to Staunton. Acting on that incredible assumption, Early sent a wire to Lexington, and from there a courier rode out ten miles west to the foot of North Mountain near Collierstown (about 18 miles east of Clifton Forge) with instructions for Fitz Lee and Imboden to immediately ride for Buchanan, some sixteen miles to the south.[71] And thus as Averell was marching north toward Covington in the predawn hours of the nineteenth, Fitz Lee and Imboden were headed in the opposite direction on a parallel course twenty miles to the east. Lee later estimated, probably correctly, that had he not been redirected to Buchanan, he could have beaten Averell to Covington by at least three hours.[72] Undoubtedly, Averell would then have met with disaster.

The local newspapers, anxious themselves to keep a handle on Averell's whereabouts, reflected the general confusion prevalent at that time among the Confederate commanders. Uncertain at first as to the correct identity of the various advancing Federal columns, the newspapers' speculations weaved in and out of the truth. That speculation had begun back on the fourteenth when the *Richmond Examiner,* confusing Averell with Scammon, noted that a Federal force had left the Kanawha for some unknown reason.[73] Two days later the paper mistook Averell for Thoburn. "Nothing official has been heard from Averell," proclaimed an article titled "Averell's Movements." "One report is that he has, after advancing towards Staunton, turned back. Another is that he never had the first idea of molesting that important mountain fastness."[74] The next day, the seventeenth, under the headline, "Important From Southwest Virginia—A Raid On The Virginia And Tennessee Railroad," the paper mistook Colonel Moor for Averell, by confirming that a force from Beverly had struck the railroad at Salem.[75] Then over the next three days, speculation ran high among several papers—the *Examiner, Richmond Dispatch, Richmond Sentinel, Lynchburg Virginian*—as to the escape route Averell planned to use. "We hardly think he [Averell] will be able to go forward in the hope of extricating himself from the meshes in which he is involved," the *Lynchburg Virginian* confidently proclaimed on the morning of the nineteenth, "but believe that he will be rich game for the men now on his track, who are burning to wipe out the disgrace of the audacious attempt of the Yankee robbers to penetrate into the heart of Virginia."[76] While the *Virginian* speculated that Averell might swing west up the Catawba toward Salt Pond in an effort to reach the Kanawha Valley,[77] the *Examiner* believed he might head south for North Carolina, striking Danville along the way and liberating "the Yankee prisoners confined there."[78] And though the Richmond paper expressed confidence "that, by whatever route he attempts to escape, he will find a lion in his path,"[79] it went on to warn that "if Averell is allowed to escape the cavalry of Virginia had better be re-organized without loss of time."[80]

As to Early's redirection of troops south toward Buchanan, the press would have a very strong reaction. "Here was committed the fatal and foolish blunder," the *Richmond Examiner* would howl with perfect hindsight on 28 December. "While Lee and Imboden were on the road to Covington, in striking distance of that place, word was sent the Yankees are marching toward Buchanan, instead of Covington. No man ought to have put credence in a statement so utterly absurd as that the enemy were going from Salem to that place. Such a statement pre-supposes Averell deliberately placing himself past escape, and therefore run raving mad. Such improbable rumors should never be entertained a moment, much less made the basis of important military movements."[81]

But on the Saturday morning of 19 December rumor and speculation were essentially all the Confederates had to go on. That morning's issue of the *Lynchburg Virginian,* for example, concluded that because the James River had risen so rapidly and dramatically over the past few days, the mountain streams to the west must be so full as to surely cut off Averell's command. "This is the most daring raid yet perpetrated by the enemy," the newspaper confessed, but then it quickly added, "we have strong hopes that he will be punished for his temerity." Confident in the inevitable swift and thorough execution of such punishment, the paper expressed an additional, fervent hope: "We sincerely trust that their fate will be a warning to other Yankee leaders who may be ambitious of emulating the example of Averill [*sic*] and Kilpatrick."[82]

But before he could be punished and made into an example for "other Yankee leaders," Averell had to be caught. Thanks, in part, to Dr. Wylie's guidance down obscure country paths, the Federal column remained undetected for several precious hours. It was not sighted till after daylight, when the painful truth finally became known to the Confederate leaders. From Nicholls at Lynchburg that morning (19th) Early finally received the startling information that Averell had not returned to Salem but had managed to cross Craig's Creek and was headed for Covington.[83]

Realizing it was probably too late to bring Fitz Lee back up in time, a frantic Early nonetheless sent him a dispatch by way of Jackson at Covington. He then went down to Millborough Depot to see if Thomas' infantry brigade "could not be thrown to some point to intercept the enemy," specifically, to go by rail down to Jackson at Covington (Walker's brigade to be left in Staunton). But he quickly abandoned that notion when he saw the dilapidated condition of the rails and cars at Millborough[84]—more of Averell's good fortune, for a full infantry brigade in Covington would certainly have caused him a great deal of trouble.

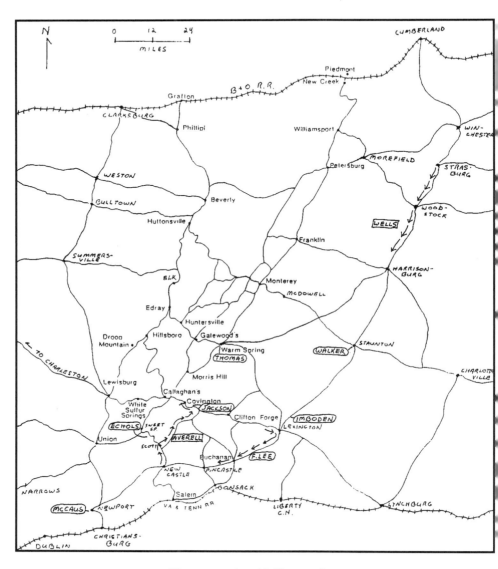

Movements, 19 December

Compiled from *Official Records Atlas,* Plate 135c, No. 1. Stephen Z. Starr,
The Union Cavalry in the Civil War. Author's notes.

"Did you send my dispatch to Fitzhugh Lee?" Early, feeling utterly helpless, anxiously wired Jackson later that day (19th). "Have you heard from him? Where is he? What is the enemy doing?"[85]

5. Covington

"Thirty miles through the forest and frost brought us to the Fincastle pike about noon of the 19th,"[86] Averell reported. Thirty miles, from the top of Potts' Mountain to the tiny, one-church settlement of Rich Patch, in about eleven hours. The journey had been tough and grueling. The lane along Barber's Creek was extremely rough, often going through dense woods, which in darkness carried its own special hazards; "the path was covered in places by fallen trees and logs," remembered Captain Rife, "over which the weary horses stumbled and sometimes fell."[87] In this way many of the animals sustained injuries too severe to allow them to go on, and they were thereby added to the already appallingly long list of fellow creatures who had had their throats slit and their carcasses left by the roadside to mark the progress of the humans who had no further use of them.[88]

But many of those humans were beginning to wish that they, too, could be simply left by the roadside. "The awful demand of nature for sleep called loud and unrelenting," Rife declared. "Hunger applied in vain for satisfaction. Cold—and so cold! A fire, a warm meal and a bed were worth millions. . . ." Rife became so exhausted that he laid his head down on his horse's neck and let his arms drape on either side. "And all around me are men and horses marching, suffering, hungering just as I am," he observed, rather sadly. "O what had become of the romance of soldiering—the beating drums, marching men, prancing horses and waving flags?" And to this rhetorical question he had his own ready answer: "That was the poetry of war; this is the bitter reality, robbed of all charm."[89]

At Rich Patch, if not sooner, Dr. Wylie's obligation ended. (Wylie went on with the column and eventually received the promised $500 in gold.[90] Despite the extenuating circumstances, and Averell's letter of exoneration written to the editor of the *New Castle Record* in 1885,[91] the people of Craig County considered Wylie a traitor and he never lived among them again. He continued, however, to lead an adventurous life. After the war he resided in Charleston, West Virginia, where he was eventually arrested for the murder of a speculator named Tift. Upon making bail, Wylie disappeared.)[92] With Covington now within reach, Averell allowed no let-up. "I had carefully calculated the possible marches of the enemy," he explained in his report, "and felt certain we could make the march through the points deemed most secure, but no halt could be made."[93]

Averell knew that with each passing mile, his chances for successfully slipping between, and past, Jones on his left and Fitz Lee on his right, increased dramatically. But he did not know that danger still lay ahead—his column was marching straight for Colonel Jackson's forces located near Covington.

Like his famous second cousin "Stonewall," thirty-eight-year-old William Lowther Jackson had been born near Clarksburg in what is now West Virginia. With dark red hair and piercing blue eyes, Jackson was a large man for his time, standing six feet tall and weighing about 200 pounds. An ardent seccessionist before the war, he had used his position as circuit judge in Parkersburg to defend Southern sympathizers, even going so far on one occasion as to get involved in a common brawl. Such behavior inevitably led to Jackson being literally run out of town by loyal Unionists. The ensuing reputation, plus a distinguished prewar career as a lawyer, commonwealth attorney, judge, state legislator, and lieutenant governor, made Jackson a popular figure among the pro-Confederates of western Virginia. As was the case with many of his Northern counterparts, influence and popularity were somehow translated into military command. Soon after the war began, Jackson was made colonel of the 31st Virginia Infantry, a regiment composed primarily of men from the trans-Allegheny. But after the disaster of Rich Mountain and the subsequent loss of western Virginia to the despised Federals, a disheartened Jackson gave up the 31st and joined the staff of his cousin Stonewall, serving with him through Fredericksburg. In February 1863, however, Congress took the risk of returning the colonel to field command by authorizing him to form a new regiment "behind enemy lines," where his popularity was still high. The new regiment, composed mostly of discharged veterans, many of whom had served in the old 31st, became the 19th Virginia Cavalry.[94] As the summer wore on, however, volunteers continued to pour in until Jackson had a brigade on his hands. In addition to the 19th, the 20th Virginia Cavalry took shape as did the two-gun battery of Warren Lurty, who was another cousin of the famous Stonewall. Furthermore, the recruits spilled over into six independent companies that would be formed early the following year into the 46th Battalion of Virginia Cavalry.

As one of the Confederacy's few politician-officers, Jackson never seemed to get the hang of field command. Though long on words—as befitted his legal and political background, his reports were sometimes near book-length—he was woefully short on providing discipline and training to his men. He apparently attained the unflattering handle "Mudwall" when Yankee soldiers carved the name on the wall of the Pocahontas County courthouse in Huntersville in August of 1863. They evidently did this by way of distinguishing Jackson, who had just stepped aside to let them pass on toward Lewisburg, from the mighty "Stonewall."[95]

Having missed the Rocky Gap triumph in August, and then being nearly destroyed on Droop Mountain by Averell in November, Jackson's men had yet to taste a real victory. Now, in defense of the Covington bridges, they stood in readiness for a vengeful rematch with Averell and his Yankees.

But even if Averell had known "Mudwall" was waiting for him, there was no turning back now—Jackson River was unfordable, he had to get to those bridges at Covington. Basically, there was no place else to go. Though the men were beaten down by fatigue and their ammunition was extremely low, there was no choice but to stay on course and fight through Jackson, if need be.

At Rich Patch the column turned due north up the Rich Patch road and headed for the James River pike, which paralleled Jackson River and connected Clifton Forge and Covington. It was eight miles to the pike, and the column would reach it across the river from the Karne farm, about seven miles east of Covington. Two miles west of the intersection was Averell's first objective—the Island Ford Bridge, which stood about six miles west of Jackson's headquarters at Jackson River Depot.[96] This area, along the Rich Patch road to the Island Ford Bridge, is where Averell would be most vulnerable. And Jackson knew he was coming.

Jackson's present assignment, given to him by Early, was to guard the bridge at Clifton Forge and the two at Covington. From the warnings sent to him from Staunton, he knew by the afternoon of the nineteenth that Averell was headed his way.[97] Why Jackson did not then destroy the bridges is a mystery. If his concern had been their preservation for the future con-venience of Confederate troop movements, he could have followed Early's suggestion and pulled up the planks and saved them for easy reinstallation once the crisis had passed.[98] In either case, it probably would have meant the end of Averell. But Jackson, reassured by the locals that the river would remain unfordable for at least another two days, preferred to hold off on any decisive action until the very last moment. At the Island Ford Bridge he posted a destruction crew of about ten Alleghany Home Guards under Captain Thompson McAllister, whom he instructed to hold himself in readi-ness to immediately fire the covered span once he received the word.[99]

Jackson considered Averell's most likely approach to be either north up the Rich Patch road or west along the pike from Clifton Forge. To deal with the threat from the east the Confederate commander built a defensive "fence" across the pike at Alum Rock, about a mile east of the Rich Patch road intersection. Behind the fence he placed about half of his command—Colonel William Arnett's 20th Virginia Cavalry and Captain Warren Lurty's section of two guns—about 300 men altogether. For the threat from Rich Patch, he sent the other half of his command, most of the 19th Virginia Cavalry, a few hundred yards down the road.[100]

Everything seemed to be covered. All except one little side path that broke off to the left of the Rich Patch road about two miles south of the pike. This obscure little lane Rich Patch residents used when traveling to Covington; they took the fork to the right when they wanted to go to Clifton Forge. For some reason, Jackson knew nothing about the side lane to the left. "[It was] some route that had never been explained to me," he testified in his report, "although I sought information from every source, and was assured that I was guarding every possible approach."[101] Though he claimed to have sent his scouts out toward Buchanan and down the Rich Patch road "as far as high water permitted,"[102] a more accurate account can probably be found in an investigative report filed the following January by Major Edward McMahon of Jones' staff. In that report Jackson is accused, among other things, of sending his scouts out no farther than four miles from his headquarters at Jackson River Depot.[103] If that were so, they would not have gone far enough to discover the side lane. Either that or the scouts did such a poor job of reconnaissance that they missed it altogether.

Averell's scouts didn't miss it. A quick reconnaissance by them revealed its great value—the path came out on the pike only about a mile east of the bridge. Word of the important find was speedily sent back down the column with the result that shortly before dark the 8th West Virginia, led by Companies A, B, D, and F, began to pour into the side lane.[104]

But the apparent advantage gained by this shortcut was almost offset by the difficulties that came with it. Passing through a deep, rocky gorge, the lane became so narrow that the column had to ride through most of it in single file, and so slippery was the surface with ice that progress slowed to a snail's pace. It was "a deep, narrow defile," recalled Frank Reader, "so narrow that it was with the greatest difficulty for anyone to pass from the rear to the front. The road was covered with ice, and it was impossible to prevent the horses from falling, and at times many of them would be down at once."[105]

When the Confederates on the Rich Patch road finally figured out what was happening, they sent word back to Jackson's headquarters on the pike. Undoubtedly chagrined to learn the Yankees were slipping by a position he had supposedly made thorough dispositions to cover, Jackson sprang into action. He ordered the detachment on the Rich Patch road to move up and attack Averell's column as it passed onto the side lane; he turned the troops around at the "fence" and started them west for the Rich Patch road intersection, and he sent his aide, Captain Charles Boyd of the engineer corps, to instruct McAllister to burn the bridge.[106]

This was a critical time for Averell, despite the newly found shortcut, for although Jackson had fewer men, the rebels were more concentrated. Averell, superb at keeping his command on the move, was less efficient about keeping it closed-up (he had paid dearly for this in August at the battle of Rocky Gap). His column was strung out for more than four miles,[107] and the wagons, under Lieutenant Alexander J. Pentacost of the quartermaster staff, and guarded by the 14th Pennsylvania, were about ten miles back.[108] The train had fallen so far behind mainly because of the poor condition of the road along Barber's Creek. The path was so rough and bumpy that to keep from tipping over, the wagons had to go very slowly with two or three men riding along on each side.[109] All of this meant, of course, that the column and the train would require a great deal of time to get through the narrow defile, time enough for Jackson, with his more concentrated forces,

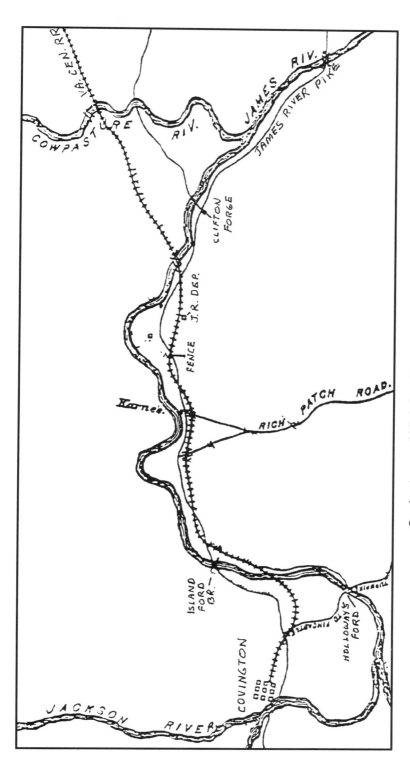

Covington and Vicinity, 19–20 December, 1863

Compiled from *Official Records*, Ser. I, V. 29, Pt. 1, p. 947. Author's notes.

to burn the bridge and inflict serious damage on the command as it came up piecemeal. (Jackson, however, would sorely miss his detachments of 250 or so men, who had yet not reached him from Pocahontas County.)[110]

Sometime after sunset, an advanced guard of three officers (including Captain Rife) and two or three men of the 8th West Virginia cautiously approached the end of the defile and looked out onto the pike. About a mile to the west they saw the Island Ford Bridge. To their great relief, the span was still intact. But to their dismay they also saw campfires with men standing about and three large piles of pine kindling—"fagots"—stacked on each side of the bridge. This could mean only one thing—destruction crews were waiting to set the bridge ablaze.[111]

No sooner had the officers lowered their binoculars and agreed on this assessment when a lone rider, moving east along the pike, approached them from out of the darkness. The man unsuspectingly rode up to the party, bid them good evening and, apparently unable in the darkness to distinguish uniform color, asked them where they were going. "Where are you going?" someone in the scouting party shot back. "I am going to Colonel Jackson," the Confederate replied without hesitation, "with a dispatch from General Jones." Almost before the hapless rider could complete his statement, he found himself staring in amazement down the barrels of six revolvers.[112]

The dispatch was an incredible find, and another instance of Averell's remarkable luck. The captured note had been sent in response to the one General Early had sent on the seventeenth to inform Jones of the move of Thomas' brigade to Warm Springs (Early unaccountably not telling him of the movement of Fitz Lee and Imboden for Lexington). The troops under Early at Staunton were the much-anticipated and longed-for reinforcements Jones had been anxiously awaiting General Lee to provide. The department commander understandably believed these troops should be sent at once to cooperate with Jackson at Covington, and thus after receiving Early's note during the night of the eighteenth, he responded immediately to urge that Thomas be sent all the way to Gatewood's via Morris Hill. He went on to say that to snare Averell he, too, was prepared to cooperate with Jackson and/or Thomas by moving off Sweet Springs and marching toward either Lewisburg or White Sulphur Springs.[113]

With this message, Jones' courier set out from Sweet Springs Mountain in the predawn darkness of the nineteenth for Covington, from where the information would be sent on to Staunton by wire. Traveling northeast along Potts' Creek, the courier followed a route that roughly paralleled Averell's and was about four miles to the west of it. Familiar with the area, the rider made good time, good enough he apparently thought, to allow for an approximately two-hour break at the home of a friend (Jo Sively) on Potts' Creek, a mere six miles from the Island Ford Bridge.[114] Thus he unknowingly timed his ride to coincide perfectly for a rendezvous with Averell's advance guard.

**1st Sgt. James H. Nesmith,
Co. F, 14th Regt., Pa. Vol. Cav.**

He was a raider in the ranks.

Mrs. Jean Beck Collection, US Army Military History Institute

The captured dispatch, and the information about the still-intact bridge, was immediately sent back down the defile to Averell. Aware at last of the danger to his command, and grateful for the now unbelievable news that Island Ford was still standing, Averell sped a staff officer forward to instruct the 8th to immediately seize the bridge.[115]

By now, around 9 p.m.,[116] Companies B, D, and F had joined Company A at the opening of the defile onto the pike.[117] (Cos. H and K brought up the extreme rear guard, behind the wagons.)[118] Upon the receipt of Averell's instructions they all formed up and slowly, cautiously rode toward the bridge. The rebel home guards, hearing the low rumble of hundreds of hooves striking the soft ground off to the west, suddenly perked up and anxiously turned toward the menacing sound. One of them picked up a torch and ran for the piles of kindling. Shots rang out. The order to charge pierced the cold night air, "and on we moved with a rush," recalled Captain Rife. The destruction crews, including the torch bearer, promptly scattered and the West Virginians thundered onto the bridge. "What a clatter of hoofs on the wooden floor," Rife observed, "and how the horses crowded on the front line."[119] The bridge was Averell's!

In the rush across the bridge Captain Rife had lost his hat. When he later had the time, he went in search of it, hoping that the bridge itself may have somehow caught the cap and saved it from the icy water below. Looking down through the planks, he was struck by how remarkably sturdy the span appeared to be, and though he did not recover his hat, he was nonetheless grateful the bridge hadn't been sabotaged in some way.[120]

Had he known, Rife could have directed his gratitude to Averell's good fortune and Jackson's incompetence. The good fortune occurred when Captain Boyd's horse tripped and fell, flinging Boyd to the ground with a serious injury that prevented him from delivering Jackson's orders to destroy the bridge. The incompetence occurred when Jackson gave such an important mission to only one man instead of an entire squad.[121]

Within moments of the 8th West Virginia's thunderous rush onto the bridge, Averell rode up to his newly won prize and took control. He assigned one of the 8th's companies to guard the span. Another he sent riding east on the pike to find a good defensive position about three-fourths of a mile down, where they were to dismount and buy some time by holding against any advance Jackson might make in this direction. The other two companies Averell sent on to Covington to seize the bridge on the west side of town. Finally, he sent three officers and six orderlies back down the side lane to close up the column and hurry it along.[122]

Jackson, meanwhile, remained ignorant of the fact that Averell was slipping right by him. Seeing no flames in the night sky, "Mudwall" kept sending riders to order the destruction of the bridge, all of whom kept falling into Yankee hands.[123] Finally suspecting something was amiss, he sent an entire company (Co. A, Captain George Downs, 19 Va. Cav.). It ran into the company Averell had posted across the pike. The Confederates rushed the position and pushed back the West Virginians, a few of whom fell into rebel hands. A hot fire fight broke out, but the blue coats stiffened and held until, after only a few minutes, the rebels broke off and retired back along the pike.[124]

At last, Jackson knew he had lost the bridge. Instead of making a direct effort to retake it, however, he sent the 20th Virginia down the Rich Patch road to join in the attack on Averell's rear.[125] But there hadn't been much of an attack there in the first place. Averell's advancing column had rather easily brushed aside the 300 or so rebels of the 19th Virginia Cavalry, which then evidently became so disorganized that most of the regiment dispersed and melted away into the darkness.[126]

Among other things, the 19th seemed to be the victim of nebulous leadership. Jackson was in nominal command, but because of his brigade responsibilities, the regiment had been turned over to Lieutenant Colonel William Thompson. Thompson, however, was presently with Echols on Sweet Springs, having ridden there three days before on a scout with 100 men. That left Major Joseph Kessler, but he was more-or-less in charge of the independent companies. Altogether, then, the 19th was now commanded by whatever senior captain was on the field, a confusing situation at best.[127]

So it was with just a few remnants of the 19th that at around midnight the 20th Virginia moved up and opened fire.[128] The Virginians had caught the very end of Averell's column: the wagon train, its escort, the 14th Pennsylvania (led by Co. A),[129] and the rear guard, consisting of "Powell's Squadron"—companies H and K of the 8th West Virginia, under Captain E.B. Powell.

Just before the fight broke out, however, Confederates posing as Federals led three of the ambulances and their unsuspecting escorts down the right fork of the road and into captivity. In this way Averell lost both his aide, Captain Leopold Markbreit, who was lying weak and exhausted in one of the wagons, and Lieutenant John McAdams of Company G, 10th West Virginia, now in charge of the expedition's ambulances.[130] A more stunning loss was Lieutenant Colonel John Polsley, who had hung back with the rear of the column and was now either on some sort of recon or he had simply gotten lost in the darkness. When the 19th Virginia Cavalry's Captain John Spriggs approached him from out of the shadows, Polsley mistook the rebel for one of his own men. Spriggs, evidently blessed with keener night vision, was quick to set the West Virginian straight. "Do you know who you are talking to?" he demanded. "Who are you?" Polsley asked, with some surprise. "I am one of Jackson's men," came the firm answer. Then putting a gun to Polsley's head, Spriggs quickly added, "Unless you surrender immediately I will blow out your brains." The 28 December issue of the *Richmond Sentinel* ended this story on a foregone note. "It is needless to say," the paper read, "that the gallant Captain was soon seen on the Colonel's fine horse."[131]

At any rate, shortly after these mishaps befell the unsuspecting Federals, a wild, confused fire fight broke out along the Rich Patch road between members of the 19th and 20th Virginia on the one hand and the 14th Pennsylvania and 8th West Virginia on the other. "We immediately took to the woods," recalled Corporal George Stover of Powell's Squadron.[132]

In the darkness and among the trees, neither side could do much harm to the other, but the Yankees were nonetheless pinned down and couldn't get away. Sporadic firing continued for some time, all the while the rest of the Federal column was safely crossing over the Island Ford Bridge.

Then, suddenly, the firing dropped off. Cautiously, the Pennsylvanians probed the woods in front and quickly discovered that the rebs had gone. Not wasting any time to analyze the situation, the surprised Federals seized the opportunity by jumping on their mounts and making for the bridge. Their chance had been granted them by Colonel Arnett when he abruptly broke off the fight and took his men back to the fence at Alum Rock.

William Wiley Arnett, the six-foot-tall twenty-four-year-old native of Marion County, West Virginia and graduate of Allegheny College in Pennsylvania, had just begun his law practice when the war broke out. He served two years in the old 31st Virginia, working his way up from private to captain of Company A. Along the way he earned such respect from the men of the trans-Allegheny that in the summer of 1863 they elected him to both the Virginia Legislature and to the command of the newly formed 20th Virginia Cavalry. Barely a month after assuming the latter post, he tasted the bitter defeat of Droop Mountain. Now facing many of those same Yankees again, Arnett preferred caution, and he broke off his fight with the Pennsylvanians.[133]

He did this, he subsequently explained, because he believed that by this time Jackson and whatever troops were with him had secured or destroyed the Island Ford Bridge, thereby forcing the Federals on the pike to turn around and head for the bridge at Clifton Forge. Hoping to cut off the Yankees, Arnett hurried his troops back up the road to the intersection, then advanced two companies (Otho Alexander's Co. K and Walker's, apparently independent co.) west along the pike to open communications with Jackson. They ran into Averell's column and were promptly driven back into the mountains. This in turn led Arnett to assume that, instead of securing the bridge, Jackson had either been cut off or destroyed. Now fearing for the safety of his own small command, Arnett fell back to the cover of the fence.[134] Such was the confusion amid the complete breakdown of communication among the Confederate commanders.

But Jackson was neither cut off nor destroyed. Despite having lost contact with virtually everyone in his command, he was stubbornly trying to resist Averell's advance. From the scattered troops running about in the darkness, he managed to grab the 20th Virginia's Major John Lady and his little command of about fifty men and place them on the heights overlooking the approach to the bridge. It was Jackson's first good move of the day, for when the formerly pinned-down Pennsylvanians tried to rush the bridge, the hot fire of these fifty turned them back and forced them to seek refuge in the defile. A second and a third try proved no more successful, leaving Lieutenant Colonel Blakely with no choice but to stay put and await rescue from Averell.[135]

They waited, and waited, until the concensus finally arose that Averell must be holding off until daylight to make his move. Having reached that hopeful conclusion, the Pennsylvanians bedded down and tried to get some sleep. Sleep, however, proved nearly impossible. Unable to build many fires for fear of being discovered by the rebels, the men spent most of their time lying shivering on the hard ground. "The air was very cold that night," remembered Lieutenant Pentacost, "but we had to sleep at a distance from our fire to avoid being shot at."[136] "The night was cold," a soldier later wrote the *Pittsburgh Gazette,* "fires could not be lighted, and our men almost perished."[137] Fortunately, the rebels, no doubt cold and miserable themselves, did not seem inclined to bother them.

Nevertheless, throughout the cold, dark night there were a number of chance encounters with the enemy. One such encounter occurred during a scout toward the pike by a party of five men—Chief Quartermaster Captain W.H. Brown, Chief of Commissary Lieutenant Koenigsberger, Hospital Steward Theo Brown, and two headquarters orderlies. After going about three-fourths of a mile, the five men abruptly pulled up in reaction to the sight of a man on horseback approaching at the head of three ambulances. The small band at first assumed the wagons were their own, but taking no chances, they drew their pistols. "Who comes there?" Captain Brown called out.

"A friend," answered the man on horseback, now only about twenty paces away.

"Are you a Confederate?" Brown continued.

"Yes," came the simple, unsuspecting answer.

"Follow us!" Brown demanded, as "we all covered him with our six-shooters."

The prize, a captain in the rebel ambulance corps, they promptly took back to the bivouac and turned over to the 14th Pennsylvania. So eager were the men to turn in their trophy, however, that they seemed to have forgotten all about the three ambulances, which continued on their way down the pike toward Alum Rock. At the bivouac of the 14th a detail of twenty men and a lieutenant was thus drawn up to go get the wagons. While the twenty men were preparing themselves for the mission, the lieutenant asked Theo Brown to show him where he had last seen the ambulances.

Brown had not been popular with most of the officers in the brigade. Since he and Averell were the only "regulars" in the command, everyone assumed the two were close friends. Thus, out of respect for their commander, many officers would offer a salute to Brown when they passed by him. But Brown, a mere hospital steward, and no acquaintance of Averell, considered it inappropriate to return the salutes and he thereby earned a reputation as "that stuck-up Regular who is too proud to acknowledge the courtesies of volunteer officers."[138] Whether the lieutenant now about to accompany Brown into the darkness felt this way about him is unknown, but the young officer was nonetheless about to gain quite an insight into the hospital steward's character, as well as his own.

With the lieutenant and two orderlies, Brown set out on his mission. After riding only about 300 yards, however, the four men heard from both sides of the road the chilling, clicking sound of numerous gun locks, then the challenge "Halt! Who goes there?"

"A friend," was the reflexive answer.

"Advance one," demanded the voice in the darkness. The game was up, or so it would seem. The desperate situation inspired Brown to quickly devise a somewhat-less-than-dignified escape plan. "You go," he said to one of the orderlies. Then while the hapless private rode forward, Brown turned his own mule around and sped back toward camp. The lieutenant and the other orderly quickly followed his example and did the same. The three got away, "but they never saw the lad who rode forward again," Brown unashamedly admitted afterwards.[139]

Meanwhile, the men had been right in their consensus—Averell had decided to wait until daylight to make his move. "A night attack is always appalling," he rationalized, "even to experienced troops."[140] A determined rescue attempt that night, however, probably would have succeeded at very little cost. Jackson's troops were widely scattered, his communications had broken down and confusion reigned throughout his command. But Averell knew none of this. He believed that the Confederates, as evidenced by their retention of the heights leading up to the span, were capable of retaking the bridge at almost any moment.[141] He decided to hold in Covington until morning.

Two of the five companies that had made the initial rush upon Island Ford Bridge had been the first of Averell's men to enter Covington, sometime around midnight, about the same time their comrades were coming under attack on the other side of the river along Rich Patch road. "Our noises and clatter soon aroused the people," Captain Rife remembered of the late-night ride into the town. Part of the noise and clatter was the result of an immediate search of all the stables, a search that yielded quite a number of horses, most of which would be put to use pulling the artillery pieces.[142]

Throughout the night Averell's men streamed into the town. At the same time, the temperature fell to three below zero, forcing many men, during the wait for the rest of their comrades to cross the river and close up, to impose themselves upon the citizenry for warmth. Though the men were "well behaved," conceded one resident, "they were not at all backward about going into the houses to escape the freezing weather."[143]

Then, just after dawn, Averell made his move at last. From Gibson's battalion he sent a squad of twenty-five men to probe across the river and open communications with Blakely. The squad, under Captain Law, crossed the bridge, now guarded by a company of the 3rd West Virginia under Captain Squires, and rode toward the defile. At about four hundred yards from the span, however, they ran into a terrific fire, opened on them by the same gang of rebels that had kept Blakely's men from getting through from the other side. Captain Law's men fell back and tried again, with no better result. With that, the discouraged bluecoats rode back over the bridge.[144]

Here Averell finally allowed a bit of his old demon, overcaution, to creep in. Like at the Rapidan nine months before, he now concluded that the Confederates across the river were too strong. He sent orders through Gibson to withdraw the troops guarding the bridge and then burn it.

It could not have been an easy decision to abandon a substantial part of his command, but Averell acted in the belief that it had become necessary to sacrifice the few in order to preserve the many. He reasoned that extreme good fortune had already saved most of his command, and he did not want to tempt that fortune by taking his men back across the river in a dangerous rescue attempt. Add to this his extreme uneasiness over the prospect that Fitz Lee or Jones were headed this way and any further delay became intolerable for him.

Major Gibson gave the job of destroying the Island Ford Bridge to Lieutenant Hoffman, who had been with Law's just-returned squad. With six men Hoffman stood several minutes at the near end of the bridge, putting off his unpleasant task until the very last moment in the slim hope that the 14th Pennsylvania might yet appear. Apparently he waited too long to satisfy Gibson, who sent a "second order—peremptory—to fire the bridge and come on immediately!" Using the stacks of kindling gathered there by the rebels, Hoffman set the span ablaze at around 8 a.m. Within moments, the structure's fiery timbers crashed into the river and floated downstream. Hoffman and his men turned away and rode on to Covington.[145] Averell, in turn, pulled the others from their refuge in the warm Covington houses, reformed the column, crossed over the bridge west of town and rode on to Callaghan's.[146]

With the sight of the smoke rising from the burning bridge, Blakely knew his situation had become extremely desperate. He also knew what he must do. The thirty wagons and ambulances left in his care were now a hopeless encumbrance. Shortly after 8 a.m. he instructed Lieutenant Pentacost to put them all to the torch. Pentacost, in turn, gave the job to his quartermaster sergeant, Elias Seaman, the same who had been the

**Capt. Rufus E. Fleming,
6th Regt. W.Va. Vol. Cav. (3rd W.Va. Mtd. Inf.)**

He was a raider in the ranks.

Roger D. Hunt Collection, US Army Military History Institute

uninvited wedding guest four days before on Potts' Mountain. Within moments, Seaman had the wagons rounded up and set afire.[147]

Going up in the flames were the command's remaining rations and all its tents, both of which Averell's men would greatly miss over the next few days.[148] (Not everything in the wagons was consumed. Hospital Steward Brown, the same who had barely saved his own skin only hours before, gallantly rescued three cases of quart bottle whiskey, which he graciously distributed among the "train men"; two of the bottles found their way into his own saddlebags.)[149] The smoke from these fires could be plainly seen by Echols' men twenty miles away on Sweet Springs Mountain.[150]

Next, Blakely had to somehow get his command across the river. Cautiously, he led the men up to the pike. Incredibly, they saw no sign of rebels, not even on the heights near the burned bridge.

Once the bridge had been destroyed, there was, of course, no need to defend it, and the rebels on the heights had withdrawn, sometime after 8 a.m.[151] Jackson's command, however, remained hopelessly disorganized. The 19th Virginia and the various home guards were strung out and scattered more than three miles away down the Rich Patch road. The 20th Virginia was three miles east on the pike at Alum Rock. Few were yet aware that so many Federals had been stranded on this side of the river.[152] This state of confusion among the Confederates gave Blakely a brief opportunity to search for a way out of his dilemma.

But the river, "swollen and full of floating ice and drift,"[153] looked terrifying. No doubt many a heart sank at the apparent hopelessness of the situation, and speculation spread among the men as to whether or not they would have to "abandon our horses and cut our way out, over the mountain, on foot."[154] Blakely, discouraged but not disheartened, sent out groups of men to scour the area for local citizens who could be of help in finding a place to cross the river. Within moments this tactic seemed to have paid off when a few soldiers began excitedly calling out from further upstream that, with the aid of a local citizen, they had found a spot that might be passable. Cautiously, one soldier, possibly from Gibson's battalion,[155] rode his horse into the river at the designated point. His comrades on shore watched in horror-struck helplessness as the horse quickly gave in to the swift current, fell over, and was swept downstream with its master, both of whom drowned. Outraged at what they perceived was a deliberate act of treachery, the soldiers on shore grabbed the helpful civilian and flung him into the water. Like those he had condemned with his act, treacherous, innocent or otherwise, the man quickly went under and was never seen again.[156]

Another civilian, however, a woman who lived near the burned bridge, gave information that most believed, or at least desperately wanted to believe, was trustworthy. Though a staunch Confederate, the woman had wilted under the threats the soldiers had made to burn her house, and told them of a place called Holloway's Ford, which she said was located two miles upstream from the burned bridge.[157]

The soldiers rushed this information to Colonel Blakely. With no choice but to act on this new and only hope, he sent a squad under Captain James Kelly to find the ford.[158]

Barely had Kelly ridden off on his new assignment when two artillery rounds came screaming in from the east—the rebels were coming down the pike!

Colonel Arnett, the smoke of the burning wagons finally alerting him to the fact that there were still a considerable number of Yankees on this side of the river, had left Alum Rock, finally reunited with Jackson, and came storming down the pike toward the burned bridge. When within range, he had ordered his two artillery pieces—twelve-pound howitzers—to open fire.[159]

The Pennsylvanians scrambled onto the pike and made a run for it to the west. The rebels, coming on fast, scooped up about twenty before running into a defensive line hastily set up by Blakely near the burned bridge under Majors John Daily and Shadrack Foley.[160] The Pennsylvanians braced themselves for a desperate struggle. Then came a surprise. Despite their numerical advantage and two pieces of artillery, the Confederates held up and sent out a party bearing a flag of truce. Captain E.B. Powell of Company K and Corporal George Stover of Company H, 8th West Virginia, rode out to meet them. The two were presented with a demand for the Federals on this side of the river to surrender within ten minutes or be fired upon. Powell, perhaps mindful of the ongoing attempt to find Holloway's Ford, shrewdly negotiated an extension to fifteen minutes, then rode back to his own line.[161] The surrender demand he carried read as follows:

Headquarters Confederate Forces,

Jackson River, Northern Va.

December 20, 1863, 8 1/2, A.M.

To the Commanding Officer Federal Forces,

Sir: The bridge is destroyed in your front, the river cannot be forded. Your retreat is cut off, and you are completely surrounded by my forces. I have directed a cessation of hostilities for fifteen minutes, and to prevent the further effusion of blood I send this, under flag of truce, and demand your immediate, unconditional surrender.

I have the honor to be very respectfully, your obedient servant,
Wm. L. Jackson,

Brig. Gen. Commanding.[162]

Here, accounts vary. Some of Blakely's veterans maintain that the colonel had not only been willing to accede to the demand but that he had gone so far as to order the roll-up of the flags and guidons, and that he had changed his mind only upon the vehement protests of his officers.[163] Others in the regiment claim that Blakely was not even aware of the surrender demand, being too far away upriver helping in the search for Holloway's Ford.[164] And yet a third group maintained that Blakely had indeed been on hand and promptly refused the rebel demand.[165] In support of this last version, the *Pittsburgh Gazette* later printed what it claimed was Blakely's reply to Jackson:

Headquarters 14th Pa. Cav.

Jackson River, West Va.

December 20, 1863

Brig. Gen. Wm. L. Jackson, Commanding Confederate Forces,

Sir: I have the honor to acknowledge the receipt of your demand for my "immediate, unconditional surrender." I admit that I am surrounded by your superior forces, on my rear, right and left flanks, and that an almost impassable gulf menaces my front, but I cannot, even under these circumstances, comply with your demand, and I will sacrifice my own life and that of every true and brave soldier under my command, before I surrender to a coward and a traitor!

With due respect, yours, etc.,

Wm. Blakely, Lieut. Col. Commanding.[166]

Unfortunately, Blakely himself left no account of the affair, either in an official report or in any known personal narrative. What is known is that the stranded command did not surrender.

And if that were because of the vehement protests of the members of the command, as some asserted, then credit for such protests must be extended to the men in the ranks. For when news of the surrender demand spread among them, they became indignant, even agitated at the prospect. "The 14th Pennsylvania Cavalry never surrenders!" someone suddenly cried out. "The 14th Cavalry doesn't know how to surrender!" another trooper quickly added. Presently, this last pronouncement was taken up in chorus by the entire rear guard, the men shouting their defiance at both the rebels and any of their own officers who might be considering capitulation.[167]

This is in sharp contrast to a rebel account, found in Major McMahon's report, which made the very dubious claim that the Yankees were so desperate and determined to surrender that it was they and not the Confederates who had sent out a flag of truce, not once but three times, only to find no one with whom to negotiate.[168] Perhaps the best refutation of this incredible claim was made by Private George H. Mowrer of Company A, when he subsequently wrote, "the boys of the 14th were not made of that kind of stuff."[169]

At any rate, the "surrender negotiations" had given Captain Kelly extra time to locate the ford. In his search for this avenue of deliverance, Kelly had gone off the road near the burned bridge and followed the rail line southwest along the river bank for about a mile to where he found a destroyed railroad bridge. He then went on a dirt path for about another mile to where the Fincastle pike came up from the south and "entered" the river— here was Holloway's Ford! Kelly sped the news of his great discovery back to an anxious Colonel Blakely, who immediately put the 14th in motion for the ford.[170]

Forty yards across with a swift current and deep water, the ford looked ominous and forbidding.[171] In point of fact, the crossing was no longer really a ford at all, in that the recent heavy rains had made it certain that a horse and rider would have to swim at least part of the way over. If a soldier was unfortunate enough to be on a worn-out or greatly weakened mount, this is when his life would face its greatest danger.

"It was a dismal scene," observed Theo Brown. "Low, leaden clouds overhead; in front a roaring, swishing torrent, carrying drift ice; behind, and for all we knew, on all sides of us, the human enemy."[172]

At the river's edge, the men stared an anxious moment at the daunting task before them. Then they heard Blakely's booming voice rise above the noise of the rushing water. "Volunteers!" he shouted, "step out and defend this fording under command of Lieutenant A.J. Pentacost!"

Twenty-eight-year-old Alexander J. Pentacost, a native of Pittsburgh, had been driven all his life by a restless nature that craved adventure. In 1859, for example, he went out to Colorado Territory to become a lone mountain man, prospecting in the Rockies. Returning home a few months later, financially poor but rich, and gratefully so, with experience, "AJ" resumed a "normal" life, becoming a machinist's apprentice. A year later, however, the war allowed him to break out of that drudgery and seek new adventures. He promptly found his way into the 2nd West Virginia, where he discovered that soldier life agreed with him, and he rose in rank to become first lieutenant in the command's quartermaster department.[173]

Now Colonel Blakely was turning to him, relieved as he was from the wagons, to guard Holloway's Ford. This meant that Pentacost would be the first to cross over, so as to set up a good covering position on the opposite side. Within moments of Blakely's call enough volunteers had stepped forward to form a squad. With Pentacost, they all plunged in. To the cheers of their anxious comrades awaiting their turn to try the water, the lieutenant and his newly formed command safely made it over.[174]

Then the rest of the men began their individual struggles with the river. Colonel Blakely stood at the riverbank anxiously watching the whole proceeding. As the men went in he occasionally called out to caution them not to look down at the rushing water. He feared that with their empty stomachs "they might be overcome by vertigo" and fall in.[175]

Nevertheless, now and then a horse and rider would break off from the struggling mass and be swept downstream to their deaths (including, perhaps, John Starks, the bridegroom taken prisoner on Potts Mountain).[176] When this happened a groan might rise up from some of those still crossing, or the victim's name might be called out in vain by a friend, but in general, "scarce a man looked at them," observed Theo Brown in horror, "since help was impossible and everyone had enough to do to look out for himself."[177]

Brown himself refused at first to go in. The day before he had been forced to shoot his regular mount when it succumbed to fatigue and illness, and he did not think that the small jackass he had replaced it with from an ambulance was capable of handling so difficult a crossing when strong horses were being swept downstream. He was considering taking refuge in the mountains when Major Daily came up with the rear guard and ordered him to cross. "In he went," Brown said of his mule, "deeper and deeper, and presently he was swimming. I had never swam a horse or a mule before, but, though I stayed in the saddle, I had sense enough to let him be the sole master of the ship, and before I could have counted 40 he was on his feet again; and if ever a mule said with his eyes 'that's no trick,' he said it."

Brown felt so grateful toward his mule that later that night he "tried to immortalize him in verse." Though his creative energies seemed to be lacking, having "found myself persona non grata with the muse; for what can be expected from a brain without sleep, a body without rest, and a stomach without food?" Brown nonetheless managed something:

> The mule's a creature of such horrid mien,
> That to be hated needs but to be seen;
> But often seen, familiar with his face,
> We first endure, then pity, then embrace.[178]

Meanwhile, at the river, hundreds of troopers were conferring on their animals an uneasy trust equal to that Brown had felt for his mule. The mass of men and beasts stretched like one undulating, living blue stream from one bank to the other. "It was a splendid sight," admitted a citizen who watched the remarkable event.[179]

Pentacost, being the first out, positioned his squad to cover the crossing until the last man got over.[180] That man was provided by Major Daily, whose command had taken several Confederate shells while holding the rear guard near the burned bridge. When the word to go finally came from Blakely, Daily broke off from the rebels and made a run for it. The Confederates came on in close pursuit, but were kept away from the river bank by the accurate fire of Pentacost's squad. Daily's men quickly and safely got across the river.[181]

Of about 500 men, all but four from the 14th and two of the stragglers from the other West Virginia regiments, had made it over.[182] This was, indeed, a truly remarkable achievement, one that owed its success not only to the obvious courage and determination of the men and their mounts, but also, one could argue, to the subtle influence of the good fortune that seemed to be following Averell, even though he had abandoned them.

Collecting themselves after their harrowing experience, the survivors followed Blakely five miles west through Covington to the next bridge— which Averell had also burned! Again, the men plunged into the rushing, freezing river. But this time there was less urgency, more organization and friendlier water. They crossed without the loss of a single man.[183] And so the last of Averell's command had slipped through Covington.

Col. William L. Jackson

Jackson was Averell's opponent at Covington.

Boyd B. Stutler Collection, West Virginia State Archives

Chapter Four

The Return to God's Country

1. The Command Reunited

Wasting no time, Blakely led his Pennsylvanians, and the two West Virginia companies, on to Callaghan's. Stopping there only long enough to close up and catch their breath, they set off in pursuit of Averell. "Our clothes were frozen and our sufferings were intense," a soldier later wrote of their condition at this time.[1] Nevertheless, the men pressed on. Following Averell's trail through the snow and mud, they rode westward at a rapid pace, unencumbered by wagons or artillery, until they finally caught up with him somewhere in the Alleghenies just before midnight on the twentieth.

Undoubtedly, when riding into Averell's camp many men had mixed feelings about having been left behind. But any bitterness they may have harbored melted away in the warm glow of the welcome extended by their comrades, whose astonishment at their arrival quickly gave way to celebration.[2] "When we arrived there," Lieutenant Pentacost fondly recalled, "the boys shouted themselves hoarse, they were so rejoiced at our escape."[3]

Colonel Blakely wanted to see Averell as soon as possible and report to him the events of the past day, but upon learning the general had retired for the night he decided to wait until next morning. The delay proved crucial. By dawn of the twenty-first, second hand sources had informed Averell of the loss of the train and of the tremendous number of men captured, and perhaps even of the rumor of Blakely's willingness to surrender. Even though he had given the 14th up for lost, as well as the train it guarded, Averell was outraged at these reports. Without waiting, or wanting, to hear Blakely's version of events, he ordered that the lieutenant colonel be relieved from duty.

The entire command had just broken camp and resumed the march when Blakely, riding at the head of the 14th, was approached by a number of headquarters orderlies, one of whom informed the Pennsylvanian that he was under arrest. Blakely was absolutely stunned. Immediately, he asked to be taken to see the general, only to be told that that was not possible. For five days Averell refused to see him. Blakely, reduced to a state of abject humiliation, finally resorted to submitting a written plea. "I did desire to save my command," he wrote the general on the twenty-sixth, "and I succeeded & every officer in the Regiment considered it as a success." Then after begging to be released from arrest until there could be a full hearing on the matter, Blakely brought the note to an emotional close. "This matter had been a source of great annoyance to me, and whilst others have been rejoicing over your recent success there has been no joy for me. If I have been guilty of crim[inal] negligence or anything else I am willing to take all the punishment that may be placed upon me. Had it not been for the cares of my family I would rather [have] been consined [*sic*] to the waves of Jackson River than suffer this humiliation."[4] Blakely would have to endure this humiliation for nearly three months until the dismissal was overturned the following March and he was returned to command.[5]

Despite his own perceived abuse at the hands of Hooker seven months before, Averell would extend this same shabby treatment to Augustus Moor, and if his authority had allowed it, he would no doubt have done the same to Scammon and perhaps even Thoburn and Wells. And Moor, suffering terribly from the "rheumatism" the recent expedition had caused to flare up, would be just as stunned as Blakely, if not more bitter. "Being a citizen nearly 30 years," the German-born colonel would protest to Averell by letter on the twenty-ninth from Beverly, "I returned from two wars[6] of the Republic respected by brother Officers & good soldiers, to my home honored by my fellow citizens—from the 3rd, to embitter forever the luck to have escaped with life. I return disgraced without warning or trial to which the murderer and the traitor is entitled, even in Russia."[7] Moor might also have reminded Averell that he had won the battle of Droop Mountain for him by executing that difficult flanking movement around the Confederate left. At any rate, Kelley eventually overruled the dismissal and restored Moor to command the following February.[8]

As to why Averell lashed out at his subordinates in this way, particularly at Colonel Blakely, a clue may be found in his post-raid report. Though Averell had undoubtedly been glad to welcome the stranded 14th back into his fold on the night of 20 December, he seemed strangely unrepentant for having left it on the other side of Jackson River, even going so far as to ease what may have been a guilty conscience by shifting the blame for the near disaster over to the 14th in general and to the regiment's commander in particular. "It was thought that had the regiment in rear been advanced steadily forward," he reported, "these captures might have been mostly prevented, and we should not have been obliged to destroy our wagons and ambulances the following day."[9] Averell thus seemed determined to allow nothing, especially his own misjudgments, to tarnish his accomplishment. His questionable treatment of Blakely and Moor, then, may have

Col. Augustus Moor, 28th Ohio Inf.

Colonel Moor led support column from Beverly to Droop Mountain.

Massachusetts Commandery, Military
Order of the Loyal Legion and the US Army Military History Institute

been a petty attempt to ease the conscience over the loss of men and materiel by shifting the blame.

Furthermore, the captures Averell referred to amounted to around 120 of his own troops, of which number only twenty-five were from the 14th Pennsylvania. The rest were distributed among the other units in such a way (38 from the 8th W.Va., 17 from the 2nd and 3rd W.Va. each, 18 from Gibson's battalion, and 5 from Ewing's battery)[10] as to indicate that straggling had been a problem throughout the command. Though not the kind of straggling associated with skulkers trying to avoid hard duty, but the type resulting from being pressed beyond one's endurance. Having driven his men to the point of near delirium, Averell had to know this. That knowledge, together with an awareness that the 14th had to mind a wagon train slowed to a snail's pace by the rough road up Barber's Creek, and the understanding that it is the commander's responsibility to keep his column closed up, denies Averell the right to lay any blame for the delay on the 14th or Colonel Blakely. After all, it was the gallant tenacity of the 14th that had helped the rest of the command to escape.

At any rate, the fate of those 120 men became the real tragedy of the Salem Raid. "There were 114 of us cooped in the station house at Jackson River Station on the morning of the 21st of December," Private J.F. Starcher, Company C, 3rd West Virginia, wrote the *National Tribune* after the war, "before we started via Staunton for Richmond and starvation." Starcher went on to claim that of those captured only three survived to see their homes again (he wrote to the *National Tribune,* in part, in an effort to discover the other two survivors). He did so only because in Richmond he cleverly avoided Andersonville by pretending to be sick and in need of treatment, and then at Libby Prison the following March he was lucky enough to be the 398th of 400 men allowed to file out the prison door to be exchanged.[11]

Unlike Private Starcher, most of the captured men were sent to Andersonville. In that chamber of horrors nearly all perished at the hands of a criminal negligence that allowed dysentery, diarrhea, typhoid, and starvation to ravage the body and destroy the mind. Then following an agonizing death came the final indignity of being flung into a nameless grave outside the prison walls.[12]

But aside from these captures that ended so horribly, Averell's losses at Covington had been light—six men wounded, seven drowned, and one missing. Jackson gave his own loss as one killed, seven wounded, and thirty missing.[13]

Averell also lost several horses, perhaps 200 in all, many of which had drowned. Another of his losses were the twenty-five or so slaves the column had acquired in Salem and an equal number it had picked up on the march through the Rich Patch Valley. Stranded at the river, these unfortunate runaways fell into the hands of Jackson, who did his civic duty by safely storing this valuable property in the jail at Covington until their owners could reclaim them.[14]

That more runaways had not flocked to the Yankees was because so many good, loyal slaves "fled to the mountains on their approach." Or so the 23 December issue of the *Richmond Examiner* would have its readers believe.[15] Anxious as it was to allay the fears of whites in this regard, the Southern press moved just as rapidly to assure white vanity that with the recapture of the slaves the "natural order" of things had been restored, an order so inherently proper that even the blacks, having learned the hard way by stepping outside its safe and preordained boundaries, had to admit it was so. "The negroes seem but too happy to have been [re]captured," professed the 28 December issue of the *Richmond Sentinel*. "[They] say the experiment is entirely satisfactory, and, if they can be forgiven, it shall never be repeated." Having taken the bait set out by the "inferiors," the newspaper then swallowed it by printing as truth the fantastic claim that, realizing their mistake, the runaways had pleaded with the Yankees to be let go so they could return to their masters, and that the Yankees had refused and even shot one of the blacks who insisted on being released.[16] The *Examiner* took the story a step further when it claimed that the negro had been shot "because he would not receive a carbine, mount a horse and follow them. They armed and mounted all they took, and employed them in guarding prisoners and as guides."[17] And to further illustrate what evils may ensue when the natural order is disturbed, the *Sentinel* reported that "One of their [slave] comrades was given a quart of whiskey [by the Yankees] and made drunk and abandoned. He was found dead on the road from the effects of the liquor & the cold."[18]

While thus reassuring its readers that with the recapture of the slaves the natural order had been restored, the Southern papers were quick to condemn the Confederate commanders who had allowed that order to be disturbed. The papers had begun to heat up as far back as the seventeenth. "It is a little singular," scorned the *Richmond Examiner* on that date, "that, with all the warnings the Government has had, from the repeated demonstrations of Averill [*sic*] and other Yankee commanders, that he should have been permitted to march from Beverly to Salem, a distance of nearly two hundred miles, without material interruption. From the day he left Beverly until he reached Salem abundance of time was given for a sufficient force to have gathered to resist his advance."[19]

"To me," wrote the *Richmond Sentinel* correspondent known as "Rambler," who filed his story on the twenty-second after traveling with Fitz Lee's column as far as Fincastle, "it seems incomprehensible how, with Gen. Echols on one side and Gen. Imboden on the other, Gen. Averill [*sic*] should have deceived and eluded both till he was entirely beyond their reach."[20]

"The story is told in a few words," scowled the *Richmond Examiner* on 28 December. "The Yankees passed through Covington and, to their great amazement, escaped. The rumor about Buchanan was the tale of some frightened fool . . . It is hardly necessary to add, the humblest private in the ranks, if he possessed sense enough to eat and drink, not only could but would have managed better."[21]

Possibly so. In the Valley, Early had been fooled by "the rumor about Buchanan." On Sweet Springs Mountain, Jones had been deceived by a false advance and huge bogus campfires. But the worst mistakes occurred where the Confederates had their greatest opportunity—Covington. There Jackson failed not only to destroy the Island Ford Bridge when he had the chance, and to locate and cover the side lane off Rich Patch road, he failed to maintain a disciplined control of his command. Moreover, on the morning of the twentieth he failed to close in on and destroy the 14th Pennsylvania, granting instead a fifteen-minute respite for the enemy to improve the time. Overall, his troop dispositions were questionable, at best, for in separating his force so widely he not only reduced his power to strike, he made sure that communication, particularly at night, would be very difficult to maintain. With poor communication came confusion, and with confusion came a breakdown in discipline, so much so that, according to the previously mentioned McMahon report, many of Jackson's men were less concerned with fighting the enemy than they were in plundering his abandoned camps and smoldering wagons. Some of Jackson's men went so far as to burglarize local citizens, and there was even one charge of rape.[22] That there was some truth to these allegations is evidenced by the petition the angry citizens of Alleghany County drew up in January to have Jackson's command kicked out of their midst. Jackson responded by issuing a circular among his officers, whereby he pleaded with them to consider the reputation of the command by enforcing strict discipline.[23]

Averell, aided by skillful planning, the determination of his men and sheer good fortune, thus took full advantage of the mistakes that even "the humblest private in the ranks" would not have committed.

2. Callaghan's to Hillsboro

With Jackson now unable to pursue because of the destroyed bridges at Covington, Averell, on the twentieth at Callaghan's, appeared to have a clear and easy shot to Beverly. But here the expedition had reached another major crossroads. Having just slipped through one vise closing in on him from east and west, Averell now believed that another was tightening its grip from north and south. Based largely on the Jones-to-Early dispatch he had captured near Covington the night before, Averell drew the reasonable conclusion that Early was shifting his considerable forces west over to Gatewood's, and that Jones was moving up from Sweet Springs to Lewisburg.[24] This meant that both the James River pike and the road up to Gatewood's and over to Huntersville, the only available routes to Pocahontas County and thence to Beverly, were blocked.

What to do? The problems, the options and the solutions were virtually the same as those Averell faced two days before at New Castle. Then as now, fighting through the enemy or swinging wide around him were both out of the question. Then as now, slipping between the rebels on an obscure and as-yet-unknown path seemed the only viable choice. Then as now, Averell was unfamiliar with this region, had no time for reconnaissance, and needed a special guide to lead his men through. Who, then, would serve him as Dr. Wylie had done?

Again, Averell's remarkable resourcefulness, and luck, came through. He called to his headquarters those few runaway slaves who were still with the column and asked if any knew of a way over the mountains to the west. When one young fellow, perhaps twelve years old, said he had learned of such a route while going to mill with his master, Averell put the lad on a horse and told him to lead the way.[25]

Averell's plan was to get over the mountains immediately to the west, enter Pocahontas County from the south, cross the Greenbrier River at Hillsboro and march thence up to Beverly.[26] It was a daring and risky plan. If the Confederates presumed to be at Gatewood's got wind of the movement, they could easily slide eighteen miles west over to Marlin's Bottom and cut it off. Likewise, from Lewisburg Jones could march up the Lewisburg road and either cut Averell off at Hillsboro or slam into his rear should the Federals get there first. Then, too, it was very risky to place so much trust in a twelve-year-old boy, though this new guide, unlike Dr. Wylie, needed no coercion and was all too happy to help the Yankees. Furthermore, unlike the trek up the relatively flat terrain along Barber's Creek to Covington, this journey promised to go into the wildest and most rugged mountains of this region. The already harsh weather was sure to be much worse there, and the physical demands required for a safe passage could very well be beyond the capacity of Averell's worn-out, frozen command. Because their tents were among the smoldering ruins of the wagons burned at Covington, the men would be rewarded after a long, hard march with having to sleep out in the open on the cold, hard ground. Moreover, the wilderness ahead offered little hope of finding sustenance for men who had had little or nothing to eat in the past several days. And finally, the intended trek promised to pass through prime bushwhack country. Indeed, the 23 December issue of the *Lynchburg Republican* would claim that an outraged farmer named Foster of Botetourt County had relentlessly trailed the column, picking off six of Averell's men before being satisfied justice had been served.[27] All-in-all, it must have seemed rash for Averell to even consider such an undertaking. But once again, he concluded that there was no other way.

Late on the morning of the twentieth, the command set out from Callaghan's. Breaking off from the James River turnpike about two miles west of town, the young runaway led the column northwest along a rough mountain path that followed Ogles Creek. After a difficult ride of about ten miles, they came to the foot of Rucker's Gap, which lay between Little Alleghany and Meadow Creek mountains on the Greenbrier County line.[28] Now began the trying ordeal of getting over the "high, rough, wild and icy

Alleghenies," as Frank Reader remembered them.[29] Some of the climbs
became so steep that Averell finally ordered the destruction of four caissons in order to increase the number of horses pulling each gun.[30] Even
so, some inclines were too slippery for the horses to gain a foothold. "It was
exceedingly hard marching," explained Private Slease, "our horses and
mules were so smooth [shod] after two weeks marching over stony, moun-
tainous roads they could scarcely stand up."[31] Many of the unfortunate
beasts fell and broke their legs. When that happened, teamsters quickly
removed the injured animals, slit their throats, then attached long ropes to
the guns and called on as many as 100 men to dismount and help pull the
pieces up the mountain. "By dint of pulling, climbing, and puffing and blowing," Lieutenant Hoffman noted in his diary, "we got our artillery over a road
which the cavalry had to go over by fits." And he added, "I must confess,
when I rode over this route, I thought the artillery was going another road."[32]

But occasionally, men, too, fell and injured themselves, sometimes
severely. Though no one slit their throats, as had been done with the horses,
some of the broken men might have preferred death to the excruciating pain
they endured while riding strapped to their mounts.[33] With no ambulances to
ride in, at least one soldier with a severely busted leg, a private in the 8th
West Virginia, had to be left behind and was captured by the enemy.[34]

In such a grueling manner, the command "moved up . . . that fearful
mountain path,"[35] and made it to the top. "How we reached the summit,"
Captain Rife recalled in amazement, "was a wonder of wonders to us all.
Only the fact that we had done it could not be denied."[36] At the summit, the
column halted briefly to close up.[37]

The climb down presented equally difficult challenges, in particular,
how to avoid losing control of the cannons. That problem was finally solved
by tying huge trees behind the guns, thereby braking the speed of their
descent.[38]

Of course, the easiest solution would have been to spike the guns
(permanently destroy their vent holes) and simply abandon them. This would
have been no great loss, as there were only four, and the back-breaking,
life-threatening labor saved would have been more than enough compensation. But to Civil War troops in general, and to commanders especially,
cannon were more than just long-range weapons (and rather inefficient
ones at that). They were symbols of victory and defiance, with almost as
much value in that regard as the regimental colors themselves. They were
concrete evidence that the command had successfully resisted the enemy
or even overwhelmed him altogether. The loss of a cannon could therefore
be cause for disgrace, while the retention of one's own piece, or the capture of the enemy's, was a mark of pride and honor. Thus Averell and his
men were determined to save those four metal tubes, even if it required
unbearable suffering to do so. "Allow me here," Lieutenant Hoffman later
wrote in his diary, "to pay lasting tribute to the brave Virginia lads who

dismounted and pushed and pulled the artillery up the hill. Such men are deserving all praise; every soldier seemed determined on saving the artillery. God bless them."[39]

After passing over Rucker's Gap with those guns and moving into Greenbrier County, West Virginia, Averell marched on westward about another five miles to the sight of present-day Neola on Anthony's Creek. The runaway's guidance probably ended here. He had done as promised, and gotten the command safely over the first range of mountains.

There was no passage over the next range. Massive Beaver Lick Mountain could only be dealt with by swinging round its lower end. Averell turned south, away from home, and marched down Anthony's Creek about six miles (on Rimel road) to the southern end of the great mountain, and went into camp at about 11 p.m.[40] In his official report, Averell made no mention of where he halted for the night of the twentieth, but if his men were able to make twenty-five miles that day, this is the area where they would have stopped. This would have also been the place, then, where the 14th Pennsylvania, following their trail through the snow and mud, caught up with them.

That night many of the men, with the cold stinging them and hunger gnawing at them, slept fitfully, if at all. "Each chilly blast," a soldier would record, "seemed pregnant with thousands of cool, prickly points, that pierced their way and seemed to be seeking for shelter beneath the very skin."[41]

With no food to end a fast that for many was now forty-eight hours long, the men rose before dawn on the twenty-first and at 4 a.m. resumed the march north up Little Creek, going alongside Slabcamp Mountain for ten miles before finally entering Pocahontas County. Weak and exhausted, but determined to win the race to Hillsboro, they pushed on another incredible eighteen miles over winding, twisting, hilly lanes—one of which one soldier estimated rose at an incredible forty-degree angle—going north and then west, to finally reach Greenbrier River about dark.[42]

They had made it—almost. Hillsboro, and the road coming up from Lewisburg and going on to Beverly, were on the other side of the river. Though many of the sleep-deprived, hungry men had walked the entire day with worn-out shoes and frozen feet,[43] the command had to make one more effort and cross the river now.

When the men looked at the Greenbrier, however, the horrors of Craig's Creek immediately came to mind; the river was up to the top of its banks. "We found the stream swollen and full of floating ice," Frank Reader later declared. "Cakes of ice ten to fifteen feet square, and heavy enough to submerge a horse, were constantly passing."[44] At about 8 p.m. the grim crossing began.[45]

As he had nobly done at Craig's Creek four days before, Averell again led by example. He tested the ford himself, and once over he directed the crossing of the rest of the column, standing on a log at the river bank until the last man got over, an exhausting process that took several hours.[46]

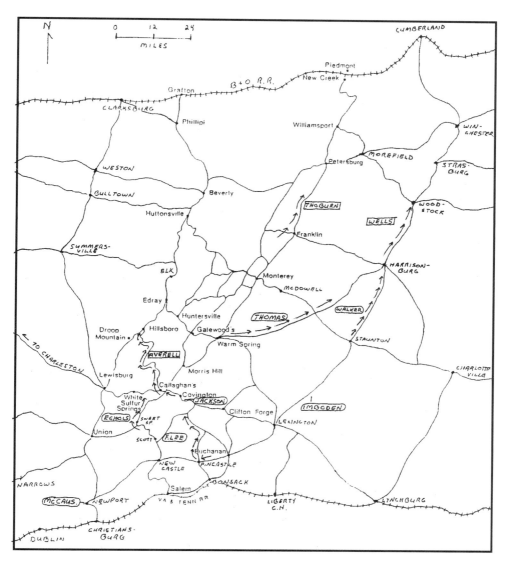

Movements, 20–21 December

Compiled from *Official Records Atlas,* Plate 135c, No. 1. Stephen Z. Starr,
The Union Cavalry in the Civil War. Author's notes.

The men, driven to near madness by now, seemed more outraged at the river than frightened by it. "The command was in no mood to hesitate," Reader declared. "Hunger, cold, exhaustion had done their utmost."[47] When the order thus came to plunge in, the men did so with an angry defiance. "Men had lost the ordinary feelings of their kind," Captain Rife testified, "bent only on taking care of self." With this anger and sense of self-preservation to sustain them, all the men safely made it over.[48]

But once across, anger and defiance gave way to relief and exhaustion. Many of the men collapsed to the ground and, despite the cold, immediately fell into a deep, almost deathlike sleep. For the most part, their officers took pity and left them alone. Soon, however, all too soon, they had to go. "When the order came to move forward," Rife observed, "it was almost impossible to get the men up and on their horses. I rode up to one after another, and by punching them with my sword aroused them and induced them to mount. Ordinary calling was useless."[49]

Then, from up ahead, shots rang out. Bushwhackers! Quickly, Captain Charles Smith formed up Company C of the 8th West Virginia and, on raw nerve and adrenaline, charged. The troublesome rebels scattered and dispersed.[50]

That night (21st), after an incredible march of about thirty miles, the exhausted men, many of whom had walked a good portion of the way, set up their camps in and around Hillsboro.[51] Once again, they had beaten the Johnnies to the punch.

3. The Confederates Give Up

Indeed, the Johnnies had all given up. But they had tried, even after Covington, to run Averell down.

When Fitz Lee rode into Buchanan back on the twentieth and finally learned, to his horror, that Averell had not returned to Salem but was headed north, he still thought it possible to snare the elusive Federal commander and immediately set out to catch him. At Fincastle that afternoon he learned of Averell's arrival in Covington and promptly turned his own horsemen in that direction, still hoping that the Federal's progress could be retarded by Echols and Jackson. But when Lee reached Callaghan's the next day (21st) he finally had to admit that his old friend, somewhere off in the Alleghenies with no possibility of being slowed down by interception, was beyond his reach. Being thus denied another "visit" with Billy Averell, Fitz Lee gave up the chase, such as it was, withdrew to Hot Springs and by Christmas his troopers were back in Mt. Crawford, having ridden more than 300 miles in twelve days with nothing to show for it except a severe depletion of strength that neither man nor beast could ill afford.[52]

Jones and Echols, too, had tried to catch Averell. Seeing the smoke rising some twenty miles in the distance from both the burning Island Ford

"Played Out"

National Tribune, 22 Sept. 1887

Bridge and the wagons Blakely had ordered destroyed, they correctly interpreted this to mean that Averell had escaped through Covington. The two rebel commanders thus came down off Sweet Springs Mountain on the twentieth and the next day started for White Sulphur Springs, where, as anticipated by Averell, they hoped to head off the Federal column on the James River pike. Upon arriving there on the twenty-second, however, they learned the Yankees had somehow slipped past them into the Little Levels of Pocahontas County far to the north.[53] And thus if Averell had not gone northwest over Rucker's Gap but used the apparently more reasonable option of marching west on the James River pike, a second battle of White Sulphur Springs could very well have been the result, with probably an even worse outcome for Averell than the battle of last August.

General Early, meanwhile, had not shifted any troops over to Gatewood's, as Averell feared he might. Disgusted with the whole affair, he brushed Averell off with the remark that "He thus succeeded in making his escape by the stupidity or treachery of a telegraph operator [J.M. Crowley, one of those who had sent reports of Averell's supposed return to Salem]."[54] Unable, or unwilling, then to go after Averell with infantry alone, Early turned his attention to the Federal troops in the Shenandoah.

When Colonel Wells finally advanced from Strasburg and occupied Harrisonburg on the nineteenth in preparation for his planned diversionary threat on Staunton, Early called up Thomas' brigade from Warm Springs and sent it the next day (20th) with Walker's brigade to get him. Wells, however, avoided disaster by pulling out and scampering back to the relative safety of Strasburg, where he arrived on the twenty-third. Early was late again.[55] (Checked by the high water of the Shenandoah River, Colonel Rosser and his Laurel Brigade were unable to swing round behind Wells.)[56]

Though unable to threaten Staunton as planned, Wells had nonetheless held out the longest of any of Averell's support columns, and, unlike Scammon and Moor, he had retreated only when confronted by superior numbers of the enemy. Wells' troops were back in their winter quarters around Harper's Ferry by Christmas Eve.[57]

Thoburn, too, had made an early "modification" of his assignment. He had pulled out of McDowell on the fifteenth in response to rumors that Imboden had been reinforced at Buffalo Gap to 5,000 men and was preparing to attack him. Retreating northwest about fifteen miles to Crab Bottom the next day, Thoburn waited there until the twentieth for the return of the strike force. But when he learned that Averell was headed for Beverly he moved on to Petersburg, arriving there on the twenty-third.[58]

Indeed, the Johnnies, and the Billies, had all given up.

4. Hillsboro to Beverly

Having learned during the November expediton that the Hillsboro area was decidedly pro-Confederate in sympathy, Averell, as was occasionally his custom when settling down in unfriendly territory, had the local men— "representatives of the Jeff Davis school," as Lieutenant Hoffman dubbed them—rounded up as a means of guarding against bushwhacking and spying. He confined them in the "Academy," the distinguished sounding name of the town's "school of higher learning." Some of these so-called prisoners recalled later that the sentinels guarding them that night (21st) were so exhausted as to be unable to remain on their feet, while other guards even went so far as to commit the grievous military sin of falling asleep while on duty.[59]

Even worse than the exhaustion was the hunger. Many of Averell's men, now without food for nearly four days, and having had very little during the three or four days before the onset of their current fast, had become like mad-ravenous wolves as they prowled the countryside for any form of sustenance they could find. The southern portion of Pocahontas County, the "Little Levels," a basin of gently rolling pastures and fertile fields extending north of Droop Mountain and so named by way of distinguishing it from the larger basin south of the mountain in Greenbrier County known as the Great Levels, was the first country they had seen for days that offered food and shelter. In their desperate struggle to survive, many men openly violated Averell's strict orders to respect private property. The people of Pocahontas County, being surprised to even see Yankees in their midst this time of year, were quite unprepared for this onslaught. "It was almost like a raid of Indians in the winter time," one resident recalled.[60] Stories abound that tell of the soldiers' near-mad search for food in an area that, by late 1863, had very little to offer.

At one house, for example, the soldiers eagerly ate all the scraps of rancid fat set aside to make soap, while at another the men ate and drank from the swill tub, which contained garbage getting ripe for the hogs. Some men were not even that "lucky." At another house three sisters saved their supply of sugar by hiding it in the lounge in the parlor, then sitting down and spreading their skirts over it until the famished soldiers had completed their search of the place and left. And at still another home a soldier was about to make off with the family's last, slender slab of bacon when the woman of the house, the wife of a Confederate soldier away on duty, frantically appealed for help from an officer passing by. The officer took pity on the woman and ordered the soldier to give up the bacon. "You be damned!" came the quick reply. But when the officer drew his revolver, the soldier dropped the bacon and ran off.[61]

In yet another episode, a half dozen boys somehow managed to secure a sizeable slab of meat, which they promptly flung into a frying pan. While the men were standing around their precious, sizzling confiscation, however, it suddenly occurred to one of them that the hot meat could also serve as a foot warmer. Agreeing with the lad that the idea was a much safer way than direct flame to thaw out frozen flesh, the men took turns applying the hot slab to their bare feet until some feeling returned. That done, the men divided the meat and consumed every bit of it, leaving nothing behind, not even a report as to what effect the foot-warming ritual had had on the flavor of the meal.[62]

Frozen feet had become a severe problem throughout the command. Not everyone was lucky enough, or resourceful enough, to have a hot meat slab at their disposal. Most had to simply endure. For some men the pain became so intense they had to cut off their boots with a knife then wrap their swollen, blackening feet in blankets. This included Averell. He wrapped his frozen feet in a "buffalo robe," but not because he had been forced to cut off his boots; his footwear had come up missing one morning, apparently stolen by one of his own men.[63]

Without boots, the men could not use the stirrup and had to walk. This, too, included Averell, who for two days hobbled along with the rest of the men, his feet bound in great "sheepskin shoes."[64] Inevitably, many men suffered permanent, horrible damage. Corporal George Stover of the 8th West Virginia, for example, would lose some toes to the cold but nonetheless feel "duly thankful that I had saved my feet."[65]

"The retreat of Napoleon's army from Moscow," Captain Rife sadly concluded, "could not have caused greater suffering than began to tell on our ranks."[66]

Worried that Fitz Lee might yet come in from the direction of Huntersville, Averell sent Gibson's battalion at 2 a.m. on the twenty-second eleven miles up to Marlin's Bottom to blockade the road going east from there. The hungry, worn-out men did not relish the prospect of the hard labor required to fell hundreds of trees. And so they were especially relieved and delighted to discover that the job had been done for them by the rebel Captain Marshall of the 19th Virginia Cavalry, who had done this back on the eleventh in the hopes of retarding Colonel Moor's advance. "Captain Marshall," Lieutenant Hoffman noted with satisfaction, "had so effectually blockaded the road . . . that we deemed it unnecessary to tumble another tree. The road was full of large trees for nearly a mile. Whether that saved us or not, I can't say, but [we] are under many obligations to Captain Marshall. Long may he—hang."[67]

On the twenty-second the command made only about fifteen miles, passing through Marlin's Bottom, to set up camp on the widow Gibson's farm near Edray. On the journey that day the rear guard had sustained "some trifling attacks," probably from bushwhackers.[68]

Many, if not most, of the men were now walking, their horses either being dead or "smooth shod, and to ride was impossible."[69] Ironically, this may have saved many of the men's lives, in that the increased muscular activity of walking generated enough heat to prevent them from slipping into severe hypothermia—a core body temperature ten degrees below normal.[70]

At Edray Averell was able to send out his first wire since the expedition began. After briefly describing the success of the mission, he proudly informed Kelley and Halleck that his men had "marched, climbed, slid and swum 355 miles since the 8th instant."[71]

That evening (22nd) Averell received a visitor, a local citizen named Alvin Clark, who had been a prisoner of the column since it passed through Hillsboro. After "debating with some of his neighbors," who had also been taken prisoner, "as to whether they ought to impose further upon the hospitality of the army," Clark acted as spokesman to plead for their release. Though he found Averell to be "very pleasant in manner and conversation," something else about his captor impressed him even more. Expecting to find a grizzled old soldier, Clark was quite surprised at Averell's youthful appearance. "He had become a household word in the mountains of West Virginia," he later explained, "and had the reputation of a most powerful and effective war lord. And he was a boy." Agreeing with Clark "that his family had more need of him than did the Union army," Averell released the prisoners.[72]

Though the command was now beyond the enemy's reach, and had entered friendly territory at last, everyone knew the remaining fifty-three miles to Beverly would not be easy. The winding, twisting, hilly, icy lanes would continue to test them right up to the very end. And again, most of the men, with their feet already frozen, would have to walk the entire distance.[73]

On the twenty-third "the glorious sun shone out clear and bright" to give "the famished, almost frozen boys hope and courage."[74] Thus sustained, the "boys," their feet frozen and bloody, their horses dying or being killed by the dozen, made twenty-two miles before stopping on the Conrad farm. But the next day, pulling the artillery by hand over a road described by many as "a glacier," they made only seven miles in eleven hours of desperate struggle. "We were slipping, sliding, skating, cursing, praying and laughing," Lieutenant Hoffman wrote, "nearly all in the same breath. The brave men pulling and tugging to bring the artillery safe home. Such falling, slipping, tumbling, and other gymnastic feats, were never performed by a mounted force in this or any other country. I saw two horses fall, and they never kicked afterwards. They fell to rise no more."[75] Finally, they stopped for the night on a farm near Elk, "where we bivouacked on the frozen, snow covered ground."

Fearful now that many of the men might freeze to death in the night, officers assigned details to go around and periodically prod them "lest they freeze," recalled Private Slease, "and pass from slumber into the sleep of death."[76] Such concern may have arisen from the sight of men becoming increasingly weak and apathetic, with signs of slurred speech and mental confusion, behavior that today would be classified as symptoms of moderate hypothermia, whereby the core body temperature has fallen to about ninety degrees Fahrenheit.[77]

From Elk, meanwhile, Averell sent couriers on to Beverly to plead for rations and supplies for the men, most of whom had now been without food for five days.[78] That same day the *Richmond Examiner* reluctantly confessed, "We are sad to say that there now exists little doubt that this venturous Yankee has, with most of his band, made good his escape."[79]

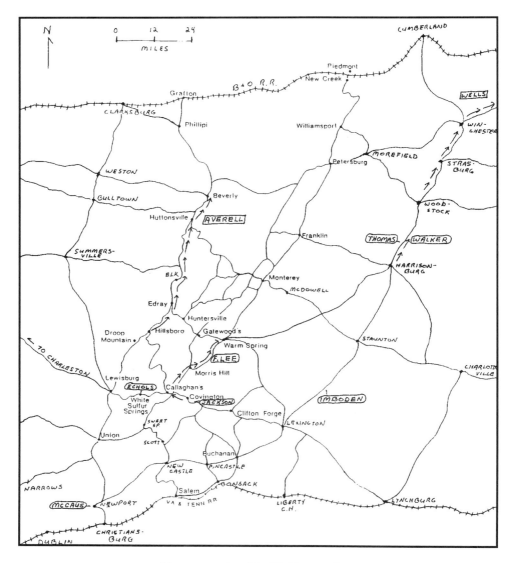

Movements, 22–25 December

Compiled from *Official Records Atlas,* Plate 135c, No. 1. Stephen Z. Starr,
The Union Cavalry in the Civil War. Author's notes.

That night Private Silas J. Clendaniel and a few of his friends in the 2nd West Virginia's Company I unknowingly, in the dark, set up their camp on a frozen frog pond. They awoke next morning to discover their blankets were frozen tight to the ice.[80]

Finally, on Christmas morning the column started out on the final leg of its long, arduous journey. Six miles out from Elk the men met the supply train from Beverly. "There never was a more joyful meeting of troops," declared Private Slease.[81] Then twelve more miles and the ragged, starving, frozen, beaten-down, magnificent command dragged itself into Beverly.

"We reentered God's country at 4 p.m. on Christmas Day," hospital steward Theo Brown declared. "A starved and wornout, but proud lot we were. . . ." The townspeople "turned out en masse to great us like heroes." Responding to the enthusiastic acclaim, Brown tried to play his part by sitting up straight in the saddle, thereby hoping to impress a pretty, "seventeen-year-old blond school marm" standing along the street. Brown's mule, however, refused to cooperate. Smelling fodder, the starving animal bolted and ran, leaving his master to feel "more like a fool than a hero." Then Brown did something that made him feel even worse than a fool: he struck the faithful animal that had saved him at Jackson River and which in gratitude he had tried to immortalize in verse. "Tell it not in Gath," he confessed in shame, "publish it not in Bethsheba; I let my clinched fist descend upon the faithful creature's sensitive ear. That was my leave taking."[82]

Brown, at least, had a mount. More than half the men entering Beverly did so on their own two legs. Of the 3,000 or so horses taken on the expedition seventeen days ago, only about 1,100 "returned from their visit to Dixie Land."[83]

"We are back home," Lieutenant Hoffman noted, simply enough. Then, as if to say the expedition had been touched by the miraculous, he added, "How we escaped is a question I cannot answer."[84]

"A more woe-begone, God forsaken lot of men and horses would be hard to describe," Sergeant Lewis Hart, Company A, 14th Pennsylvania, wrote in his diary on Christmas Day. "Some were without boots or shoes; some without trousers or shirts, others without coats or clothes of any kind, covered only with pieces of blanket or corn sacks, having burned their clothes off hovering around fires after swimming streams or rivers in zero weather."

Hart's comrade, Private Slease, would never forget that Christmas Day when "we drew rations, cooked, ate, slept, and thanked God that through the hardships and perils, threatened death and imminent danger, we were still alive and permitted to look into each other's faces."[85]

At long last, the Salem Raid was over.

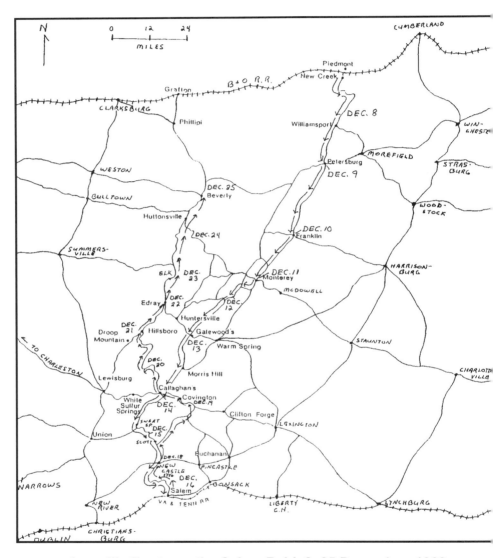

Averell's Route on the Salem Raid, 8–25 December, 1863

Compiled from *Official Records Atlas,* Plate 135c, No. 1. Stephen Z. Star
The Union Cavalry in the Civil War. Author's note

CHAPTER FIVE

The Judgment

1. Fame and Praise

"If our people cannot catch raiders," the *Richmond Examiner* growled on 24 December, "we think it would be advisable for them to take some measures to keep them out." Then the paper caustically added, "They had better not let Averell into any more traps."[1]

On Christmas Day the *Examiner* vented even more sarcasm when it expressed the opinion that no new information about Averell will be forthcoming "until we hear his glorious account of his achievements through the Northern papers. Our people have not done anything that they particularly care to talk about."[2]

Southerners did not have long to wait to hear "through the Northern papers" of Averell's "glorious achievements." The dailies ran stories on it almost immediately. The *Wheeling Intelligencer,* for example, characterized the raid as "the great cavalry feat of the war," and it went on to assert that "The march was a most incredible one and outrivals all the romances of border war in legendary times . . . All honor to the heroic sufferers who encountered and overcame its many perils." In trying to promote some comprehension of those perils, the paper urged its readers to "think of the weather. Think of men swimming rivers these days with no change of clothing. Think of the worn out condition of their poor bodies at the end of each of those days of desperate marching: how meagerly their cravings for food and warmth were supplied." Then the paper concluded with the grand claim that, "History records many wonders, but none, that we know of, surpassing in extent, danger, difficulty and success this one of Gen. Averill's [*sic*] heroic band."[3] Among papers with less regional interest, the *New York Express* declared that "The praises of Averill [*sic*] are justly upon all lips,"[4] while the prestigious *Harper's Weekly* made the raid its 16 January cover story.[5] All of this in turn led to Averell being deluged with praise and congratulations.

"[Your achievement]," wrote seventy-six-year-old L.P. Balch, a War of 1812 veteran and a proud witness of Washington's Farewell Address, "will send you down to posterity as the rival of Moreau, in his retreat through the Black Forest."[6]

"I am desirous of adding your portrait to my extensive collection of distinguished Americans," wrote another admirer (Edward Anthony), one of many such requests from around the country for autographs and photos.[7]

Journalists, too, suddenly wanted to know more about the Great Raider. *Harper's* asked for a biography as did the *Washington Chronicle,* and a portrait sitting was arranged with Mathew Brady in New York.[8]

There even swept in a wave of concern for Averell's "frosted feet." "Rub them with Ethanol Oil," one letter advised.[9] Another recommended "rubbing them with Onion (cut horizontally) dipped in common fine salt & holding them to fire and to dry ice, but not so near as to materially increase the pain." Speaking from experience, having "lost nearly all my toe nails in the frost of 1851," the concerned writer added, "I have also found a poltice of corn meal to relieve them."[10]

Praise even came in from as strange and far away a place as Libby Prison in Richmond. Taking advantage of rebel permission for officers to send out one letter a month from the prison, Averell's aide, Lieutenant Leopold Markbreit wrote on 15 January to ask his recent commander to work for his exchange. But the lieutenant also added, "You are regarded both in and outside this prison as our best Cavalry Genl. The reception of the 'Averell raiders' by the Libby prisoners was highly flattering."[11] (In subsequent letters sent the following months, both Markbreit and Lieutenant Colonel Polsley pleaded with Averell to do what he could to facilitate their exchange; in late April Markbreit, Polsley, Koenigsberger, and one other officer had been placed in close confinement as hostages for four Confederate officers being held on Johnson Island. Shortly afterwards, Polsley was transferred to Charleston, S.C., where he was supposedly "placed under the fire of the Guns of the United States Troops then being used against said place." He was finally exchanged on 26 August, but his health was "so thoroughly broken down from Scurvy and disease of urinary organs," that he never recovered and died shortly after the war, in Dec. 1866.)[12]

And despite the horrors they suffered, the men in Averell's command seemed to worship him all the more. "The gigantic exertions made by the rebels to catch us," Lieutenant Hoffman wrote shortly after the raid, "and the coolness which Gen. Averill manifested in evading the traps set for his brigade, is beyond parallel. Long may he wave over the hills and dales of West Virginia. He is a terror to all rebels . . . West Virginia is under many obligations to the War Department for sending them a man who is not afraid to fight."[13]

Washington rewarded Averell with promotion, to date from 15 December 1863, to the rank of brevet colonel in the Regular Army, "for gallant and meritorious services during the Salem Expedition in Virginia."[14]

Many of his friends, however, thought he deserved much more. John Goode went directly to the president "to say that you was the best Cavalry Officer they ever had in the Potomac Army and that you should be made a Major Genl. The President replied that you should be. I then asked why you was transferred and you would laugh to know the reason he gave telling a good story to fit the case which I will repeat when we meet again."[15] Alas, that story appears to have been lost to posterity.

Addressing him as "My Dear Raider," another friend named Frank urged Averell to take full advantage of his current acclaim by going to Washington and hobbling around on crutches so as to play on the sympathies of the town. "William," Frank pleaded on 9 February, "keep the Raid before the people if you don't some lucky dog will smash a Rail Road while Congress is in Session and your daring exploit will be forgotten."[16] William, however, preferred to go home to Bath, being granted a twenty-day leave to recover from the frost bite he had suffered on the raid. The town feted him like a hero and gave a dinner in his honor at the Park Hotel, where he delivered a speech describing the recent daring exploits of his command.[17]

Frank needn't have worried, however. The raid was kept before the people, at least for a time. Indeed, largely because of Averell's 26 December dispatch from Beverly, wherein he told Halleck his command had "marched, climbed, slid and swum 355 miles," the raid had caught the public's imagination. The declaration became a catch-phrase throughout the capital. "I find that our great December raid & its results," an officer wrote Averell at the end of February, "is yet the Subject of conversation in Hotels, Street Cars & Social Circles. The rhetorical conclusion of your dispatch to Haleck [sic] has passed into a conversationalism & the persistent use of it is often."[18] So often, apparently, that it even turned up in the papers as a rhyme:

> By marching and riding,
> By swimming and sliding,
> By thawing and freezing,
> By dodging and squeezing,
> By fasting and waking,
> By hoping and quaking,
> We went down to Salem,
> And tore up the railin'.[19]

And another unknown admirer circulated this:

> Now my kind rebels no use for to talk.
> For Averell he is now the cock of the walk.
> For when he goes raiding by night and by day,
> If you'l take my advice, you'l keep out of his way.
> If you had been present when on the last raid,

To have seen the great conduct of Averell's brigade,
They being well mounted and horses that are tough,
Hurrah for your railroad, we'll soon tear it up.[20]

Alas, Averell's fifteen minutes of fame abruptly ended in March when a new hero, not one who had merely "smashed a Rail Road," but who had taken "the Gibraltar of the West," came to town—Ulysses S. Grant.

2. The Cost

Until that eclipse, however, Averell nobly took efforts to make sure the men of his command received their proper share of the acclaim. "The officers and men undertook all that was required of them," he reported on the last day of 1863, "and endured all the sufferings from fatigue, and cold with extraordinary fortitude, even cheerfulness. The march of 400 miles, which was concluded at Beverly, was the most difficult I have seen performed."[21]

This was not the simple boasting of a proud commander, for the "march of 400 miles" may have been the most difficult anyone at the time had ever seen performed, and it may be that, when considered as a whole, the expedition, in terms of its physical demands, its daring and audacious execution, and the results it achieved, was the most remarkable of its kind in the entire war.

The physical demands were unparalleled. Only the toughest and most determined could have endured the cold, the rain, the rugged mountains, the icy streams and rivers, the days without food, the nights without sleep and the constant stress that comes with knowing that the enemy—whether a lone bushwhacker or an entire division of regulars—may appear at any moment. All this is in sharp contrast to the more renowned John Hunt Morgan raid into Indiana and Ohio during the pleasant summer days of July, wherein the rebel raiders had plenty of food, good weather and flat, easy terrain—but were captured nonetheless.

The plan for the Salem Raid, with its various diversionary movements, was sound. Its execution by Averell, despite, or perhaps because of the shortcomings of the various diversionary movements that were intended to help him, was bold and audacious, even brilliant. When two hundred miles from their base, and with the enemy closing in all around, the men made it through only by the most determined efforts, sheer good fortune and inspired leadership. "Not less than 12,000 men were maneuvered to effect my capture," Averell boasted in his dispatch sent from Beverly on the twenty-sixth, "but when they thought it most certain, it was found Early was late."[22]

But what had Averell actually achieved? "The results of this combined movement have been highly satisfactory and important," General Kelley reported to Washington, "inflicting a loss on the enemy of not less than 400 men, an immense amount of provisions, material, and machinery, and the cutting off for a number of weeks of his most important line of communication."[23] All this was basically, though not entirely, true. As evidenced by an item printed in the *Wheeling Daily Register* 1 January 1864, which read, "the President of that road [Va. & Tenn.] gave notice that it is again in running order to Bristol, in Tennesse," it would appear the rail line through Salem was down for only about two weeks, not "a number of weeks."[24] Nonetheless, two weeks is an agonizing length of time to a hungry army waiting for food at the other end of the line. Longstreet's troops couldn't live off the land, for eastern Tennessee was already stripped bare. Thus with the interruption of the rail line and the immense loss of supplies and provisions, Longstreet's men must have been severely affected by the Salem Raid. Numerous reports submitted at different command levels at year's end indicate as much. Nearly all make frequent reference to the ragged and starving condition of their respective troops, who in turn resorted to straggling and plundering in alarming numbers.[25]

General Jones, however, would have his superiors in Richmond believe that the raid had actually benefited the Confederate cause. "The railroad was rather improved than injured by the raid," he reported, "as the few small bridges burned were in such condition that they were scarcely safe, and would require rebuilding very soon."[26] But Jones conveniently made no mention of the strain placed on the iron-poor Confederacy to replace fifteen miles of track. Nor was he or any other Confederate commander willing to openly admit that one of the most significant results of the raid had been the notice served of the increasingly dangerous capacity of the Union cavalry.

But at what cost? Of the more than 3,000 horses that set out on the expedition, less than half survived the trip "to Dixie Land." The comparatively few horses captured along the way provided small compensation.[27] Simple arithmetic indicates that a sizable portion of Averell's command walked into Beverly on Christmas Day. Company A of the 14th Pennsylvania, for example, had but nine horses left at the end of the raid.[28] Because of the shortage of horses throughout the command, most of the prisoners, 116 of some 200, had to be let go "on account of their inability to walk."[29] (The prisoners Averell kept were shipped on the thirtieth to Wheeling, where one observer was of the opinion that "They were about as rough looking customers as we have yet had the pleasure of seeing." They were sent the next day to Camp Chase.)[30]

The human loss was appalling. Averell placed his total casualties at 138[31] (see appendix 2 for details), of which some 120 were captured. Of the last, however, a bare handful survived the horrors of Andersonville and Libby prisons.[32] And of the 2,000 or so men who made it back to Beverly on Christmas Day, many suffered permanent damage to their toes, feet, hands and health in general. "Many of the old veterans are still alive," a local historian wrote in 1897, "and not a few of them attribute their broken constitutions to the terrible hardships endured during the twenty days occupied in that raid; now drenched with rain; now climbing mountains and dragging cannon by hand in cold so intense that cattle froze to death in the fields."[33]

In applying for disability pensions long after the war, many veterans cited the hardships endured on the Salem Raid as the cause of their current afflictions. Twenty-eight-year-old Sergeant John McVey of the 8th West Virginia's Company A would prove to be a typical example. During the retreat from Rocky Gap in August of '63, a horse had fallen on the young McVey, leaving his legs, hips, and back banged up and severely bruised. He had barely recovered from these aggravations when the exposures incurred on the Salem Raid caused them to flare up with such ferocity that he never fully recovered. "He was hardly able to go round," a fellow soldier testified twenty-five years later about how McVey appeared at the end of the raid. McVey's pension application, in turn, claimed that he suffered from "Rhematism [arthritis] of limbs, affecting hips, and legs, contracted about December 1863, from hardships & exposures on the Salem Raid."[34]

"Hundreds of broken down constitutions," Frank Reader wrote of the raid many years after the war, "attest to this day its severity."[35] There was no better proof of this than Reader's regimental commander, Lieutenant Colonel Alexander Scott. On the Salem Raid, Scott had been especially diligent in looking after the welfare of his men, and he was a constant inspiration to them. But he paid dearly. During the raid he contracted a cold so severe as to shatter his health and finally cause his death in 1870, at age forty-nine.[36]

3. Epilogue

In his "victory dispatch" sent to Washington from Beverly on 26 December, Averell asked Commander in Chief Halleck for a special favor. "The clothing of my men has been ruined in this expedition by being torn, burned [from men huddling around campfires],[37] wet, and frozen, and I request that the Quartermaster Department be directed to make them a New Year's gift of a new suit throughout."[38] At a time when every soldier in the army was being held to a strict account for the clothing and equipment issued to him, even being required on occasion to pay for lost or damaged items, this was a most unusual request. Never before in the war had a proposition like this, on such a grand scale, been presented to the War Department, whose fiscally conscious bureaucracy was ever vigilant against setting undesirable precedents. But Averell obviously believed that "my noble soldiers," by their exemplary courage, "remarkable fortitude," and endurance of suffering "without murmur," were entitled to such special consideration.

Halleck and Secretary of War Edwin Stanton agreed. In honor of what Averell's men had achieved, and in sympathy for what they had endured, they issued on 30 December Special Order No. 518: "The quartermaster department will issue gratis, to each man of Gen. Averell's command, one pair of shoes, and a suit of clothing, to replace those lost and worn out in his recent expedition."[39] At a time when medals were still relatively rare in the army, this remarkable gesture was akin to being awarded a badge of honor. And that honor became more special as it remained unique throughout the war.[40]

But Averell's men had more suffering to endure before receiving their New Year's gift. The Salem Raid still carried a certain momentum that had not yet allowed the masses involved to come to a complete rest, and in this sense, the expedition was not quite finished. Suspecting that Early and Fitz Lee, both still in the Shenandoah, might attempt "some retaliatory operations," Averell obtained Kelley's approval to get the command into the Valley as quickly as possible. Thus after only a single, though very welcome, day of rest, Averell's men marched out of Beverly early on the cold morning of the twenty-seventh. Still wearing ragged clothing, still without tents, and with most of the men still walking—again in a heavy, cold rain—they marched north eighteen miles to Belington. The next day they trudged another nineteen miles to camp within five miles of Webster. There they met a concerned citizen from Clarksburg, who had "stepped aboard the cars this morning and ran down to see the boys and learn how such a wonderful, rapid and almost super-human raid and march in mid-winter . . . had left the command." In a letter to the editors of the *Wheeling Intelligencer,* the citizen described how he found the boys "encamped—if without a single tent could be called a camp—in a monstrous big meadow, with nothing but old mother earth under them, with here and there a sprinkle of hay, and naught above but the canopy of heaven." Both heartened and saddened by what he saw, the writer, who signed his report with the letter "B," concluded that "The men, as far as I observed, appeared cheerful, and not a murmur escaped a single lip, although many were more or less frozen, and some it was feared would lose their feet by amputation." Two days before at Beverly another citizen had made a similar assessment regarding the condition of Averell's command, with the added impression that the general was extremely well liked by the men. "Gen. Averill is the man for us," he quotes them in a letter to the editors of the *Intelligencer,* "he doesn't like rebels, and isn't afraid to sit on the ground and eat broiled meat like a soldier."[41]

On the twenty-ninth these more or less frozen men marched into Webster, where trains were waiting to carry them east to Martinsburg at the northern end of the Shenandoah.[42] Though relieved from the agony of the march, few could say they enjoyed their train ride. The weather was so cold that the men, huddled together in box cars, could not eat—their bread and rations had become frozen solid. Then at Martinsburg the men "went into camp without tents or covering of any kind," recalled Frank Reader, "and suffered severely. Fuel was scarce, and there was really no condition of comfort."[43] On the thirty-first, however, the "condition of comfort" improved dramatically when the men received their New Year's gifts. "No necessity," Averell acknowledged, "was ever more pressing, or more promptly supplied; no charity more timely, or more gratefully received."[44]

Meanwhile, Averell had been right about the Confederates undertaking "some retaliatory operations." With the current lull along the Rappahannock,

General Lee believed he could leave his troops in the Shenandoah and put them to further use there. He instructed Early to send the cavalry on a raid northwest into Hardy and Hampshire counties in order to gather in much-needed supplies for the Army of Northern Virginia. Early brought Fitz Lee's two brigades up from Mt. Crawford, gave them one day of rest, then on the thirty-first he sent them with Rosser's brigade on a ride toward Morefield. They managed to capture a few head of cattle and a supply train of about ninety wagons, but the extremely harsh weather, the icy roads, and the exhausted condition of the men soon compelled the Confederates to turn back and return to the Valley. Already worn down, bedraggled and frozen, Fitz Lee's and Rosser's men suffered terribly on this last excursion.[45]

This, then, was another major effect of the Salem Raid: that fully one half of the Army of Northern Virginia's cavalry, three of six brigades, had been worn down to an extremely dangerous level at a time when every effort was needed to prepare for the all-important and certain-to-be-desperate spring campaign in the East. The army commander admitted as much when he complained to President Davis on 2 January that "the cavalry [are] worn down by their pursuit of Averell."[46] And whereas Averell's men received their "New Year's gifts" and were eventually supplied with fresh mounts, the Confederacy could not afford to extend such generosity to its troopers.

Yet another effect of the Salem Raid was Jubal Early's loss of confidence in the Confederate cavalry. On this latest assignment in the Valley, Early had developed contempt for Imboden's command, disdain for Rosser's, and he was left relatively unimpressed with the accomplishments of Fitz Lee. All of this would combine to form in him a distrust for his own cavalry that would have disastrous consequences in the Shenandoah Valley campaign of the following summer.[47]

Conversely, many Confederates had gained from the Salem Raid a new respect for the Union cavalry in general and for Averell and his men in particular. Chief among those Confederates was General Lee himself. "The main cause of his [Averell's] success," he wrote Jones in February 1864, "appears to me at this distance to be owing to the terror with which he has inspired the troops."[48] Many of those troops readily agreed with Lee. "Deserters and refugees are coming in daily," Colonel Moses Hall, Union commander at Beverly, wrote Kelley on 30 January. "They also state that General Averell is a terror to them; more so than even Stonewall Jackson was to us. A rumor of his approach is equal to death to them. His departure from West Virginia would be joyful news to them."[49] And in keeping with the theme of "terror," the *Wheeling Intelligencer* flatly asserted on 28 December that "Averill is said to be as great a terror now to the rebels along and beyond the border counties of the New State as ever Morgan was to the people of Kentucky."[50] Indeed, Captain Rife's preraid assessment of Averell's command now seemed even more appropriate: the Salem Raid "had made the name of Averell and his raiders both famous and to be feared in all Western Virginia from the Virginia & Tennessee Railroad to the Ohio River."[51]

Moreover, these opinions would prove quite durable. "It was said of him," a local historian wrote of Averell many years after the war regarding the effects of the Salem Raid, "that his cavalry moved like a whirlwind and struck like a thunderbolt. He soon became a terror of the confederate [*sic*] outposts from Winchester to the Tennesse line."[52]

Combined with the victory at Droop Mountain, the Salem Raid did much to restore Averell's reputation and he was promptly returned to division command, though not with the Army of the Potomac. On 31 December the Department of West Virginia was reorganized and Averell's oversized brigade was made into the Fourth Division[53] (the infantry and Keeper's battery made up the First Brigade; Gibson's battalion and the 14th Pa. Cav. formed the Second Brigade; the three West Virginia regiments and Ewing's battery composed the Third Brigade).[54] Furthermore, on 26 January Averell's West Virginia regiments could at last drop the designation "mounted infantry"; they had now, in a sense, "graduated" to their true title of cavalry. The 2nd, 3rd, and 8th became, respectively, the 5th, 6th, and 7th West Virginia Cavalry.[55]

But despite their new titles, the three regiments were left with their old infantry, Enfield muskets. Averell sought to redress this "injustice" by submitting a request for Spencer carbines to the new commander in chief himself, Lieutenant General U.S. Grant, who had replaced Halleck in March. In an interview with Averell in April, Grant professed sympathy but claimed there was little he could do. The regiments would have to make do with their muskets.[56]

Grant, no doubt, had precious little time to consider the supply problems of three West Virginia regiments. He was all-consumed with developing his grand strategy for the upcoming spring campaign. His plan was like none other seen in the war. Virtually every Union command, including the Department of West Virginia, was to simultaneously take the offensive. As such, Grant wanted his involved departments to be led by proven field commanders, not administrators. This meant that Kelley, who had not led troops since Philippi, had to go. On 29 February Grant replaced him with Franz Sigel.[57]

Within his grand strategy, Grant assigned the Department of West Virginia a specific role that was to be executed by a plan not unlike the one Averell had developed for the Salem Raid. While Meade advanced farther into Virginia, Sherman into Georgia, and Butler up the James, troops from the department were to launch a two-pronged assault—one from Harper's Ferry up the Shenandoah Valley, the other from Charleston toward the Virginia & Tennessee Railroad.[58]

Since its arrival at Martinsburg in late December, Averell's brigade, now the Fourth Division, had been positioned on a line of outposts stretching from the Shenandoah River to Back Creek, and it was generally responsible for patrolling an area within a radius of sixty miles from Martinsburg.[59] In late April, the vaunted command was broken up.

Co. G, 7th W.Va. Cav. (8th W.Va. Mtd. Inf.)

Boyd B. Stutler Collection,
West Virginia State Archives

Because of his invaluable experience and proven ability, Averell was chosen to lead the department's cavalry on the expedition to the Virginia & Tennessee. He was therefore reassigned to Charleston as commander of the Second Cavalry Division. He took with him the 5th and 7th West Virginia Cavalry and 14th Pennsylvania Cavalry, leaving behind forever the infantry, the 6th West Virginia Cavalry, Gibson's battalion, and the batteries of Ewing and Keeper.[60]

As part of an overall strike force of some 6,100 men of all arms under the command of George Crook, who had replaced Scammon, Averell's division set out from Charleston on 2 May. In a tough, six-day march over rugged terrain, the division gave exemplary service; Averell displayed considerable personal gallantry and won high praise from Crook for his conduct and leadership. While Crook's infantry won a victory at Cloyd's Mountain five miles north of Dublin on the eighth, Averell's men destroyed the bridge at Blacksburg, a critical span on the Virginia & Tennessee. (Averell had been slightly wounded in the head on 10 May at Cove Mountain Gap.)[61] But these accomplishments lost much of their luster when Sigel, leading the drive up the Shenandoah, was decisively beaten on the fifteenth at New Market.[62]

Grant replaced Sigel with David Hunter, who promptly launched another drive up the Shenandoah on 26 May, the objective this time being Lynchburg. Averell's division was brought east to join in. Despite an impressive victory 5 June at Piedmont, and the subsequent burning of the Virginia Military Institute at Lexington, Hunter lost his nerve, failed to take Lynchburg, and by 1 July he had fallen back into the Alleghenies. In explaining his failure, however, he complained bitterly to Grant about "that fellow Averell."[63] But Grant, apparently seeing through this attempt to avoid taking responsibility, kept Averell and replaced Hunter. As with Hooker the year before, however, the seeds of doubt had again been planted. It marked the beginning of the end for Averell.

Hunter was succeeded by Crook, whose command in turn became part of the Valley Army of Philip Sheridan. This was another unfortunate turn for Averell. He did not get along with Sheridan, either because the new commander held alleged "past failures" against him, or because Averell, preferring "to row my own boat," did not work his way into Sheridan's inner circle of cronies. At any rate, Sheridan appointed Alfred Torbert, Averell's junior in rank, to the command of all the cavalry in the Shenandoah. Averell's complaint to the War Department at this affront did not endear him to Sheridan, who seemed determined from then on to remove him at the first opportunity. Though "Little Phil" was put off in this desire by Averell's victory near Morefield in August, when more than 400 Confederates were captured at a loss of only twenty-eight men, his resolve to remove him stiffened when Averell, once again, did not follow up the victory but fell back to safety. Sheridan's chance finally came when Averell failed to vigorously pursue the beaten Confederates at Fisher's Hill on 22 September.

Though he protested, and General Early's report concurred, that the Confederates were not the disorganized mob Sheridan believed them to be, Averell did seem in this last campaign to lack that remarkable determination and brilliant drive he had shown on the Salem Raid, almost as though he were mentally weary and physically drained.[64] Perhaps he had not yet fully recovered from the relapse that spring, aggravated by the head wound, of the fever he had contracted on the Peninsula more than two years before. Or perhaps Averell had finally outlived his usefulness as a commander. Like McClellan, his organizational skills had proved invaluable when they were most needed early in the war. And like McClellan, Averell had to eventually give way to a new type of warfare, whereby endless training and preparation were put aside in favor of decisive action and success at-almost-any-cost. On the Salem Raid, Averell's remarkable drive, determination and spirit of sacrifice seemed to mark a transition from the old school to the new type of warfare, but in the Shenandoah the following summer his old caution and reserve resurfaced, for whatever reason, to ultimately do him in. At any rate, his military career was over.

Averell was stunned. So were the men of his command. The 27 September issue of the *New York Herald* claimed Averell's dismissal "caused a universal feeling of amazement in the army." The article went on to describe Averell's farewell to his command: "Averill's [*sic*] division officers and men exhibited their devotion to him by the most marked demonstrations. The officers, who seemed to love him as an elder brother, shed tears at his departure, and as the general rode along the lines for the last time the men greeted him with the most enthusiastic cheers and many expressions of affection."[65]

Likewise, had the magnificent troops Averell had commanded on the Salem Raid entered the twilight of their military careers. Only the 14th Pennsylvania Cavalry went on with Sheridan to his final triumphs in the Shenandoah and in eastern Virginia. The other units finished out the war as they had begun it—on outpost duty, guarding the state they had done so much to help create.[66]

For the rest of his life, Averell remained very bitter about his removal from command; it hurt him more than bullets or illness could ever have. He blamed the politicians.

Though he admired Lincoln, who, despite the dismissal, promoted him on 13 March 1865 to brevet major general, Averell detested politicians in general and the Republican administration in particular. He accused it of deliberately and unnecessarily prolonging the war in order to benefit the party. The most convincing evidence of this, in his mind, was the appointment of politicians to command in the field. Such thinking unfortunately led Averell to believe that during the war the government had been rife with conspiracies set up to deal with potential threats to party power. Chief among the conspirators, in Averell's eyes, was Secretary of War Stanton. Chief among the victims was General McClellan, whom Averell greatly admired. With this sort of logic guiding him, Averell could only conclude that he, too, a life-long Democrat, had been on the administration's list of political victims.[67]

After the war, Averell served as the U.S. consul general in Montreal from 1866 to 1869. He then went into business, a field in which his keen intellect and creative energies produced a number of successful inventions, including a system of asphalt pavement, the "Averell insulating conduits" for wires and conductors, and a method of making cast steel direct from iron ore in one operation. On 24 September 1885, the fifty-three-year-old Averell finally ended his bachelorhood by marrying the English widow Kezia Hayward Browning. They produced no children.

Averell never forgot the soldiers who served with him in the war. He led many veterans organizations, whose members held him in the highest regard. Of the many speeches he gave at their gatherings, a frequent topic was the Salem Raid.

Upon his reinstatement in the U.S. Army by a special act of Congress in 1888, Averell was placed on the retired list and assumed the post of assistant inspector general of Soldiers Homes. He held this job for ten years, finally retiring in 1898. He died in Bath, New York on 3 February 1900.[68]

To the end of their days, Averell and many of his "noble soldiers" regarded the Salem Raid as a major highlight of their military experience, and as one of the more significant accomplishments of their entire lives.[69]

"How bittersweet those memories are," wrote one old veteran long after the war. "Yet, terrible as that Mid-winter raid in the Alleghanies was, not one of us that would not go through it again if he could. And what can not a man do when do he must?"[70]

APPENDIX 1

Order of Battle

Union Forces

Department of West Virginia—Brigadier General Benjamin F. Kelley
First Division—Brigadier General Jeremiah C. Sullivan

First Brigade—Colonel George D. Wells

Starting from Harper's Ferry

34 Mass. Inf.—Lt. Col. William S. Lincoln	591 men
12 W.Va. Inf.—Maj. William B. Curtis	401 men
17 Ind. Btty—Capt. Milton L. Miner	77 men
1 W.Va. Lt. Art. Btty A—Capt. George Furst	32 men
Total:	1,101 men

Cavalry Brigade—Colonel William H. Boyd

Starting from Charlestown

1 Conn. det.—Maj. Erastus Blakeslee
Md. Bn. (Potomac Home Guards)—Maj. Henry A. Cole
2 Md. Co. F (Potomac Home Guards)—Capt. Norvel McKinley
6 Mich. Co. M—Capt. Harvey H. Vinton
1 N.Y.—Maj. Timothy Quinn
21 Pa. 5 cos. A, D, F, G, I—Maj. Charles F. Gillies
22 Pa. 1 Bn.—Maj. B. Mortimer Morrow
Total: c. 700 men

Second Division—Colonel James A. Mulligan

Second Brigade—Colonel Joseph Thoburn

Starting from Beverly

1 W.Va. Inf.—Lt. Col. Jacob Weddle
14 W.Va. Inf.—Capt. Jacob Smith

21 Pa. Cav. 5 cos. (Ringgold Cav.) B, C, E, H, K—Capt. James Y. Chesrow
1 Ill. Lt. Art. Btty L 1 section—Capt. John Rourke
Total: c. 700 men

Third Division—Brigadier General Eliakim P. Scammon
Second Brigade—Colonel Carr B. White
Starting from Fayette County

12 Ohio Inf.—Lt. Col. Jonathon D. Hines
91 Ohio Inf.—Col. John H. Turley
1 Ohio Btty 2 sections—Capt. James R. McMullen
Total: c. 1,000 men

Third Brigade—Brigadier General Alfred N. Duffie
Starting from Charleston

34 Ohio Mtd. Inf.—Capt. Luther Furney
2 W.Va. Cav.—Lt. Col. David Dove
3 W.Va. Cav. 3 cos.—Capt. George M. McVicker
Total: c. 1,000 men

First Separate Brigade—Brigadier General William W. Averell
Starting from New Creek

2 W.Va. Mtd. Inf.—Lt. Col. Alexander Scott
3 W.Va. Mtd. Inf.—Lt. Col. Francis W. Thompson
8 W.Va. Mtd. Inf.—Col. John H. Oley
14 Pa. Cav.—Lt. Col. William Blakely
Gibson's Bn. 6 cos.—Maj. Thomas Gibson
Co. A 1 W.Va. Cav.—Capt. Harrison H. Hogan
Cos. E, F and H 3 W.Va. Cav.—Capt. Lot Bowen
Co. C 16 Ill. Cav.—Capt. Julius Jaehne
3rd Ind. Ohio—Capt. Frank Smith
1 W.Va. Lt. Art. Btty G 4 guns—Capt. Chatham T. Ewing
Total: c. 2,500 men

First Separate Brigade—detachment—Colonel Augustus Moor
Starting from Beverly

28 Ohio Inf.—Col. Augustus Moor
10 W.Va. Inf.—Col. Thomas M. Harris
Total: c. 1000 men
Grand Total: c. 8,000 men

Confederate Forces

Department of Western Virginia & East Tennessee—Major General Samuel Jones
Echols' Brigade—Brigadier General John Echols
Starting from Lewisburg

22 Va. Inf.—Col. George S. Patton
23 Va. Bn. Inf.—Lt. Col. Clarence Derrick
26 Va. Bn. Inf.—Lt. Col. George Edgar
Partisan Rangers—Capt. W.D. Thurmond
Va. Btty—Capt. George B. Chapman
Va. Btty—Capt. T.E. Jackson
14 Va. Cav. of Jenkins' Brigade—Col. J.A. Gibson
Total: c. 1,500 men

McCausland's Brigade—Colonel John McCausland
Starting from Narrows

36 Va. Inf.—Maj. T. Smith
60 Va. Inf.—Col. B.H. Jones
Va. Btty—Capt. Thomas A. Bryan
17 Va. Cav. of Jenkins' Brigade—Maj. F.F. Smith
Total: c. 1,600 men

Jackson's Brigade—Colonel William L. Jackson
Starting from the Huntersville Line

19 Va. Cav.—Lt. Col. William P. Thompson
20 Va. Cav.—Col. William W. Arnett
Va. Btty—Capt. Warren S. Lurty
Det. of 6 independent cos.
Total: c. 900 men
Total for Jones' command: c. 4,000 men

Valley District—Major General Jubal Early
Northwest Brigade—Brigadier General John D. Imboden
Starting from Harrisonburg

62 Va. Mtd. Inf.—Col. George H. Smith
18 Va. Cav.—Col. George W. Imboden
41 Va. Cav. Bn.—Maj. Robert White
2 Md. Cav. Bn.—Maj. H.W. Gilmore
Va. Btty—Capt. John H. McClanahan
Total: c. 1,500 men

Army of Northern Virginia—General Robert E. Lee
Cavalry Corps—Major General J.E.B. Stuart
Lee's Division—Major General Fitzhugh Lee
Starting from Charlottesville
W.H.F. Lee's Brigade—Colonel John R. Chambliss

9 Va. Cav.—Col. R.L.T. Beale
10 Va. Cav.—Col. James L. Davis
13 Va. Cav.—Col. James R. Chambliss

Wickham's Brigade—Brigadier General W.C. Wickham

1 Va. Cav.—Col. R.W. Carter
2 Va. Cav.—Col. Thomas T. Munford
3 Va. Cav.—Col. T.H. Owen
4 Va. Cav.—Lt. Col. W.H. Payne
Total: c. 1,800 men

Hampton's Division—Major General Wade Hampton
Rosser's Laurel Brigade—Brigadier General Thomas L. Rosser
Starting from Fredericksburg

7 Va. Cav.—Col. R.H. Dulany
11 Va. Cav.—Col. O.R. Funsten
12 Va. Cav.—Col. A.W. Harmon
35 Va. Cav. Bn.—Lt. Col. E.V. White
Total: c. 800 men

Third Corps—Lieutenant General A.P. Hill
Wilcox's Division—Major General Cadmus Wilcox
Thomas' Brigade—Brigadier General E.L. Thomas
Starting from Orange C.H.

14 Ga. Inf.—Col. Robert W. Folsom
35 Ga. Inf.—Col. B.H. Holt
45 Ga. Inf.—Col. Thomas J. Simmons
49 Ga. Inf.—Col. S.T. Player

Heth's Division—Major General Henry Heth
Walker's Brigade—Brigadier General H.H. Walker

40 Va. Inf.—Col. J.M. Brockenbrough
47 Va. Inf.—Col. R.M. Mayo
55 Va. Inf.—Col. W.S. Christian
40 Va. Inf.
22 Va. Inf. Bn.—Lt. Col. E.P. Taylor
Total: c. 3,000 men
Grand Total: c. 11,100 men

APPENDIX 2

Losses in Averell's Brigade During the Salem Raid

Sources

West Virginia Troops: Reader; Compiled Service Records on Microfilm at the National Archives in Washington, D.C.
Pennsylvania Troops: Bates; Slease.
Ohio Troops: Reid; Adj. Gen. Report.
Illinois Troops: Adj. Gen. Report.

All those listed below were captured near Covington, Va. 19–20 Dec. 1863, unless otherwise specified. Though thoroughly researched, the list is by no means complete. Not included are the dozens, perhaps hundreds of cases of frostbite.

2nd West Virginia Mounted Infantry (21)

Name	Rank	Co.	Age	Comments
Ammon, Jesse	Pvt.	I	20	died in Andersonville.
Burskell, John	Pvt.	H	—	fate unknown.
Creel, Edward B.	Pvt.	B	20	exchanged 11-64.
Deems, Jeremiah	Pvt.	K	33	died in Andersonville 9-18-64.
Garnet, Abraham	Pvt.	H	27	died in Andersonville 8-21-64.
Garton, William	Cpl.	I	35	died in Andersonville 10-10-64.
Halpin, John	Pvt.	D	22	died in Andersonville 5-2-64.
Kay, James M.	Pvt.	E	26	exchanged 11-64.
McClary, Thomas	Pvt.	E	27	paroled 3-21-64.
McGurgen, Peter	Pvt.	D	19	died in Andersonville 9-22-64.
Matlick, Jacob G.	Pvt.	B	22	exchanged 11-18-64.
Miller, Conrad	Pvt.	C	32	died in Andersonville 8-27-64.
Nolte, Anton	Pvt.	C	31	died in Belle Isle, Richmond 3-16-64.
Poggneur, Ernst	Pvt.	C	35	fate unknown.
Sexton, Lindley	Pvt.	K	24	paroled 2-26-65.

Name	Rank	Co.	Age	Comments
Snyder, George	Pvt.	F	36	paroled 4-16-64.
Stafford, William E.	Pvt.	B	24	exchanged 11-20-64.
Walton, Joseph	Pvt.	D	28	paroled 4-18-64.
Warwick, Edward	Pvt.	D	20	died in Andersonville 4-4-64.
West, Thomas F.	Pvt.	K	26	died in Millen, Ga.
Woods, John	Pvt.	D	20	"Feet frozen on Salem Raid"

3rd West Virginia Mounted Infantry (22)

Name	Rank	Co.	Age	Comments
Bishoff, Jacob C.	Pvt.	C	24	died in Andersonville 8-13-64.
Bowermaster, Simon R.	Pvt.	D	21	died in Andersonville 6-23-64.
Buckmire, William	Pvt.	H	—	fate unknown.
Channing, James	Cpl.	H	21	exchanged 11-64.
Collins, Charles	Pvt.	C	21	died in Andersonville 7-25-64.
Davis, Sanderson	Pvt.	B	19	died in Andersonville 4-30-64.
Hammer, Samuel	Pvt.	K	28	died in Andersonville 8-8-64.
Hartley, Isaac S.	Pvt.	I	25	died in Andersonville 8-12-64.
Hiller, William	Pvt.	D	36	died in Andersonville 4-15-64.
Horan, Edward C.	Pvt.	G	27	died in Andersonville 7-25-64.
Kantner, William H.	2 Lt.	H	25	wounded by horse falling.
McClain, William R.	Pvt.	E	23	survived captivity.
Moore, John	Pvt.	K	23	escaped form Andersonville 7-5-64.
Nichols, James	Pvt.	B	26	died in Andersonville 1-17-65.
Pugh, Louis	Pvt.	I	28	died in Andersonville 8-8-64.
Schiller, Charles	Pvt.	A	25	died in Andersonville 7-19-64.
Snider, Samuel	Pvt.	D	21	died in Andersonville 8-5-64.
Starcher, John	Pvt.	C	22	exchanged 11-64.
Starr, Benjamin	Cpl.	K	21	shot in leg near Franklin 12-10.
Steetler, Joseph N.	Pvt.	B	30	died in Andersonville 6-25-64.
Williams, John E.	Pvt.	G	21	wounded and cap; paroled.
Wilson, John	Pvt.	B	29	died in Andersonville 9-2-64.

8th West Virginia Mounted Infantry (36)

Name	Rank	Co.	Age	Comments
Adams, Thomas H.	Pvt.	K	43	exchanged 11-30-64.
Ballinger, Andrew	Sgt.	D	27	died in Andersonville 10-5-64.
Carr, William	Pvt.	B	39	died in Andersonville 4-4-64.
Casdorph, Caleb	2Lt.	A	25	exchanged 3-1-64.
Casdorph, William H.	Pvt.	A	22	died in Richmond 3-11-64.
Casto, Jesse C.	Pvt.	E	30	died in Andersonville 5-11-64.
Cobb, John M.	Pvt.	C	32	died at Belle Isle 7-17-64.

Name	Rank	Co.	Age	Comments
Curcus, Richard	Pvt.	E	31	died in Andersonville 11-2-64.
Dent, John W.	Pvt.	A	22	died in Andersonville 9-11-64.
Edens, Clarkson Sr.	Pvt.	A	22	died in Richmond 4-5-64.
Forth, Robert	Pvt.	D	30	died in Andersonville 10-4-64.
Foster, Seth	Pvt.	A	21	died in Andersonville 8-29-64.
Fowler, Joseph	Pvt.	E	22	died in Richmond 2-27-64.
Gregg, Andrew	Capt.	H	38	paroled 1-19-64.
Hagar, Charles	Pvt.	G	29	died in Richmond 4-15-65.
Harper, William A.	Pvt.	H	28	fate unknown.
Haynes, Samuel	Pvt.	A	25	fate unknown.
Hunter, George W.	Pvt.	A	22	died in Andersonville 4-6-64.
Kirkpatrick, William	Pvt.	D	20	died in Andersonville 9-11-64.
Kittle, Andrew J.	Pvt.	A	—	paroled 4-16-64.
Males, Robert	Pvt.	H	32	fate unknown.
Murphy, Jeremiah	Pvt.	D	20	died in Andersonville 5-27-64.
Pauley, Jesse J.	Pvt.	C	20	died in Andersonville 8-17-64.
Payne, Mitchell	Cpl.	H	35	died in Andersonville 8-14-64.
Petry, John	Pvt.	G	25	died in Andersonville 4-29-64.
Polsley, John J.	Lt Col	—	33	exchanged 8-3-64.
Scott, Zachariah	Sgt.	D	39	died in Andersonville 5-31-64.
Simmons, John J.	Pvt.	F	31	died in Richmond 4-4-64.
Smith, John W.	Pvt.	G	25	died in Andersonville 8-17-64.
Taylor, John H.	Pvt.	D	20	died in Andersonville 9-13-64.
Tyree, Granville	Pvt.	H	32	died in Andersonville 8-9-64.
Welcher, John	Pvt.	G	27	died in Camp Sumter, Ga. 10-15-64.
Whiting, William A.	Pvt.	F	19	died in Andersonville 5-25-64.
Williams, Owens	Cpl.	A	24	died in Richmond 3-9-64.
Workman, Benjamin H.	Pvt.	B	20	exchanged 11-64.
Wristan, Patterson	Pvt.	H	22	fate unknown.

14th Pennsylvania Cavalry (29)

Name	Rank	Co.	Age	Comments
Bonewell, William W.*	Pvt.	G	—	died in Andersonville 9-26-64.
Crawford, Matthew*	Pvt.	G	—	died in Andersonville 7-30-64.
Crawford, Michael*	Pvt.	K	—	died in Andersonville 10-29-64.
Cumberland, T.S.*	Pvt.	B	—	died in Andersonville 8-12-64.
Dunbar, John*	Pvt.	M	—	died in Andersonville 8-6-64.
Furlow, Seth E.*	Pvt.	G	—	died in Andersonville 8-21-64.
Golbert, Adam F.*	Pvt.	C	—	died in Andersonville 10-20-64.
Heenter, James*	Pvt.	M	—	died in Andersonville 10-20-64.
Hefflefinger, V.S.*	Pvt.	K	—	died in Andersonville 7-28-64.
Hicks, John F.*	Pvt.	A	—	died in Andersonville 10-2-64.

Name	Rank	Co.	Age	Comments
Johnston, Adrian	Pvt.	E	—	drowned in Jackson River 12-20-63.
Larrison, Wallace*	Pvt.	C	—	died in Andersonville 8-4-64.
Lewis, John	Pvt.	L	—	died in Andersonville 10-26-64.
Loughry, Andrew P.*	Pvt.	E	—	died in Andersonville 9-30-64.
McEwen, Charles*	Pvt.	C	—	died in Andersonville 7-3-64.
Mackerel, James*	Pvt.	K	—	died in Andersonville 8-3-64.
Maxwell, Samuel*	Pvt.	B	—	died in Andersonville 10-15-64.
Miller, Hamlin*	Pvt.	I	—	died in Andersonville 8-5-64.
Murphy, William W.	Capt.	G	—	shot through the arm 12-20-63.
Neeman, John	Pvt.	F	—	died in Andersonville 7-18-64.
Pratt, Thomas*	Pvt.	I	—	died in Andersonville 7-28-64.
Seiberts, Edward	Pvt.	E	—	drowned in Jackson River 12-20-63.
Smith, Woodbury*	Pvt.	E	—	died in Andersonville 8-6-64.
Stricker, Frederick*	Pvt.	C	—	died in Andersonville 8-9-64.
Thatler, Robert*	Pvt.	C	—	died in Andersonville 10-10-64.
Tingley, Samuel*	Pvt.	B	—	died in Andersonville 10-6-64.
Vandergrift, Amos	Pvt.	A	—	no further record.
White, Samuel	Pvt.	B	—	died in Andersonville 8-7-64.
Wildeman, E.A.*	Pvt.	G	—	died in Andersonville 10-17-64.

*Bates gives no indication of where these men were captured, but it seems a fair assumption that they were taken near Covington.

Gibson's Independent Cavalry Battalion (15)

Name	Rank	Co.	Age	Comments
3 W.Va. Cav.				
Cork, John D.	Cpl.	E	21	paroled 11-19-64.
Hamrick, Robert	Pvt.	E	20	paroled 11-29-64.
Morris, Isaac M.	Pvt.	E	24	died in Andersonville 5-13-64.
Vanscoy, Adam	Cpl.	E	29	died in Andersonville 5-16-64.
3 Ind. Ohio Cav. Co.				
Dottling, George	Cpl.	—	26	died in Millen, Ga. 11-4-64.
Fischer, Charles	Pvt.	—	30	no further record.
Freehauf, George	Pvt.	—	24	died in Andersonville 5-26-64.
Homan, John W.	Pvt.	—	25	survived and mustered out.
Hugel, John	Pvt.	—	29	died in Andersonville 6-16-64.
Meyer, B.L.	Pvt.	—	20	died in Andersonville 9-11-64.
Meyer, Lawrence	Pvt.	—	27	no further record.
Pfirman, Valentine	Pvt.	—	29	died in Richmond 9-18-64.
Schneider, Augustus	Cpl.	—	28	no further record.
16 Ill. Cav.				
Hanson, Nicholas	Pvt.	C	—	fate unknown.
Peterson, Charles	Pvt.	C	—	drowned in Craig's Creek 12-17-63.

Battery G 1st West Virginia Light Artillery

Name	Rank	Age	Comments
Deiffenbaugh, Jeremia	Cpl.	37	died in Andersonville 7-14-64 (paroled?).
Grubb, John	Pvt.	29	fate unknown.
Guest, James P.	Pvt.	22	paroled 11-18-64.
Hobaugh, John	Pvt.	21	paroled 11-20-64.
McGillvary, Farquhar	Pvt.	28	paroled 11-23-64.

Losses as stated in Averell's report of 31 December 1863

2 W.Va. Mtd. Inf.
1 sergeant wounded; 1 corporal & 16 privates captured near Covington.

3 W.Va. Mtd. Inf.
1 corporal wounded while on picket near Franklin; 1 corporal &
16 privates captured near Covington.

8 W.Va. Mtd. Inf.
1 private suffered a broken leg & was captured 21 Dec.; 3 officers,
1 sergeant, 4 corporals, & 29 privates captured near Covington.

14 Pa. Cav.
6 privates drowned; 5 privates wounded, 1 corporal & 24 privates
captured near Covington.

Gibson's Bn.
1 private drowned & 1 missing; 5 corporals & 13 privates captured
near Covington.

Ewing's Btty
1 corporal & 4 privates captured near Covington; 2 privates captured
near Hillsboro 23 Dec.

Total
3 officers, 2 sergeants,14 corporals, 119 privates; =138.

Appendix 3

Dates, Routes, & Distances

CR=County Road

Date	Miles	Journey	Route
Dec. 8	18	New Creek, Mineral Co., W.Va. to about 7 miles north of Williamsport.	U.S. 220 south & southeast 13 miles to Burlington, then CR 11 south 5 miles.
9	25	Williamsport to Petersburg, Grant Co., W.Va.	CR 11 south 3 miles to Grant Co. ine, then CR 5 south 18 miles to W.Va. 42, then 4 miles south to Petersburg.
10	32	Petersburg to near Franklin, Pendleton Co., W.Va.	U.S. 220 south 12 miles to Pendleton Co. line, then 20 miles on to Franklin.
11	23	Franklin to Monterey, Highland Co., Va.	U.S. 220 south 15 miles to Highland Co. line, then 8 miles on to Monterey.
12	12	Monterey to near Mill Gap, Highland Co.	U.S. 220 south 4 miles to Va. 84 at Bulltown (Vanderpool), then 3 miles west, then south 5 miles to Mill Gap.
13	20	Mill Gap to Gatewood's (Mountain Grove), Bath Co., Va.	Va. 84 south 2 miles to CR 600, then 5 miles south to Bath Co. line, then 13 miles south to Gatewood's (Mountain Grove).
14	24	Gatewood's to Callaghan's, Alleghany Co., Va.	CR 600 south (Morris Hill rd.— route interrupted by present day Lake Moomau).

147

Date	Miles	Journey	Route
Dec. 15	42	Callaghan's to New Castle, Craig Co., Va.	Va. 159 (Dunlap's Creek rd.) south 12 miles to Crows, then Va. 311 (Kanawha Trail) south 6 miles to Sweet Sp., Monroe Co., W.Va., then 4 miles to top of Sweet Sp. Mtn., then 9 miles to top of Potts,' then 11 miles on to New Castle.
16	30	New Castle to Mason's Cove, Roanoke Co., Va.	Va. 311 (Catawba Valley rd.) south 14 miles to top of North Mtn., then 9 miles east and south to Salem, Roanoke Co., Va., then Va. 311 north 7 miles to Mason's Cove.
17	8	Mason's Cove to 8 miles south of New Castle	Va. 311 (Catawba Valley rd.) north to foot of North Mtn.
18	24	8 miles south of New Castle to Barber's Creek rd.	Va. 311 north 8 miles to New Castle, then 10 miles north to top of Potts,' then 6 miles back south to CR 611 (Barber's Creek rd.).
19	36	Barber's Creek rd. to Covington, Alleghany Co., Va.	CR 611 (Barber's Creek rd.) north 5 miles to CR 617 (Jamison Mtn. rd.), then north 10 miles to Alleghany Co. line, then north 1 mile to CR 618 (Upper Rich Patch rd.), then north 2 miles to CR 616 (Rich Patch rd.), then north 5 miles to Rich Patch, then 7 miles to Island Ford Br., then 6 miles west on CR1101 to Covington.
20	29	Covington to Anthony's Creek, Greenbrier Co., W.Va.	U.S. 60 west 8 miles to CR 661 (Ogles Creek rd.), then north 8 miles to CR 781 (Rucker Gap rd.), then north 2 miles to top of Rucker's Gap and CR 14 in Greenbrier Co., W.Va., then west 5 miles to W.Va. 92 at Neola, then south 6 miles to CR 16 (Alvon rd.).
21	28	Anthony's Creek to Hillsboro, Pocahontas Co., W.Va.	CR 16 west 1 mile to Little Creek rd. then north 10 miles to CR 21 in Pocahontas Co., then 14 miles north and west to CR 27, then 3 miles west to Hillsboro.

Date	Miles	Journey	Route
22	15	Hillsboro to near Edray, Pocahontas Co.	US 219 north
23	22	Edray to the Conrad farm, Pocahontas Co.	US 219 north
24	7	Conrad farm to Elk, Randolph Co., W.Va.	US 219 north
25	18	Elk to Beverly, Randolph Co.	US 219 north
Dec. 8–25	411	New Creek to Beverly	

NOTES

CHAPTER ONE
THE SUMMONS

1. H.E. Matheny, *Major General Thomas M. Harris* (Parson, W.Va.: McClain Printing Co., 1963), p. 63 (hereafter cited as Matheny).
2. Patricia Faust, ed., *Historical Times Illustrated Encyclopedia of the Civil War* (New York: Harper & Row Publishers, 1986), p. 410 (hereafter cited as Faust).
3. United States War Department, *War of the Rebellion: A Compilation of the Official Records of the Union and Confederate Armies*, 128 vols. (Washington: U.S. Government Printing Office, 1880–1901), Series I, vol. 29, pt. 2, p. 473 (hereafter cited as OR; all references are from Series I).
4. Boyd B. Sutler, *West Virginia in the Civil War* (Charleston, W.Va.: Education Foundation, Inc., 1963), pp. 1–48 (hereafter cited as Sutler); Stan Cohen, *The Civil War in West Virginia* (Missoula, Mont. Gateway Printing & Litho, 1976), pp. 1–38 (hereafter cited as Cohen).
5. Stephan Z. Starr, *The Union Cavalry in the Civil War*, 3 vols. (Baton Rouge: The Louisiana State University Press, 1979), vol. 1, pp. 151–56 (hereafter cited as Starr; all references are from vol. 1).
6. Theodore F. Lang, *Loyal West Virginians From 1861 to 1865* (Baltimore: The Deutsch Publishing Co., 1895), pp. 101–7 (hereafter cited as Lang); OR, vol. 25, pt. 1, pp. 90–137; pt. 2, pp. 246–60; John H. McNeil, "The Imboden Raid and its Effects," *Southern Historical Society Papers*, vol. 34, pp. 294–307 (hereafter cited as McNeil).
7. Starr, pp. 155–56; OR, vol. 25, pt. 2, pp. 170–71.
8. OR, vol. 25, pt. 2, pp. 170–71, 176, 502.
9. Ibid., p. 502; Francis Smith Reader, *History of the Fifth West Virginia Cavalry, Formerly the Second Virginia, and Battery G First West Virginia Light Artillery* (New Brighton, Pa.: Daily News, 1890), p. 200 (hereafter cited as Reader); Lang, p. 355.
10. Faust, p. 636; Lang, pp. 105–7.
11. Robert B. Boehm, "The Unfortunate Averell," *Civil War Times Illustrated*, Aug. 1966, p. 30 (hereafter cited as Boehm).
12. Reader, p. 197.
13. Edward K. Eckart and Nicholas J. Amato, eds., *Ten Years in the Saddle: The Memoir of William Woods Averell 1851–1862* (San Rafael, Calif.: Presidio Press, 1978), pp. 1–24 (hereafter cited as *Ten Years*); William Woods Averell Papers, 1836–1910, New York State Library, Albany (hereafter cited as Averell Papers), Biographical Sketch, p. 3.
14. *Ten Years*, pp. 24–25, 39.
15. Ibid., p. 65.

16. Ibid., pp. 1–4.
17. Ibid., pp. 90–203; Averell Papers, Biographical Sketch, p. 2.
18. *Ten Years*, pp. 126–27.
19. Ibid., pp. 80, 203–8, 211.
20. Ibid., pp. 242–43.
21. Ibid., pp. 258–71.
22. Ibid., pp. 1–7; Faust, pp. 31–32; Lang, pp. 353–55; Reader, pp. 196–99.
23. Terry Lowry, *Last Sleep: The Battle of Droop Mountain* (Charleston, W.Va.: Pictorial Histories Publishing Co., Inc., 1996), p. 10 (hereafter cited as Lowry).
24. Capt. Jacob M. Rife, 8 W.Va. Mtd. Inf., "Averell's Raid," *The National Tribune*, 8 Sept. 1887 (hereafter cited as Rife, *NT*); Boehm, p. 30.
25. *Ten Years*, p. 385.
26. Ibid., p. 5.
27. Boehm, pp. 30–32; Faust, pp. 31–32, 411; Lang, pp. 353–54; Reader, pp. 196–99; *Ten Years*, pp. 388–89; Starr, p. 157.
28. OR, vol. 25, pt. 2, p. 502; Lang, p. 107.
29. Lang, p. 108.
30. Ibid.
31. Ibid., p. 109.
32. Frederick M. Dyer, *A Compendium of the War of the Rebellion*, 2 vols. (Dayton, Ohio: The National Historical Society in cooperation with The Press of Morningside Bookshop, 1978), vol. 2, p. 1656 (hereafter cited as Dyer; all references are from vol. 2); Lowry, pp. 11–12.
33. Lowry, pp. 12–13; Rife, *NT*, 8 Sept. 1887.
34. Lowry, p. 13; Dyer, p. 1657.
35. Lowry, pp. 14–15; Samuel T. Wiley, *History of Monongalia County, West Virginia* (Kingwood, W.Va.: Preston Publishing Co., 1883), pp. 529–31.
36. Lowry, pp. 15–16; Dyer, p. 1663; Rife, *NT*, 8 Sept. 1887.
37. Averell Papers, box 2, various letters from Oley to Averell.
38. OR, vol. 27, pt. 2, pp. 209–10; Matheny, p. 61.
39. *Ten Years*, p. 388.
40. Ibid., p. 59.
41. Ibid., p. 355.
42. Ibid., p. 348.
43. Lang, p. 109; Rife, *NT*, 8 Sept. 1887.
44. OR, vol. 27, pt. 3, pp. 449–50; Matheny, p. 63; Dyer, p. 383.
45. OR, vol. 27, pt. 3, p. 350.
46. OR, vol. 25, pt. 2, p. 502.
47. Faust, pp. 788–89.
48. Oren F. Morton, *A History of Pendleton County, West Virginia* (Franklin, W.Va.: pub. by the author, 1910), pp. 107–16, 411–29; Officers of the Pocahontas County Historical Society, *History of Pocahontas County, West Virginia 1981* (Marlinton, W.Va.: Pocahontas County Historical Society, Inc., 1982), pp. 35–40; Otis K. Rice, *A History of Greenbrier County* (Parsons, W.Va.: McClain Printing Co., 1986).
49. OR, vol. 27, pt. 3, p. 960.
50. McNeil, pp. 294–302; Richard L. Armstrong, *The 19th and 20th Virginia Cavalry* (Lynchburg, Va.: H.E. Howard, Inc., 1994), pp. 1–22 (hereafter cited as Armstrong).
51. OR, vol. 27, pt. 3, pp. 941–42.
52. Ibid., pt. 2, pp. 805–16; Matheny, p. 62.
53. OR, vol. 27, pt. 2, pp. 205–6, 209–10.
54. OR, vol. 29, pt. 1, p. 39.
55. Ibid., pp. 31–65.

56. Eugene Wise Jones, *Lieutenant Colonel John F. Polsley 7th West Virginia Regiment 1861–1865* (Master's thesis: University of Akron, 1949), p. 70 (hereafter cited as *Polsley*); Reader, p. 207; Boehm, p. 33.
57. OR, vol. 29, pt. 1, pp. 498–549.
58. *Ten Years*, p. 234.
59. Starr, pp. 163–64.
60. *Ten Years*, p. 420.
61. Ibid., pp. 1–2.
62. Ibid; Boehm, p. 33; Starr, p. 164.
63. OR, vol. 29, pt. 2, p. 473.

CHAPTER TWO
THE STRIKE SOUTH

1. OR, vol. 29, pt. 2, p. 517; In preparation of the story published in the *National Tribune*, 8 Sept. 1887, Capt. Rife maintained that he received a letter from Gen. Kelley, who claimed that Secretary of War Stanton had summoned him to Washington to discuss the feasibility of a strike at the Va. & Tenn. RR. In this letter, according to Rife, Kelley further claimed that in consultation with Stanton and Halleck, all agreed on the importance of such a strike, but that Halleck, fearful of the great risks involved, refused beforehand to accept blame if the strike failed, though he was willing to allow Kelley to reap all the credit and praise if it succeeded. Though this story seems rather implausible—there is no record of such a meeting, for one thing—both Reader and Slease used it in their respective accounts of the Salem Raid.
2. Ibid., pt. 1, p. 933.
3. Ibid., p. 926.
4. Letter of Sgt. B.F. Hughes, Co. F, 3 W.Va. to wife, Ellen, 7 Dec. 1863. Civil War Misc. Papers, item 1021, West Virginia Collection, West Virginia University, Morgantown.
5. Ibid.; Rife, *NT*, 8 Sept. 1887.
6. *Wheeling Intelligencer*, 12 Dec. 1863.
7. OR, vol. 29, pt. 1, p. 926; Rife, *NT*, 22 Sept. 1887—In response to this article Averell wrote that Kelley had nothing to do with the planning, nor did he know where Longstreet's supplies were located, but directed him (Averell) to find them by his own way.
8. 22 Va. Inf. under Col. George S. Patton, 26 Va. Bn. under Lt. Col. George M. Edgar, 23 Va. Bn. under Lt. Col. Clarence Derrick, the Va. battery of Capt. Beirne Chapman, 14 Va. Cav. under Col. J.A. Gibson.
9. 60 Va. Inf. under Col. B.H. Jones, 36 Va. Inf. under Maj. T. Smith, the Va. battery of Capt. Thomas Bryan, 17 Va. Cav. under Maj. F.F. Smith.
10. 19 Va. Cav. under Lt. Col. William P. Thompson, 20 Va. Cav. under Col. William W. Arnett, the Va. battery of Capt. Warren S. Lurty, 6 independent dismounted companies. Near Huntersville was Capt. J.W. Marshall with Co. I, 19 Va. Cav., and at Mill Point was Lt. Col. Thompson with Capt. William L. McNeel's Co. F, 19 Va. Cav., and the unattached company of Capt. Jarvis.
11. 18 Va. Cav. under Col. George W. Imboden, 41 Bn. Va. Inf. under Maj. Robert White, 62 Va. Mtd. Inf. under Col. George H. Smith, 2 Bn. Md. Cav. under Maj. H.W. Gilmore, the Va. battery of Capt. John H. McClanahan.
12. OR, vol. 29, pt. 1, pp. 950–51; pt. 2, p. 857; Rife, *NT*, 8 Sept. 1887.
13. OR, vol. 29, pt. 1, pp. 920–21, 926; pt. 2, pp. 550–52.
14. Ibid., pt. 2, p. 552.
15. OR, vol. 31, pt. 1, pp. 454–63.
16. 34 Ohio Mtd. Inf. under Capt. Luther Furney, 2 W.Va. Cav. under Lt. Col. David Dove, 3 companies of the 3 W.Va. Cav. under Capt. George W. McVickers.
17. Col. Carr B. White's 2nd Brigade, consisting of the 12 Ohio Inf. under Lt. Col. Jonathon D. Hine, 91 Ohio Inf. under Col. John A. Turley, and 4 guns of the 1 Ohio Battery under Capt. James R. McMullen.

18. OR, vol. 29, pt. 1, p. 940; pt. 2, pp. 614–16.
19. Lowry, p. 26.
20. OR, vol. 29, pt. 2, p. 550.
21. 1 W.Va. Inf. under Lt. Col. Jacob Weddle, 14 W.Va. Inf. under Capt. Jacob Smith, Battery L, 1 Ill. Lt. Art. under Capt. John Rourke.
22. OR, vol. 29, pt. 1, pp. 920, 926–27; pt. 2, p. 616; Boehm, p. 34; Reader, p. 222; Sutler, p. 259.
23. OR, vol. 29, pt. 1, p. 926; pt. 2, p. 552; Jeremiah Sullivan was Brigadier General Benjamin Franklin Kelley's son-in-law.
24. Ibid., pt. 1, p. 926.
25. Ibid.
26. Cecil D. Eby, Jr., ed., *A Virginian in the Civil War: The Diaries of David Hunter Strother* (Chapel Hill, N.C.: The University of North Carolina Press, 1961), p. 209.
27. OR, vol. 29, pt. 2, p. 524.
28. Ibid., pt. 1, p. 931.
29. Ibid., p. 926.
30. William Davis Slease, *The Fourteenth Pennsylvania Cavalry in the Civil War* (Pittsburgh: Art and Engraving Printing Co., 1915), pp. 15–24 (hereafter cited as Slease); George H. Mowrer, *History of the Organization and Service, During the War of the Rebellion, of Co. A 14th Pennsylvania Cavalry* (privately printed by the author, 1890s), pp. 2–10 (hereafter cited as Mowrer); Samuel P. Bates, *History of Pennsylvania Volunteers 1861–65,* 5 vols. (Harrisburg, Pa.: B. Singerly Printers, 1869), vol. 2, pp. 851–53 (hereafter cited as Bates; all references are from vol. 2); Dyer, pp. 1565–66; Lowry, pp. 16–21.
31. Lowry, pp. 21–23.
32. Lang, p. 317; Reader, pp. 199–202; Dyer, p. 1660.
33. Cpl. and Chief Bugler C.E. Shank, 8 W.Va. Mtd. Inf., "General Averell's Salem Raid," *The National Tribune,* 27 Sept. 1883 (hereafter cited as Shank, *NT*).
34. Rife, *NT*, 8 Sept. 1887.
35. Edward G. Longacre, *Mounted Raids of the Civil War* (Lincoln, Nebr.: The University of Nebraska Press, 1975), p. 15 (hereafter cited as Longacre); Letter of Sgt. B.F. Hughes, Co. F, 3 W.Va. to wife, Ellen, 7 Dec. 1863, Civil War Misc. Papers, item 1021, West Virginia Collection, West Virginia University, Morgantown.
36. Polsley, pp. 74, 79–80.
37. Slease, p. 114.
38. Lang, p. 370.
39. Slease, p. 114.
40. Reader, p. 222; Rife, *NT*, 8 Sept. 1887; Diary of Lt. N.N. Hoffman of Gibson's battalion as printed in *The Wheeling Intelligencer,* 7 Jan. 1864 (hereafter cited as Hoffman diary).
41. Rife, *NT*, 8 Sept. 1887.
42. Slease, p. 114; according to David Scott Turk, *The Union Hole: Unionist Activity and Local Conflict in Western Virginia* (Baltimore: Heritage Books, Inc., 1994), p. 68 (hereafter cited as Turk), a few of the men were quite familiar with some of the enemy territory they were going into. Pvts. David R. Noble, Co. A, 8 W.Va., and William G. Ballard of Co. H, 8 W.Va., for example, were from Monroe County.
43. Longacre, pp. 13–16.
44. Rife, 8 Sept. 1887.
45. OR, vol. 29, pt. 1, p. 926.
46. *Ten Years*, p. 337.
47. Diary of Cpl. George Washington Ordner, Co. B, 2 W.Va. Mtd. Inf. Ordner Family Papers. West Virginia University, Morgantown (hereafter cited as Ordner diary.)
48. Hoffman diary.
49. Ibid.; Slease, p. 115.

50. Ibid.; OR, vol. 29, pt. 1, p. 927; C.J. Rawling, *History of the First Regiment Virginia Infantry* (Philadelphia: J.B. Lippincott Co., 1887), p. 154 (hereafter cited as Rawling).
51. Sgt. John W. Elwood, 22 Pa. Cav., *Elwood's Stories of the Old Ringgold Cavalry 1847–1865* (Coal Center, Pa.: pub. by the author, 1914), p. 175 (hereafter cited as Elwood); Ordner diary; Reader, p. 222; Rawling, p. 154.
52. Hoffman diary.
53. OR, vol. 29, pt. 1, p. 932; *Adjutant General's Report of the State of West Virginia for 1864* (Wheeling: John Frew, Public Printer, 1865), p. 649.
54. OR, vol. 29, pt. 1, p. 927; Ordner diary; Reader, p. 223; Rawling, p. 154; Hoffman diary.
55. Rife, *NT*, 8 Sept. 1887.
56. Reader, p. 222.
57. Ibid., pp. 90–95; Lowry, p. 13.
58. Rife, *NT*, 8 Sept. 1887.
59. OR, vol. 29, pt. 1, p. 931; The Compiled Service Records on microfilm at the National Archives in Washington, D.C., indicate that ten men were detached from the 8 W.Va. and assigned to accompany Thoburn.
60. Ibid., pp. 927, 957; Elwood, p. 176; Rawling, p. 154,
61. Rife, *NT*, 8 Sept. 1887.
62. Slease, p. 115.
63. Rawling, p. 154.
64. Reader, p. 222.
65. OR, vol. 29, pt. 1, p. 927; Major George B. Davis, *The Official Military Atlas of the Civil War* (New York: Arno Press, Crown Publishers, Inc., 1978), plate 135c, no. 1 (hereafter cited as OR Atlas).
66. Ibid.
67. Reader, p. 223; Rife, *NT*, 8 Sept. 1887.
68. OR, vol. 29, pt. 1, p. 927; OR Atlas, plate 135c, no. 1.
69. OR, vol. 29, pt. 1, p. 927; Reader, p. 223; Rawling, p. 154.
70. Calvin Price, "The Salem Raid," *Pocahontas Times*, 26 Apr. 1923.
71. Reader, p. 223.
72. Rife, *NT*, 8 Sept. 1887.
73. OR, vol. 29, pt. 1, p. 957.
74. Reader, p. 223.
75. Hoffman diary.
76. OR, vol. 29, pt. 1, p. 927; Ordner diary.
77. Rife, *NT*, 8 Sept. 1887.
78. OR, vol. 29, pt. 1, p. 950.
79. Ibid., pp. 927, 934, 950; Hoffman diary.
80. *Mosby's Manual of Clinical Nursing*, 2nd. ed. (St. Louis: The C.V. Mosby Company, 1989), p. 1653 (hereafter cited as Mosby); OR, vol. 29, pt. 1, p. 27; Reader, p. 223; Hoffman diary.
81. OR, vol. 29, pt. 1, p. 927.
82. Ibid., p. 943; pt. 2, p. 852.
83. Faust, p. 404.
84. OR, vol. 29, pt. 1, p. 943.
85. Ibid., pt. 2, p. 552—Based on the dispatch Kelley sent Halleck on 8 Dec., wherein he informed the commander in chief that Averell would "strike the raiload in Botetourt and Roanoke Counties," it is reasonable to assume that Averell originally intended to hit both Bonsack's and Salem.
86. Ibid., pt. 1, pp. 927, 959.
87. Rife, *NT*, 8 Sept. 1887.
88. OR, vol. 29, pt. 1, p. 927.
89. Ibid.; OR Atlas, plate 135c, no. 1.

90. Ibid.; Reader, p. 223; Slease, p. 116; Hoffman diary.

91. OR, vol. 29, pt. 1, p. 927; OR Atlas, plate 135c, no. 1.

92. Stewart Sifakis, *Who Was Who in the Civil War* (New York: Facts on File Publications, 1988), p. 571.

93. Diary of James Ireland, Co. A, 12 Ohio Inf., VFM 2304, Ohio Historical Society, Columbus.

94. OR, vol. 29, pt. 1, pp. 922–23, 939–40.

95. Ibid., pp. 922–23, 935; According to the Compiled Service Records on microfilm at the National Archives in Washington, D.C., one of the Droop Mountain casualties picked up by Moor was Pvt. Joseph Hagar, Co. B, 8 W.Va., who had been wounded in the leg and left behind at Hillsboro.

96. Ibid., p. 927.

97. Ibid.

98. Ibid.; Ruth Woods Dayton, *Greenbrier Pioneers and Their Homes* (Charleston, W.Va.: West Virginia Publishing Co., 1942), pp. 351–52.

99. 591 men of the 34 Mass. Inf. under Col. George D. Wells, 402 men of the 12 W.Va. Inf. under Maj. William B. Curtis, 77 men of the 17 Ind. Battery under Capt. Melton Miner, about 700 men of the 1 N.Y. Cav. under Maj. Timothy Quinn of Col. William H. Boyd's Brigade, and 32 men of Battery A, 1 W.Va. Lt. Art. under Capt. Furst.

100. OR, vol. 29, pt. 1, pp. 935–37; pt. 2, p. 615.

101. Ibid., pt. 1, p. 927.

102. Rife, *NT*, 8 Sept. 1887.

103. Reader, pp. 68, 111.

104. Jane Johnston and Brenda Williams, eds. and comps., *Hard Times 1861–1865*, 3 vols. (New Castle, Va.: pub. by authors, 1987), vol. 1, p. 171 (hereafter cited as *Hard Times*; all references are from vol. 1).

105. Ibid.; Reader, pp. 223–224; This incident may have been alluded to in the 21 Dec. issue of the *Richmond Examiner*, wherein it cited a dispatch filed by a correspondent from Lynchburg on the nineteenth: "On Tuesday night [15 Dec.] they surprised and fired into the camp of Captain White, on Catawba creek, and captured seventeen men and about one hundred horses, which were being recuperated."

106. Reader, p. 224.

107. *Hard Times*, p. 171; Michael West, *30th Battalion Virginia Sharpshooters* (Lynchburg, Va.: H.E. Howard, Inc., 1994), pp. 65–66, 274.

108. Ordner diary; OR Atlas, plate 135c, no. 1.

109. OR, vol. 29, pt. 1, p. 927.

110. Turk, pp. 62–64.

111. Slease, p. 118; 1860 Federal Census.

112. Rife, *NT*, 8 Sept. 1887.

113. Ibid; Reader, pp. 224–25.

114. OR, vol. 29, pt. 1, p. 933; Rife, *NT*, 8 Sept. 1887.

115. Reader, p. 223.

116. Rife, *NT*, 8 Sept. 1887.

117. Ibid.

118. Boehm, p. 35.

119. OR, vol. 29, pt. 1, pp. 927–28; Reader, pp. 58, 92, 229. Shirley belonged to Co. H. One of the surrendered was supposedly a Capt. Tomlinson.

120. OR, vol. 29, pt. 1, p. 928; Reader, p. 225.

121. Rife, *NT*, 22 Sept. 1887.

122. Norwood C. Middleton, *Salem: A Virginia Chronicle* (Salem, Va.: Salem Historical Society, Inc., 1986), pp. 29–76, 440 (hereafter cited as *Salem*).

123. Ibid., pp. 77–79.

124. Thomas D. Mays, "The Lost Generation: The Roanoke College Community During the 'Late Unpleasantness' 1861–1865" (Salem, Va.: A Seminar Paper Submitted to The History Department of Roanoke College, 1988), pp. 3, 23 (hereafter cited as Mays);

Millard K. Bushong, *Old Jube* (Boyce, Va.: Carr Publishing Co., 1955), pp. 163–64 (hereafter cited as *Old Jube*).

125. *Lynchburg Virginian*, 22 Dec. 1863; Letter of J.J. Moorman to Gov. John Letcher, 18 Dec. 1863 (Letters to the Governor, Archives Division, Virginia State Library and Archives, Richmond; hereafter cited as Moorman letter).
126. *Lynchburg Virginian,* 22 Dec. 1863.
127. *Richmond Sentinel*, 28 Dec. 1863.
128. Ibid.
129. Mays, p. 24.
130. OR, vol. 29, pt. 2, pp. 875–76.
131. Moorman letter.
132. Salem, p. 86; Mays, p. 24; *Richmond Dispatch*, 18 Dec. 1863.
133. *Lynchburg Virginian*, 22 Dec. 1863; Moorman letter.
134. Rife, *NT*, 8 Sept. 1887.
135. Ibid.; *Lynchburg Virginian*, 22 Dec. 1863.
136. Rife, *NT*, 22 Sept. 1887.
137. *Wheeling Intelligencer*, 13 Jan. 1864.
138. OR, vol. 29, pt. 1, p. 925.
139. Salem, p. 81.
140. OR, vol. 29, pt. 1, p. 928; pt. 2, pp. 877, 880; *Lynchburg Virginian*, 22 Dec. 1863.
141. *Richmond Dispatch*, 18 Dec. 1863; *Lynchburg Virginian*, 22 Dec. 1863.
142. OR, vol. 29, pt. 1, p. 928.
143. Reader, p. 225.
144. OR, vol. 29, pt. 1, p. 928.
145. Rife, *NT*, 22 Sept. 1887.
146. OR, vol. 29, pt. 1, p. 928.
147. Hoffman diary.
148. OR, vol. 29, pt. 1, p. 969.
149. Rife, *NT*, 8 Sept. 1887.
150. Ibid.
151. *Richmond Examiner*, 28 Dec. 1863; Moorman letter.
152. Rife, *NT*, 22 Sept. 1887.
153. Ibid.
154. *Lynchburg Virginian*, 19 Dec. 1863.
155. *Lynchburg Virginian*, 22 Dec. 1863; Moorman letter.
156. OR, vol. 29, pt. 1, p. 928.
157. Ibid.
158. *Lynchburg Virginian*, 19 and 22 Dec. 1863; Moorman letter.
159. Rife, *NT*, 22 Sept. 1887.
160. *Lynchburg Virginian*, 22 Dec. 1863.
161. Moorman letter.
162. Rife, *NT*, 8 Sept. 1887.
163. *Lynchburg Virginian*, 19 and 22 Dec. 1863.
164. *Richmond Examiner,* 28 Dec. 1863.
165. OR, vol. 29, pt. 1, p. 928; *Lynchburg Virginian*, 19 Dec. 1863; Moorman letter.
166. OR, vol. 29, pt. 1, p. 928.
167. Ibid; *Lynchburg Virginian*, 22 Dec. 1863.
168. OR, vol. 29, pt. 1, p. 928.

CHAPTER THREE
THE GREAT ESCAPE

1. OR, vol. 29, pt. 1, pp. 943–51.
2. Ibid., pp. 941–43, 971.

3. Ibid., p. 971.
4. Ten Years, pp. 49, 386; Douglas S. Freeman, *Lee's Lieutenants,* 3 vols. (New York: Charles Scribner's Sons, 1944), vol. 3, p. xlii (hereafter cited as Freeman); William C. Davis, ed., *The Confederate General,* 6 vols. (Washington, D.C.: The National Historical Society, 1991), vol. 4, pp. 36–39 (hereafter cited as *Confed. Gen.*); Faust, p. 429.
5. OR, vol. 29, pt. 1, p. 970; Jubal Anderson Early, Frank E. Vandiver, ed., *War Memoirs* (Bloomington, Ind.: University of Indiana Press, 1960), p. 326 (hereafter cited as Vandiver).
6. OR, vol. 29, pt. 2, p. 876.
7. Freeman, vol. 3, p. XXX; *Confed. Gen.,* vol. 2, pp. 89–90; Faust, p. 233.
8. OR, vol. 29, pt. 1, p. 970; Vandiver, p. 327.
9. Rife, *NT,* 22 Sept. 1887; Faust, pp. 378–79; *Confed. Gen.,* vol. 3, pp. 137–41.
10. Vandiver, p. 328.
11. OR, vol. 29, pt. 1, p. 970; Vandiver, p. 328.
12. Reader, p. 225.
13. Boehm, pp. 30, 35.
14. W.P.A. Workers' Writers' Program, *Roanoke: Story of County and City* (Roanoke, Va.: School Boards of Roanoke City and County, 1942), p. 107 (hereafter cited as *Roanoke*); *Roanoke Collegian,* June 1875.
15. *Richmond Examiner,* 28 Dec. 1863.
16. *Lynchburg Virginian,* 22 Dec. 1863.
17. *Richmond Sentinel,* 28 Dec. 1863.
18. OR Atlas, plate 135c, no. 1; Reader, p. 225.
19. OR, vol. 29, pt. 1, p. 928.
20. Hoffman diary.
21. Reader, p. 225.
22. Ibid., p. 226; Boehm, p. 35; Rife, *NT,* 22 Sept. 1887.
23. Reader, pp. 225–26.
24. Elwood, p. 177; Reader, roster.
25. Reader, p. 226.
26. *Adjutant General's Report for the State of Illinois 1861–1866* (Springfield: Phillip Bros., 1901), vol. 8, p. 532.
27. *Hard Times,* p. 169.
28. OR, vol. 29. pt. 1, pp. 928–29.
29. Rife, *NT,* 8 Sept. 1887.
30. Reader, p. 88.
31. Hoffman diary.
32. *Hard Times,* p. 169.
33. Military Service and Pension Records of Martin Hope, National Archives, Washington, D.C.
34. OR, vol. 29, pt. 1, pp. 933–34.
35. *Hard Times,* p. 169.
36. Rife, *NT,* 22 Sept. 1887.
37. Reader, p. 226.
38. Ibid.
39. Sgt. and Chief Bugler C.E. Shank, 8 W.Va. Mtd. Inf., "General Averell's Salem Raid," *The National Tribune,* 27 Sept. 1883; Shanks' compiled service and pension records on microfilm at the National Archives, Washington, D.C.
40. Rife, *NT,* 22 Sept. 1887.
41. Ibid.; OR, vol. 29, pt. 1, p. 924; Reader, p. 226.
42. OR, vol. 29, pt. 1, p. 929.
43. *Hard Times,* p. 170.
44. Ibid.; OR, vol. 29, pt. 1, p. 964.

45. *Hard Times*, pp. 169–70.
46. Rife, *NT*, 22 Sept. 1887.
47. Philip Wayne Rhode, "Descendents of Thomas Love of Lynchburg and Amherst Co. Va." *The Virginia Genealogist,* vol. 35, pp. 193–94.
48. Ordner diary.
49. OR, vol. 29, pt. 1, pp. 944, 949; Lowry, p. 38.
50. OR, vol. 29, pt. 1, pp. 952, 970–71.
51. Ibid., p. 965.
52. Ibid., p. 945.
53. Terry Lowry, *The 22nd Virginia Infantry* (Lynchburg, Va.: H.E. Howard, Inc., 1988), p. 54 (hereafter cited as 22nd Va.).
54. OR, vol. 29, pt. 1, p. 929.
55. Ibid.
56. A.S. Johnston, *Captain Beirne Chapman and Chapman's Battery* (n.p.), p. 17 (hereafter cited as Johnston).
57. 1860 Federal Census of Craig Co., Va., on microfilm at the National Archives, Washington, D.C.
58. Johnston, p. 17; Rife, *NT*, 22 Sept. 1887.
59. OR, vol. 29, pt. 1, p. 929; Rife, *NT*, 22 Sept. 1887.
60. OR, vol. 29, pt. 1, pp. 929, 945, 949.
61. 22nd Va., p. 54.
62. Reader, pp. 229–30. Bower was captured later, probably near Covington on the night of 19 Dec., but during the confusion of an attack on Averell's rear, probably on the same night, he managed to escape by pretending to join in the charge.
63. Rife, *NT*, 22 Sept. 1887.
64. Ibid.; OR, vol. 29, pt. 1, pp. 944, 949.
65. OR, vol. 29, pt. 1, p. 929.
66. Rife, *NT*, 22 Sept. 1887; *Hard Times,* pp. 172–73. Averell's men apparently did not leave Scott's Tavern unscathed. After their departure, Mrs. Scott submitted to the county a statement of her losses, totalling some $17,000. Her list is included here as an interesting example of what Averell's men found worth using or taking: 5 pr blankets, 5 white coverlids, 10 pr cotton sheets, 8 pillows & bolsters, 1 mattress & 5 long table cloths, 1 doz. fine knives & forks, $^1/_2$ doz. chairs, 1 lot earthen & glass ware, 1 skillet, 3 ovens & 2 bakers, damage to cooking stoves, 2 coffee pots 7 12 tin cups, 1 bucket, 1 tub & 1 churn, 16 large turkeys, 50 chickens, 30 lbs tallow, 1 bbl pickles, 2 overcoats, 700 bu. corn, 50 bu. oats, 60 bu. wheat, 6 tons hay, 1 straw tick, 20 bu. potatoes, 4 horses, 2 mules, 2000 rails burnt, 3500 lbs salt pork, 1000 lbs beef, 2 sets wagon harness, 3 gal. brandy, 1 bbl flour, $^1/_2$ set blacksmith tools.
67. OR, vol. 29, pt. 1, p. 949.
68. Ibid., pt. 2, p. 878; Rife, *NT*, 22 Sept. 1887.
69. OR, vol. 29, pt. 2, p. 880.
70. Vandiver, p. 329.
71. Ibid.; OR, vol. 29, pt. 1, p. 970.
72. OR, vol. 29, pt. 1, p. 972.
73. *Richmond Examiner,* 14 Dec. 1863.
74. *Richmond Examiner,* 16 Dec. 1863.
75. *Richmond Examiner,* 17 Dec. 1863.
76. *Lynchburg Virginian,* 19 Dec. 1863.
77. *Lynchburg Virginian,* 23 Dec. 1863.
78. *Richmond Examiner,* 19 Dec. 1863.
79. *Richmond Examiner,* 21 Dec. 1863.
80. *Richmond Examiner,* 22 Dec. 1863.
81. *Richmond Examiner,* 28 Dec. 1863.

82. *Lynchburg Virginian,* 19 Dec. 1863.
83. Vandiver, p. 329.
84. Ibid.; OR, vol. 29, pt. 1, p. 970.
85. OR, vol. 29, pt. 1, p. 966.
86. Ibid., p. 929.
87. Rife, *NT,* 22 Sept. 1887.
88. *Lynchburg Virginian,* 24 Dec. 1863.
89. Rife, *NT,* 22 Sept. 1887.
90. Johnston, p. 18.
91. *Hard Times,* p. 171.
92. Rife, *NT,* 22 Sept. 1887.
93. OR, vol. 29, pt. 1, p. 929.
94. Faust, p. 392; McNeil, pp. 303–4.
95. McNeil, pp. 303–4; Lowry, p. 47.
96. Based on measurements made by the author.
97. OR, vol. 29, pt. 1, pp. 964–66.
98. Ibid., p. 963.
99. Ibid., p. 952; Armstrong, p. 43.
100. Ibid.
101. OR, vol. 29, pt. 1, p. 952.
102. Ibid.
103. Ibid., p. 946.
104. Rife, *NT,* 22 Sept. 1887.
105. Reader, pp. 226–27.
106. OR, vol. 29, pt. 1, p. 952.
107. Ibid., p. 930.
108. Reader, p. 226.
109. Ibid.
110. OR, vol. 29, pt. 1, p. 952.
111. Rife, *NT,* 22 Sept. 1887; letter of Josiah Davis, Co. F, 3 W.Va. Mtd. Inf., George R. Latham Papers, West Virginia State Archives, Charleston (hereafter cited as Davis letter).
112. Ibid.
113. OR, vol. 29, pt. 1, pp. 929–30, 944.
114. Ibid., p. 946.
115. Rife, *NT,* 22 Sept. 1887.
116. OR, vol. 29, pt. 1, p. 929.
117. Rife, *NT,* 22 Sept. 1887.
118. Cpl. George Stover, Co. H, 8 W.Va. Mtd. Inf., "Averell's Salem Raid," *The National Tribune,* 28 April 1904 (hereafter cited as Stover, *NT*).
119. Rife, *NT,* 22 Sept. 1887; Davis letter.
120. Rife, *NT,* 22 Sept. 1887.
121. OR, vol. 29, pt. 1, p. 954.
122. Ibid., p. 929.
123. Ibid., p. 952.
124. Ibid., pp. 930, 952.
125. Ibid., pp. 952–53.
126. Ibid., pp. 929, 953.
127. Ibid., pp. 951–52; Lowry, p. 49.
128. OR, vol. 29, pt. 1, p. 968.
129. Bates, p. 853; Slease, p. 120.
130. Rife, *NT,* 22 Sept. 1887; Reader, p. 227; *Wheeling Intelligencer,* 31 Dec. 1863 and 6 Jan. 1864.

131. *Richmond Sentinel,* 28 Dec. 1863—story filed 22 Dec. by correspondent known as "Rambler."

132. Stover, *NT.*

133. Robert K. Krick, *Lee's Colonels: A Biographical Register of the Field Officers of the Army of Northern Virginia* (Dayton, Ohio: Morningside House, 1992), p. 38; Lowry, p. 51.

134. OR, vol. 29, pt. 1, p. 968.

135. Ibid., p. 953.

136. Reader, p.121.

137. *Pittsburgh Gazette,* 11 Jan. 1864.

138. Hospital Steward Theo. V. Brown, "With Averell On His Raid to Salem, December, 1863—Privations and Hardships of a Nine Days' March," *The National Tribune,* 30 July 1903 (hereafter cited as Brown, *NT).*

139. Ibid.

140. OR, vol. 29, pt. 1, p. 931.

141. Ibid., pp. 924, 931.

142. Rife, *NT,* 22 Sept. 1887.

143. Oren F. Morton, *A Centennial History of Allegheny County Virginia* (Dayton, Va.: J.K. Ruebush Co., 1923), pp. 49–50.

144. OR, vol. 29, pt. 1, p. 931; Hoffman diary.

145. Hoffman diary.

146. OR, vol. 29, pt. 1, p. 931; Rife, *NT,* 22 Sept. 1887.

147. Reader, p. 121.

148. Brown, *NT.*

149. Ibid.

150. OR, vol. 29, pt. 1, p. 942.

151. Ibid., p. 953.

152. Ibid., pp. 953, 968.

153. Reader, p. 227.

154. *Pittsburgh Gazette,* 11 Jan. 1864.

155. OR, vol. 29, pt. 1, p. 932.

156. Reader, p. 227.

157. Ibid.; OR, vol. 29, pt. 1, p. 953.

158. Reader, p. 227.

159. OR, vol. 29, pt. 1, p. 968; Lowry, p. 52.

160. Reader, p. 227; Bates, p. 851.

161. Stover, *NT;* Reader, p. 228.

162. *Pittsburgh Gazette,* 11 Jan. 1864.

163. M.J.C., Co. C, 14th Pa. Cav., "Here's a Comrade Who Won't Whitewash Col. Blakely," *The National Tribune,* 27 Dec. 1894—M.J.C. goes on to say that most of the credit for engineering the regiment's escape should go to Capt. Kerr of Co. C and to Capt. Wakefield of Co. D.

164. Slease, p. 121.

165. As inferred by the *National Tribune* article cited in note 163.

166. *Pittsburgh Gazette,* 11 Jan. 1864.

167. Slease, p. 121.

168. OR, vol. 29, pt. 1, p. 946.

169. Mowrer, p. 11.

170. OR, vol. 29, pt. 1, p. 947.

171. Brown, *NT.*

172. Ibid.

173. Reader, pp. 111, 222.

174. Ibid., pp. 122, 228.

175. Brown, *NT.*

176. Reader, p. 228.
177. Brown, *NT.*
178. Ibid.
179. Rife, *NT,* 22 Sept. 1887.
180. Reader, p. 228.
181. Ibid.; OR, vol. 29, pt. 1, pp. 968–69.
182. OR, vol. 29, pt. 1, p. 932; *Pittsburgh Gazette,* 11 Jan. 1864.
183. Reader, p. 228.

CHAPTER FOUR
THE RETURN TO GOD'S COUNTRY

1. *Pittsburgh Gazette,* 11 Jan. 1864.
2. OR, vol. 29, pt. 1, p. 924; Reader, p. 228; Mowrer, p. 11; Bates, p. 854.
3. Reader, p. 122.
4. Averell Papers, box 2, folder 8.
5. Averell Papers, Averell scrapbook, box 27; that there was no lingering hard feelings between the two officers is evidenced by the fact that by the 1880s "General" William Blakely was president of the "Averell Association," an organization dedicated to honoring the veterans who had served in Averell's various commands.
6. The Seminole War of 1837 and the Mexican War.
7. Averell Papers, box 2, folder 8.
8. Averell Papers, Averell diary, box 12, folder 7.
9. OR, vol. 29, pt. 1, p. 931.
10. Ibid., p. 932.
11. J.F. Starcher, Co. C, 3 W.Va. Mtd. Inf., "Captured on the Salem Raid," *The National Tribune,* 27 Sept. 1883.
12. Military Service Records on microfilm at the National Archives, Washington, D.C.
13. OR, vol. 29, pt. 1, pp. 932, 954.
14. Ibid., p. 954; *Lynchburg Virginian,* 26 Dec. 1863.
15. *Richmond Examiner,* 23 Dec. 1863.
16. *Richmond Sentinel,* 28 Dec. 1863.
17. *Richmond Examiner,* 23 Dec. 1863.
18. *Richmond Sentinel,* 28 Dec. 1863.
19. *Richmond Examiner,* 17 Dec. 1863.
20. *Richmond Sentinel,* 28 Dec. 1863.
21. *Richmond Examiner,* 28 Dec. 1863.
22. OR, vol. 29, pt. 1, p. 946.
23. Armstrong, p. 47.
24. OR, vol. 29, pt. 1, p. 931.
25. Reader, p. 228; Rife, *NT,* 22 Sept. 1887.
26. OR, vol. 29, pt. 1, p. 931.
27. *Lynchburg Virginian,* 23 Dec. 1863.
28. OR, vol. 29, pt. 1, pp. 931, 945; Rife, *NT,* 22 Sept. 1887; Reader, p. 228.
29. Reader, p. 228.
30. OR, vol. 29, pt. 1, p. 924.
31. Slease, p. 122.
32. Hoffman diary.
33. Slease, p. 122; Rife, *NT,* 22 Sept. 1887; Reader, p. 228.
34. OR, vol. 29, pt. 1, p. 932.
35. Reader, p. 228.
36. Rife, *NT,* 22 Sept. 1887.
37. Slease, p. 122.
38. Hu Maxwell and H.L. Swisher, *History of Hampshire County, West Virginia* (Morgantown, W.Va.: A. Brown Boughner, Printer, 1897), p. 225 (hereafter cited as Hampshire County).

39. Hoffman diary.
40. OR, vol. 29, pt. 1, p. 931; OR Atlas, plate 135c, no. 1; Davis letter.
41. *Wheeling Intelligencer*, 30 Dec. 1863.
42. OR Atlas, plate 135c, no. 1; Slease, p. 122; Hoffman diary; Davis letter.
43. Slease, p. 122.
44. Reader, p. 228.
45. Slease, p. 122.
46. Ibid.; Reader, p. 228.
47. Reader, p. 229.
48. Ibid.; Rife, *NT*, 22 Sept. 1887.
49. Rife, *NT*, 22 Sept. 1887.
50. Ibid.
51. OR, vol. 29, pt. 1, p. 931; OR Atlas, plate 135c, no. 1.
52. OR, vol. 29, pt. 1, pp. 971–72.
53. Ibid., pp. 949–50.
54. Vandiver, p. 331.
55. Ibid., pp. 331–32; OR, vol. 29, pt. 1, pp. 939, 970.
56. OR, vol. 29, pt. 1, p. 970.
57. Ibid., p. 923.
58. Ibid.; Elwood, p. 177; Samuel Clark Farrar, *Twenty Second Pennsylvania Cavalry and Ringgold Battalion* (Pittsburgh: The New Werner Co., 1911), p. 145.
59. William T. Price, *Historical Sketches of Pocahontas County* (Marlinton, W.Va.: Price Brothers, Publishers, 1901), pp. 605–6 (hereafter cited as Price); Hoffman diary.
60. *Pocahontas Times*, 26 April 1923.
61. Price, pp. 599–600; *Pocahontas Times*, 4 May 1899.
62. *Wheeling Intelligencer*, 1 Jan. 1864.
63. Averell Papers, Averell scrapbook, box 27; at a meeting of the Averell Association in the 1880s, the question was jokingly put to Averell, "who stole your boots?"
64. *Wheeling Intelligencer*, 6 Jan. 1864.
65. Stover, *NT*.
66. Rife, 8 Sept. 1887.
67. Hoffman diary.
68. OR, vol. 29, pt. 1, p. 931; Ordner diary.
69. Bates, p. 854.
70. Mosby, p. 1653.
71. OR, vol. 29, pt. 1, p. 925.
72. *Pocahontas Times*, 26 April 1923.
73. Brown, *NT*; OR, vol. 29, pt. 1, p. 931.
74. Slease, p. 123.
75. Hoffman diary.
76. Slease, p. 123; OR, vol. 29, pt. 1, p. 931; Ordner diary.
77. Mosby, p. 1653.
78. OR, vol. 29, pt. 1, p. 931; Rife, *NT*, 22 Sept. 1887; Reader, p. 229.
79. *Richmond Examiner*, 24 Dec. 1863.
80. Reader, pp. 96, 230.
81. Slease, p. 123.
82. Brown, *NT*.
83. Ibid.
84. Hoffman diary.
85. Slease, pp. 123–24.

CHAPTER FIVE
THE JUDGMENT

1. *Richmond Examiner*, 24 Dec. 1863.

2. *Richmond Examiner*, 25 Dec. 1863.
3. *Wheeling Intelligencer*, 24 and 25 Dec. 1863.
4. As reported in the *Wheeling Intelligencer*, 29 Dec. 1863.
5. *Harper's Weekly*, 16 Jan. 1864.
6. Averell Papers, box 2, folder 9, L.P. Balch to Averell, 12 Jan.1864.
7. Averell Papers, box 2, folder 9, Edward Anthony to Averell, 11 Jan. 1864.
8. Averell Papers, box 2, folder 8, L.P. Balch to Averell, 16 Jan. 1864.
9. Averell Papers, box 2, folder 10, Frank to Averell, 9 Feb. 1864.
10. Averell Papers, box 2, folder 7, William Strickler to Averell, 7 Jan. 1864.
11. Averell Papers, box 2, folder 13.
12. Averell Papers, box 2, folder 10, Markbreit to Averell, 15 May 1864; box 2, folder 13, Polsley to Averell, 5 May 1864; John J. Polsley Papers, Ms. 82-274, folder 4, physician's affidavit dated 30 Sept. 1868, West Virginia State Archives, Charleston.
13. Hoffman diary.
14. Averell Papers, box 16, folder 9.
15. Averell Papers, box 2, folder 10, John Goode to Averell, 8 Feb. 1864.
16. Averell Papers, box 2, folder 10, Frank to Averell, 9 Feb. 1864.
17. Averell Papers, box 2, folder 10.
18. Averell Papers, box 2, folder 10, William Stevens to Averell, 28 Feb. 1864.
19. Brown, *NT*.
20. *Ten Years*, p. 395.
21. OR, vol. 29, pt. 1, pp. 931–32.
22. Ibid., p. 925.
23. Ibid., p. 923.
24. Angus James Johnston II, *Virginia Railroads in the Civil War* (Chapel Hill, N.C.: The University of North Carolina Press, 1961), p. 188; *Wheeling Daily Register*, 1 Jan. 1864.
25. OR, vol. 31, pt. 1, pp. 517–37.
26. OR, vol. 29, pt. 1, p. 945.
27. Ibid., p. 925; Brown, *NT*.
28. Mowrer, p. 11.
29. OR, vol. 29, pt. 1, p. 925.
30. *Wheeling Intelligencer*, 1 Jan. 1864.
31. OR, vol. 29, pt. 1, p. 932.
32. Military Service Records on microfilm at the National Archives in Washington, D.C; Reader, pp. 197-237; Bates, pp. 858–60.
33. Hampshire County, p. 219.
34. McVey's compiled service and pension records on microfilm at the National Archives, Washington, D.C.
35. Reader, p. 230.
36. Ibid., p. 33.
37. Bates, p. 854.
38. OR, vol. 29, pt. 1, p. 925.
39. Ibid., p. 932; Reader, p. 122.
40. Bates, p. 854.
41. *Wheeling Intelligencer*, 1 Jan. 1864.
42. OR, vol. 29, pt. 1, p. 932; Ordner diary.
43. Reader, p. 236.
44. OR, vol. 29, pt. 1, p. 932.
45. Ibid., p. 889; vol. 33, p. 43.
46. OR, vol. 33, p. 1061.
47. Freeman, vol. 3, pp. 326–27.

48. OR, vol. 33, p. 1141.
49. Ibid., p. 446.
50. *Wheeling Intelligencer*, 28 Dec. 1863.
51. Rife, *NT*, 8 Sept. 1887.
52. Hampshire County, p. 213.
53. OR, vol. 29, pt. 1, p. 595.
54. OR, vol. 33, p. 481.
55. Ibid.; Reader, p. 237.
56. *Ten Years*, p. 392.
57. OR, vol. 33, p. 618.
58. Faust, p. 146.
59. *Ten Years*, p. 393.
60. OR, vol. 37, pt. 1, p. 557.
61. *Ten Years*, p. 395.
62. Boehm, p. 35; Faust, p. 146.
63. Boehm, p. 35.
64. Ibid.; *Ten Years*, pp. 397–400.
65. *Ten Years*, p. 400.
66. Dyer, pp. 1481, 1565, 1658, 1660.
67. *Ten Years*, pp. 315–16.
68. Ibid., pp. 409–15.
69. Ibid., pp. 329–30.
70. Brown, *NT*.

BIBLIOGRAPHY

Manuscript Collections

William Woods Averell Papers 1836–1910. New York State Library, Albany.

Ireland Papers. Diary of James Ireland, Co. A, 12 Ohio Infantry. Ohio Historical Society, Columbus, Ohio. VFM 2304.

Jones, Eugene Wise. *Lieutenant Colonel John J. Polsley 7th West Virginia Regiment 1861–1865.* Master's Thesis. University of Akron, 1949.

George R. Latham Papers. West Virginia University, Morgantown.

Letters to the Governor. Letter of J.J. Moorman to Gov. John Letcher, 18 Dec. 1863. Library of Virginia, Richmond.

Mays, Thomas D. "The Lost Generation: The Roanoke College Community During the 'Late Unpleasantness' 1861–1865." A Seminar Paper Submitted to The History Department of Roanoke College, Salem, Va., 1988.

Ordner Family Papers. West Virginia University, Morgantown.

John J. Polsley Papers. West Virginia State Archives, Charleston.

John J. Polsley Papers. West Virginia University, Morgantown.

Books

Adjutant General's Report for the State of Illinois 1861–1866. Springfield: Phillip Bros., 1901.

Adjutant General's Report of the State of West Virginia for 1864. Charleston, W.Va.: John Frew, Public Printer, 1865.

Armstrong, Richard L. *19th and 20th Virginia Cavalry.* Lynchburg, Va.: H.E. Howard, Inc., 1994.

Avery, Clara A. *The Averell-Averill-Avery Family—A Record of the Descendants of William and Abigail Averell of Ipswich, Massachusetts.* 2 vols. Cleveland: Press of Evangelical Publishing, 1914.

Bates, Samuel P. *History of Pennsylvania Volunteers 1861–65.* 5 vols. Harrisburg, Pa.: B. Singerly, Printers, 1869.

Bushong, Millard K. *Old Jube.* Boyce, Va.: Carr Publishing Company, 1955.

Cohen, Stan. *The Civil War in West Virginia: A Pictorial History.* Missoula, Mo.: Gateway Printing & Litho., 1976.

Davis, Maj. George B. *The Official Military Atlas of the Civil War.* New York: Arno Press, Crown Publishers, Inc., 1978.

Davis, William C., ed. *The Confederate General.* 6 vols. Washington, D.C.: The National Historical Society, 1991.

Dayton, Ruth Woods. *Greenbrier Pioneers and Their Homes.* Charleston, W.Va.: West Virginia Publishing Co., 1942.

Dyer, Frederick M. *A Compendium of the War of the Rebellion.* 2 vols. Dayton, Ohio: The National Historical Society in cooperation with The Press of Morningside Bookshop, 1978.

Early, Jubal Anderson. *War Memoirs.* Edited by Frank E. Vandiver. Bloomington, Ind.: Indiana University Press, 1960.

Eby, Cecil D., Jr., ed. *A Virginia Yankee in the Civil War: The Diaries of David Hunter Strother.* Chapel Hill: The University of North Carolina Press, 1961.

Eckart, Edward K., and Nicholas J. Amato, eds. *Ten Years in the Saddle: The Memoir of William Woods Averell 1851–1862.* San Rafael, Calif.: Presidio Press, 1978.

Elwood, Sgt. John W. *Elwood's Stories of the Old Ringgold Cavalry 1847–1865.* Pub. by the author, Coal Center, Pa., 1914.

Evans, Clement A., ed. *Confederate Military History.* 13 vols. Atlanta: The Confederate Publishing Company, 1898.

Farrar, Samuel Clark. *Twenty Second Pennsylvania Cavalry and Ringgold Battalion 1861–1865.* Pittsburgh: The New Werner Co., 1911.

Faust, Patricia, ed. *Historical Times Illustrated Encyclopedia of the Civil War.* New York: Harper & Row Publishers, 1986.

Freeman, Douglas S. *Lee's Lieutenants.* 3 vols. New York: Charles Scribner's Sons, 1944.

Johnston, Albert S. *Capt. Beirne Chapman and Chapman's Battery.* Union, W.Va.: The Monroe Watchman, 1905.

Johnston, Angus James II. *Virginia Railroads in the Civil War.* Chapel Hill: The University of North Carolina Press, 1961.

Johnston, Jane, and Brenda Williams, eds. and comps. *Hard Times 1861–1865.* 3 vols. New Castle, Va.: pub. by authors, 1987.

Krick, Robert K. *Lee's Colonels: A Biographical Register of the Field Officers of the Army of Northern Virginia.* Dayton, Ohio: Morningside House, 1992.

Lang, Theodore F. *Loyal West Virginians From 1861–1865.* Baltimore: Deutsch Publishing Company, 1895.

Longacre, Edward G. *Mounted Raids of the Civil War.* Lincoln, Nebr.: The University of Nebraska Press, 1975.

Lowry, Terry. *Last Sleep: The Battle of Droop Mountain.* Charleston, W.Va.: Pictorial Histories, Inc., 1996.

————. *The 22nd Virginia Infantry.* Lynchburg, Va.: H.E. Howard, Inc., 1988.

Matheny, H.E. *Major General Thomas Maley Harris.* Parsons, W.Va.: McClain Printing Company, 1963.

Maxwell, Hu, and H.L. Swisher. *History of Hampshire County West Virginia.* Morgantown, W.Va.: A. Brown Boughner, Printer, 1897.

Middleton, Norwood C. *Salem: A Virginia Chronicle.* Salem, Va.: Salem Historical Society, Inc., 1986.

Moore, Frank, ed. *The Rebellion Record.* 12 vols. New York: D. Van Nostrand, Publisher, 1865.

Mosby's Manual of Clinical Nursing, 2nd. ed. St. Louis: The C.V. Mosby Company, 1989.

Morton, Oren F. *A Centennial History of Allegheny County Virginia.* Dayton, Va.: J.K. Ruebush Co., 1923.

————. *A History of Pendleton County, West Virginia.* Franklin, W.Va.: pub. by the author, 1910.

Mowrer, George H. *History of the Organization and Service, During the War of the Rebellion, of Co. A 14th Pennsylvania Cavalry.* pub. by the author, 1890s.

Ohio Roster Commission. *Roster of Ohio Soldiers in the War of the Rebellion 1861–65.* Cincinnati: Valley Publishing- Manufacturing Co., 1866.

Osborne, Charles C. *Jubal: The Life and Times of General Jubal A. Early, C.S.A., Defender of the Lost Cause.* Chapel Hill, N.C.: Algonquin Books, 1991.

Phillips, David L. ed., *War Stories: Civil War in West Virginia.* Leesburg, Va.: Gauley Mount Press, 1991.

Pocahontas County Historical Society, Inc. *History of Pocahontas County, West Virginia 1981.* Marlinton, W.Va.: Pocahontas County Historical Society, Inc., 1982.

Price, William T. *Historical Sketches of Pocahontas County.* Marlinton, W.Va.: Price Brothers, Publishers, 1901.

Rawling, C.J. *History of the First Regiment Virginia Infantry.* Philadelphia: J.B. Lippincott, Co., 1887.

Reader, Francis Smith. *History of the Fifth West Virginia Cavalry, Formerly the Second Virginia, and Battery G, First West Virginia Light Artillery.* New Brighton, Pa.: Daily News, 1890.

Reece, Jasper W. *Report of the Adjutant General for the State of Illinois, 1861–1865.* Springfield, Ill.: Phillip Bros., State Printers, 1901.

Reid, Whitelaw. *Ohio in the War.* 2 vols. Cincinnati: Moore, Wilstach & Baldwin, 1868.

Rice, Otis K. *A History of Greenbrier County.* Parsons, W.Va.: McClain Printing Co., 1986.

Sifakis, Stewart. *Who Was Who in the Civil War.* New York: Facts on File Publications, 1988.

Slease, William Davis. *The Fourteenth Pennsylvania Cavalry in the Civil War, A History of the Fourteenth Pennsylvania Volunteer Cavalry from its Organization until the Close of the Civil War, 1861–1865.* Pittsburgh: Art Engraving and Printing Co., 1915.

Starr, Stephen Z. *The Union Cavalry in the Civil War.* 3 vols. Baton Rouge: Louisiana State University Press, 1979.

Sutler, Boyd B. *West Virginia in the Civil War.* Charleston, W.Va.: Education Foundation, Inc., 1963.

Taylor, Frank H. *Philadelphia in the Civil War, 1861–1865.* Philadelphia: Dunlop Printing Co., 1913.

Turk, David Scott. *The Union Hole: Unionist Activity and Local Conflict in Western Virginia.* Baltimore: Heritage Books, Inc., 1994.

Turner, Ronald R. *7th West Virginia Cavalry.* Manassas, Va.: The Print House Press, 1979.

United States War Department. *War of the Rebellion: A Compilation of the Official Record of the Union and Confederate Armies.* 128 vols. Washington: U.S. Government Printing Office, 1880–1901.

West, Michael. *30th Battalion Virginia Sharpshooters.* Lynchburg, Va.: H.E. Howard, Inc., 1994.

W.P.A. Workers' Writers' Program. *Roanoke: Story of County and City.* Roanoke, Va.: School Boards of Roanoke City and County, 1942.

Wiley, Samuel T. *History of Monongalia County, West Virginia.* Kingwood, W.Va.: Preston Publishing Company, 1883.

Woodward, Harold R., Jr. *Defender of the Valley: Brigadier General John D. Imboden, C.S.A.* Berryville, Va.: Rockbridge Publishing Co., 1996.

Newspapers

Brown, Theo. (Hospital Steward). "With Averell On His Raid to Salem, December, 1863—Privations and Hardships of a Nine Days' March." *The National Tribune.* 30 July 1903.

Harper's Weekly. 16 Jan. 1864.

J., M.C. (Pvt. Co. C, 14 Pa. Cav.). "Here's a Comrade Who Won't White-wash Col. Blakely." *The National Tribune.* 27 Dec. 1894.

The Lynchburg Republican. 23 Dec. 1863.

The Lynchburg Virginian. Various reports. 18–26 Dec. 1863.

Pittsburgh Gazette. 30 Dec. 1863 and 11 Jan. 1864.

Price, Andrew. "The Salem Raid." *The Pocahontas Times.* 4 May 1899.

Price, Calvin W. "The Salem Raid." *The Pocahontas Times.* 26 April 1923 and 25 Aug. 1927.

The Richmond Daily Dispatch. 18 Dec. 1863.

The Richmond Examiner. Various reports. 14–28 Dec. 1863.

The Richmond Sentinel. 28 Dec. 1863.

Rife, Jacob M. (Capt., 8 W.Va. Mtd. Inf.). "Averell's Raid." *The National Tribune.* 8 and 22 Sept. 1887.

The Roanoke Collegian. June 1875.

Shank, C.E. (Chief Bugler, 8 W.Va. Mtd. Inf.). "General Averell's Salem Raid." *The National Tribune.* 27 Sept. 1883.

Starcher, J.F. (Co. C, 3 W.Va. Mtd. Inf.). "Captured on the Salem Raid." *The National Tribune.* 27 Sept. 1883.

Stover, George. (Cpl. Co. H, 2 W.Va. Mtd. Inf.). "Averell's Salem Raid, Narrow Escapes and Terrible Hardships on the Return." *The National Tribune.* 28 April 1904.

Swetnam, George. "The Fourteenth Cavalry." *The Pittsburgh Press.* 8 Oct. 1961.

Wheeling Daily Register. 1 Jan. 1864.

Wheeling Intelligencer. Various reports. 12 Dec. 1863 through 13 Jan. 1864.

Magazines and Journals

Boehm, Robert B. "The Unfortunate Averell." *Civil War Times Illustrated* Aug. 1966.

McNeil, John H. "The Imboden Raid and Its Effects." *Southern Historical Society Papers,* vol. 34.

Rhodes, Philip Wayne. "Descendants of Thomas Love of Lynchburg and Amherst Co., Virginia." *The Virginia Geneologist,* vol. 35.

Index

First names are listed where known.